CCNP™ Routing
The Cram Sheet

This Cram Sheet contains the distilled key facts about *CCNP Routing Exam*. Review this information right before you enter the test room, paying special attention to those areas where you feel you need the most review. You can transfer any of these facts onto a blank sheet of paper before beginning the exam.

SCALABLE INTERNETWORKS

1. Router roles:
   - *Core*—At the top of your internetwork hierarchy
   - *Distribution*—In the midsections of your hierarchy, providing connectivity from the core backbone to the individual sites
   - *Access*—At the bottom of the hierarchy, providing end-user access to internetwork resources
2. Compression is best utilized on low-speed serial links.

ROUTING PROTOCOL OVERVIEW

3. Routing protocol metrics:
   - *OSPF*—Cost (based on bandwidth)
   - *EIGRP*—Bandwidth, delay, load, reliability, and MTU
4. Administrative distance is the believability of a route learned by a particular routing protocol:
   - *OSPF* —110
   - *EIGRP*—90
   - *Directly connected*—0
   - *Static route*—0 or 1 for administrative distance with static routes depends on whether a next hop address is specified (1) or an outbound interface (0).

- Use the **distance** command to manipulate administrative distance from the **config-router** prompt

IP ADDRESSING USING VLSM

5. VLSM
   - Routing protocol must be capable of passing the prefix in routing updates to support VLSM.
   - RIP and IGRP do not support VLSM.
   - OSPF does support VLSM.
   - EIGRP support for VLSM must be enabled (**no auto-summary** under the EIGRP configuration).
   - Further subdivides the address space.
   - Mask for serial links is 255.255.255.252 to provide for only two hosts.
6. Route summarization:
   - Find a common bit boundary in the sequence of network addresses.
   - Count the number of bits the addresses have in common to create the prefix.
   - Use the command **area <*number*> range <*network address* > <*prefix* >** for OSPF route summarization. This command is entered under the OSPF configuration.
   - Use the command **ip summary-address eigrp <*as number* > <*network address*>**

47. The command **line vty 0 4** will move you to the virtual terminal configuration prompt.

48. IP helper addresses should be placed on the inbound interface that will be receiving the broadcast to be forwarded.

49. Required information for tunnel configuration:
    - *Tunnel source*—The outbound interface through which to depart this router.
    - *Tunnel destination*—The next logical hop IP address where the tunnel terminates.
    - *Tunnel mode*—The definition of the mode used to encapsulate the traffic to be carried. **tunnel mode gre ip** is the command to set it to generic route encapsulation.
    - *Encapsulated protocol attributes*—Includes IPX network number, AppleTalk, cable range, and zone.

OPTIMIZING ROUTING UPDATES

50. Static routes:
    - **ip route <*dest.network*> <*dest. netmask*> <*next hop addr I out int* > <*distance* >**
    - Specifying outbound interface sets administrative distance to 0 and automatically redistributes.
    - Specifying next hop address sets administrative distance to 1 and requires manual redistribution.
    - Manipulating administrative distance to a high number so that the dynamic route will show and use the static route as a backup is called a *floating static route*.

51. Default route:
    - Use the **ip default network <*network address* >** command to set on each router.
    - Use **ip route 0.0.0.0 0.0.0.0 <*out int I next hop address* >** to set static default route.

52. Stopping routing updates:
    - Use the **passive interface <*int* >** command to force a routing protocol to stop sending updates.
    - Use distribute lists with access lists to filter routes.

IP ADDRESSING

53. IP addressing:
    - Routing decision is based on longest match of routing table entry to destination address.
    - *Class A* —1 to 126.
    - *Class B* —128 to 191.
    - *Class C* —192 to 223.
    - To find number of subnets created or number of hosts per subnet, use the 2^x-2 formula.
    - Subnet address is derived through *logical AND* process.

54. Private internetwork space:
    - *Class A* —10.0.0.0 to 10.255.255.255
    - *Class B* —172.16.0.0 to 172.31.255.255
    - *Class C* —192.168.0.0 to 192.168.255.255

CORIOLIS™
Certification Insider Press

- Use the **area <*number*> stub no-summary** command on the ABR to create totally stubby area.
- Use the **area <*number*> stub** command on internal routers to tell them they're part of a stub area.
- Do not configure area 0 as a stub area.

22. Virtual links must be configured on areas that cannot connect directly to area 0.

23. Show commands:
- **show ip protocols**—Shows active routing protocols
- **show ip ospf neighbor**—Shows neighbor database

EIGRP

24. Routes for IP, IPX, and AppleTalk.

25. Metric is composite of bandwidth, delay, load, reliability, and MTU.

26. Best route is called *successor* or *current successor*. Selected based on lowest feasible distance.

27. Second best route is called *feasible successor*. Advertised distance of this route must be lower than feasible distance of best route to be considered a feasible successor.

28. Automatic redistribution between EIGRP and IGRP if AS numbers are same.

29. Use the **ip summary-address eigrp <*as number*> <*network address*> <*prefix*>** command on the outbound interface to configure summarization.

30. Show commands:
- **show ip eigrp neighbors**—Displays the EIGRP IP neighbor table.
- **show ip eigrp topology**—Displays the EIGRP IP topology table.
- **show ip route**—Displays the IP routing table.

BGP OPERATION

31. Use BGP to connect to ISP when you need multiple exit points or when specified by ISP.

32. EBGP is a BGP connection to an external AS, whereas IBGP is a BGP connection within the local AS.

33. Use a default route to point your AS to the ISP rather than redistributing.

34. BGP uses TCP to ensure guaranteed delivery of routing updates.

35. A peer group is a group of BGP neighbors that share the same update policies.

36. When load-balancing, BGP only operates properly if it's receiving identical updates from the same provider.

37. BGP uses route maps for route filtering.

38. A route reflector is based on the idea of specifying a concentration router to act as a focal point for internal BGP sessions. Multiple BGP routers can peer to a central router, and then multiple route reflectors can peer together.

39. A BGP confederation is based on the concept that an AS can be broken into multiple sub-ASes.

TRAFFIC MANAGEMENT

40. IP standard access lists:
- Filter only on source IP address.
- Use list numbers between 1 and 99.

41. IP extended access lists:
- Filter on source IP address, destination IP address, protocol, and port number.
- Use list numbers between 100 and 199.

42. A wildcard mask is the inverse value of a subnet mask. To find an appropriate wildcard mask for a specific subnet, change the binary value of each bit in the subnet mask. For example, a subnet mask of 255.255.255.240 would use a wildcard mask of 0.0.0.15.

43. Standard access lists should be placed as close as possible to the destination of the filtered traffic.

44. Extended access lists should be placed as close as possible to the source of the filtered traffic.

45. Any traffic not specifically permitted by an access list is denied. The last line of all access lists is an implicit **deny**.

46. A static route specifying an outbound interface of null 0 is a good alternative to access lists.

prefix for EIGRP route summarization. This command is entered on the outbound interface that will be advertising the summary route. Enter the command **no auto-summary** under EIGRP to support summarization.

7. Network Address Translation (NAT) is used to convert private internal IP addresses to public external IP addresses, which should exist in your registered space.

SCALABLE ROUTING PROTOCOLS

8. Distance-vector routing protocols:
   - RIP
   - RIP v.2
   - IGRP

9. Link-state routing protocols:
   - OSPF
   - IS-IS

10. Advanced distance-vector routing protocols:
   - EIGRP

11. Classful routing protocols do not support VLSM.

12. Classful routing protocols:
   - RIP
   - IGRP

13. Classless routing protocols (which do support VLSM):
   - RIP v.2
   - OSPF
   - IS-IS
   - EIGRP

OSPF

14. OSPF is a link-state routing protocol.

15. Developed to overcome RIP limits:
   - Fast convergence.
   - No hop count limit.
   - Support for VLSM.
   - Metric is cost based on bandwidth.
   - Efficient routing updates via multicast.

16. Uses Hello protocol to establish neighbor relationship.

17. DR election:
   - Highest priority is DR.
   - Second highest priority is BDR.

   - Router ID used to break tie on priority.
   - Router ID is highest IP address or IP address of Loopback 0 interface.
   - Election of DR/BDR will occur only on broadcast media (such as Ethernet and token ring).

18. Routing updates:
   - Routing updates sent to DR and BDR if present via 224.0.0.6.
   - DR forwards routing updates to other OSPF routers via 224.0.0.5.
   - If no DR/BDR, simply forward update to neighbor(s).
   - Routing updates, called *LSAs*, are disseminated in flooding fashion.

19. Required information for OSPF neighbors:
   - Neighbor ID
   - Area ID
   - Router priority
   - DR IP address
   - BDR IP address
   - Authentication type
   - Authentication password
   - Stub area flag

20. OSPF router designations:
   - *Internal router*—Any router with all interfaces in one area
   - *Area border router*—Any router with interfaces in multiple areas
   - *Backbone router*—Any router with an interface in area 0
   - *Autonomous system boundary router*—Any router with a connection to an external autonomous system

21. Stub areas:
   - *Stub area*—Contains only one exit point (via the ABR to area 0), all intra-area routes, summary routes to other areas, and a default route.
   - *Totally stubby area*—Contains only one exit point (via the ABR to area 0), all intra-area routes, and a default route. It contains no external routes or summary routes.
   - All routers in stub or totally stubby area must agree that the area is a stub.

CCNP™
Routing

Eric McMasters
Brian Morgan
Mike Shroyer

CCNP™ Routing Exam Cram

Limits of Liability and Disclaimer of Warranty

The author and publisher of this book have used their best efforts in preparing the book and the programs contained in it. These efforts include the development, research, and testing of the theories and programs to determine their effectiveness. The author and publisher make no warranty of any kind, expressed or implied, with regard to these programs or the documentation contained in this book.

The author and publisher shall not be liable in the event of incidental or consequential damages in connection with, or arising out of, the furnishing, performance, or use of the programs, associated instructions, and/or claims of productivity gains.

Trademarks

Trademarked names appear throughout this book. Rather than list the names and entities that own the trademarks or insert a trademark symbol with each mention of the trademarked name, the publisher states that it is using the names for editorial purposes only and to the benefit of the trademark owner, with no intention of infringing upon that trademark.

The Coriolis Group, LLC
14455 N. Hayden Road
Suite 220
Scottsdale, Arizona 85260

(480)483-0192
FAX (480)483-0193
www.coriolis.com

Library of Congress Cataloging-in-Publication Data
McMasters, Eric.
    CCNP routing exam cram / by Eric McMasters, Brian Morgan, and Mike Shroyer.
        p. cm.
    Includes index.
    ISBN 1-57610-633-0
    1. Electronic data processing personnel--Certification.
2. Telecommunication--Switching systems--Examinations--Study guides.   I. Morgan, Brian (Brian Edward).   II. Shroyer, Mike.   III. Title.

QA76.3. M3262   2000
004.6'2--dc21
                                                    00-043139
                                                        CIP

Printed in the United States of America
10 9 8 7 6 5 4 3 2 1

President and CEO
Keith Weiskamp

Publisher
Steve Sayre

Acquisitions Editor
Shari Jo Hehr

Marketing Specialist
Cynthia Caldwell

Project Editor
Karen Swartz

Technical Reviewer
Brian Morgan

Production Coordinator
Wendy Littley

Cover Designer
Jesse Dunn

Layout Designer
April Nielsen

The Coriolis Group, LLC • 14455 North Hayden Road, Suite 220 • Scottsdale, Arizona 85260

ExamCram.com Connects You to the Ultimate Study Center!

Our goal has always been to provide you with the best study tools on the planet to help you achieve your certification in record time. Time is so valuable these days that none of us can afford to waste a second of it, especially when it comes to exam preparation.

Over the past few years, we've created an extensive line of *Exam Cram* and *Exam Prep* study guides, practice exams, and interactive training. To help you study even better, we have now created an e-learning and certification destination called **ExamCram.com**. (You can access the site at **www.examcram.com**.) Now, with every study product you purchase from us, you'll be connected to a large community of people like yourself who are actively studying for their certifications, developing their careers, seeking advice, and sharing their insights and stories.

I believe that the future is all about collaborative learning. Our **ExamCram.com** destination is our approach to creating a highly interactive, easily accessible collaborative environment, where you can take practice exams and discuss your experiences with others, sign up for features like "Questions of the Day," plan your certifications using our interactive planners, create your own personal study pages, and keep up with all of the latest study tips and techniques.

I hope that whatever study products you purchase from us—*Exam Cram* or *Exam Prep* study guides, *Personal Trainers*, *Personal Test Centers*, or one of our interactive Web courses—will make your studying fun and productive. Our commitment is to build the kind of learning tools that will allow you to study the way you want to, whenever you want to.

Help us continue to provide the very best certification study materials possible. Write us or email us at learn@examcram.com and let us know how our study products have helped you study. Tell us about new features that you'd like us to add. Send us a story about how we've helped you. We're listening!

Visit ExamCram.com now to enhance your study program.

Good luck with your certification exam and your career. Thank you for allowing us to help you achieve your goals.

Keith Weiskamp
President and CEO

Look for these other products from The Coriolis Group:

CCNP Remote Access Exam Cram
By Craig Dennis and Eric Quinn

CCNP Remote Access Exam Prep
By Barry Meinster

CCNP Routing Exam Prep
By Bob Larson, Corwin Low, and Paulden Rodriguez

CCNP Support Exam Cram
By Matthew Luallen

CCNP Support Exam Prep
By Gina Galbraith and Sean Odom

CCNP Switching Exam Cram
By Richard Deal

CCNP Switching Exam Prep
By Sean Odom and Doug Hammond

This book is dedicated to my wife Sally and my son Shane, who was born while working on this book. Their love and patience has given me the insight to life's true goals and rewards.
—Eric McMasters

ҙ

This book is dedicated to my wife Beth and my daughters Emma and Amanda for their patience in putting up with me during its production. Also included in this dedication is Michelle Smith. Her willingness to give a kid a chance so long ago made this possible.
—Brian Morgan

ҙ

This book is dedicated to my wife Dianne, whose love and support makes all things possible.
—Mike Shroyer

ҙ

About the Authors

Eric McMasters is a Cisco Certified Network Professional (CCNP) and a Cisco Certified Design Professional (CCDP) working for Sprint PCS as a Senior Network Systems Engineer in Lenexa, Kansas. Eric has been involved in communications over the past ten years and has spent the last four years working in the network field, focusing on Cisco products and solutions.

Prior to working for Sprint PCS, Eric spent nine years in the U.S. Air Force as a Communications Control System Technician working with various communications systems. His first six years were spent dealing with mobile communications and setting up mobile/deployable communications networks utilizing various satellite and wide-band technologies. Eric's last three years in the Air Force were spent working with multiple networking technologies, which was his first introduction to Cisco equipment. During this time Eric achieved his Cisco Certified Network Associate (CCNA) and Cisco Certified Design Associate (CCDA) certifications. During his nine years in the Air Force, Eric was stationed around the world, including England, South Korea, Panama, and Saudi Arabia.

Currently Eric is working on varying projects within Sprint PCS to ensure that new product releases are supported on the production network. Eric is also an active member of an Internet Cisco studygroup, located at **www.groupstudy.com**.

Eric is married to Sally and is the proud father of a new three-month-old baby boy. Eric and his family currently reside in Overland Park, Kansas.

Brian Morgan is a CCIE (#4865) as well as a CCSI for Chesapeake Network Solutions. He has been instructing for nearly four years and in the networking industry for over ten years. During that time he has taught Cisco Dial Access Solutions boot camp classes for the internal Service Provider Tiger Teams. The classes he teaches for Chesapeake are ICRC, ACRC, ICND, BSCN, CVOICE, and CATM.

Prior to teaching, Brian spent a number of years with IBM in Network Services, where he attained MCNE, ECNE, and MCSE certifications. He was involved with a number of larger LAN/WAN installations for many of IBM's Fortune 500 companies.

Brian is the proud father of five-year-old fraternal twin girls (Emma and Amanda) and husband to Beth. His greatest hobby is spending time with the family.

Mike Shroyer is President of J.M. Shroyer Associates, Inc. (JMSAI), a 20-year old, Denver-based data communications consulting company. He has over 35 years experience at all levels in the computer field. Mike is a Cisco Certified Internet Expert (CCIE #2280) and Certified Computer Professional (CCP). As a Certified Cisco Systems Instructor (CCSI), Mike has worked as a contract instructor for Geo Train, Inc. and its predecessor, Protocol Interface, Inc. for over five years. Among the Cisco courses he has taught are Introduction to Cisco Router Configuration (ICRC), Advanced Cisco Router Configuration (ACRC), Cisco Campus ATM (CATM), Cisco Internetwork Design (CID), and Introduction to Cisco Works Configuration (ICWC).

Mike has lectured and consulted extensively in the United Sates, Europe, and Asia on Internetworking, SNA, network security and audit of data networks, Unix, C language programming, and other technical topics. In addition to his consulting practice, Mike has taught for the University of Denver in its Masters in Computer Science program for Metropolitan State College.

Mike is married to Dianne and lives in Denver, Colorado.

Acknowledgments

First of all I would like to thank Brian Morgan and Mike Shroyer for all their hard work on *CCNP Advanced Cisco Router Configuration Exam Cram*, which set the groundwork for this book. Their work and perseverance have made my job during this revision much more enjoyable. Second, I would like to thank Jeff Kellum, who invited me to participate in the project and got me started on the right track. I would also like to thank the production team, who kept me headed in the right direction, even though I wanted to stray once in awhile. Many thanks to Brian Morgan, who offered his time and knowledge to assist me in various areas of this edition and provided excellent feedback as the technical editor. Your help was appreciated more than you can imagine.

I would like to thank everyone at Coriolis who worked on this project: Karen Akins Swartz, Project Editor; Bart Reed, Copy Editor; and Wendy Littley, Production Coordinator. This project would never have succeeded without them, and they deserve more credit than anyone. I would like to express my appreciation to Jesse Dunn for the cover design and April Nielsen for the layout design, as well as those involved in marketing this book. These guys are the best people that anyone could ever ask to work with.

Finally, I would like to thank two people from my prior life in the Air Force who had a great deal of influence on my technical development. David Bright was a coworker who, like myself, was just learning the ropes, but his ambition to learn everything that he could motivate me to do the same. Our many experiments on the production network were a great learning tool (don't do this on your production network), and provided me the confidence that I needed. Mike Cohen is a prodigy who had a photographic memory and knew how to implement his ideas with the best of him. Without Mike, I would never have started reading all of the networking books that I have. He also motivated me to start pursuing the Cisco certifications and provided good advice on many of my ideas. To both of you—I thank you, and my family thanks you.

—*Eric McMasters*

I would like to thank Eric McMasters for his work on this book and Mike Shroyer for putting in some long hours in writing as a co-author of *CCNP Advanced Cisco Router Configuration Exam Cram*. Special thanks to GeoTrain Corporation (especially Guy, Marty and Dolores) for their on-going support of me and my professional development. Thanks to Bill Wagner for providing a sounding board for my frustrations and ideas. He is and has been a good friend to my family and me. A great deal of work went into this book from its writing, to its final production. I want to say thanks to the Coriolis team of editors and production personnel.

—*Brian Morgan*

First and foremost, I want to thank Brian Morgan and Eric McMasters. I also want to thank the many people who have helped along the way by carrying on intense discussions, answering difficult questions, and contributing great ideas for this book.

I wish to thank our Coriolis editors and the rest of the team at The Coriolis Group, including Keith Weiskamp, for publishing our book.

—*Mike Shroyer*

Contents at a Glance

Table of Contents

Introduction

Welcome to *CCNP Routing Exam Cram*! This book aims to help you get ready to take—and pass—the Cisco career certification test 640-503, "Routing 2.0". This Introduction explains Cisco's certification programs in general and talks about how the *Exam Cram* series can help you prepare for Cisco's career certification exams.

Exam Cram books help you understand and appreciate the subjects and materials you need to pass Cisco career certification exams. *Exam Crams* are aimed strictly at test preparation and review. They do not teach you everything you need to know about a topic (such as the ins and outs of managing a Cisco router implementation). Instead, we (the authors) present and dissect the questions and problems we've found that you're likely to encounter on a test. We've worked from Cisco's own training materials, preparation guides, and tests, and from a battery of third-party test preparation tools. Our aim is to bring together as much information as possible about Cisco certification exams.

Nevertheless, to completely prepare yourself for any Cisco test, we recommend that you begin your studies with some instructor-led classroom training. You should also pick up and read one of the many study guides available from Cisco or third-party vendors, including The Coriolis Group's *Exam Prep* series. We also strongly recommend that you install, configure, and fool around with the Internetwork Operating System (IOS) software or environment that you'll be tested on, because nothing beats hands-on experience and familiarity when it comes to understanding the questions you're likely to encounter on a certification test. Book learning is essential, but hands-on experience is the best teacher of all!

The Cisco Career Certification Program

The Cisco Career Certifications program is relatively new on the internetworking scene. The best place to keep tabs on it is the Cisco Training Web site, at **www.cisco.com/training/**. Before Cisco developed this program, Cisco Certified Internetwork Expert (CCIE) certification was the only available Cisco certification. Although CCIE certification is still the most coveted and prestigious certification that Cisco offers (possibly the most prestigious in the internetworking industry), lower-level certifications are now available as stepping stones on the

Table 1 Cisco Routing and Switching CCNA, CCNP, and CCIE Requirements

CCNA

Only 1 exam required	
Exam 640-507	Cisco Certified Network Associate 2.0

CCNP*

All 4 exams are required	
Exam 640-503	Routing 2.0
Exam 640-504	Switching 2.0
Exam 640-505	Remote Access 2.0
Exam 640-506	Support 2.0

* You need to have your CCNA before you become a CCNP.

CCIE

1 written exam and 1 lab exam required	
Exam 350-001	CCIE Routing and Switching Qualification
Lab Exam	CCIE Routing and Switching Laboratory

road to the CCIE. The Cisco Career Certifications program includes several certifications in addition to the CCIE, each with its own acronym (see Table 1). If you're a fan of alphabet soup after your name, you'll like this program:

Note: Within the certification program, there are specific specializations. For the purposes of this book, we will focus only on the Routing and Switching track. Visit www.cisco.com/warp/public/10/wwtraining/certprog/index.html for information on the other specializations.

➤ *Cisco Certified Design Associate (CCDA)*—The CCDA is a basic certification aimed at designers of high-level internetworks. The CCDA consists of a single exam (640-441) that covers information from the Designing Cisco Networks (DCN) course. You must obtain CCDA and CCNA certifications before you can move up to the CCDP certification.

➤ *Cisco Certified Network Associate (CCNA)*—The CCNA is the first career certification. It consists of a single exam (640-507) that covers information from the basic-level class, primarily Interconnecting Cisco Network Devices (ICND). You must obtain CCNA certification before you can get your CCNP and CCDP certifications.

➤ *Cisco Certified Network Professional (CCNP)*—The CCNP is a more advanced certification that is not easy to obtain. To earn CCNP status, you must be a CCNA in good standing. There are two routes you can take to obtain your CCNP. For the first route, you must take four exams: Routing (640-503), Switching (640-504),

Remote Access (640-505), and Support (640-506). For the second route, you must take the Foundation (640-509) and Support (640-506) exams.

Although it may seem more appealing on the surface, the second route is more difficult. The Foundation exam contains more than 130 questions and lasts almost 3 hours. In addition, it covers all the topics covered in the Routing, Switching, and Remote Access exams.

Whichever route you choose, there are four courses Cisco recommends that you take:

➤ *Building Scalable Cisco Networks (BSCN)*—This course corresponds to the CCNP Routing exam.

➤ *Building Cisco Multilayer Switched Networks (BCMSN)*—This course corresponds to the CCNP Switching exam.

➤ *Building Cisco Remote Access Networks (BCRAN)*—This course corresponds to the CCNP Remote Access exam.

➤ *Cisco Internetworking Troubleshooting (CIT)*—This course corresponds to the CCNP Support exam.

Once you have completed the CCNP certification, you can further your career (not to mention beef up your resume) by branching out and passing one of the CCNP specialization exams. These include:

➤ *Security*—Requires you to pass the Managing Cisco Network Security exam (640-422).

➤ *LAN ATM*—Requires you to pass the Cisco Campus ATM Solutions exam (640-446).

➤ *Voice Access*—Requires you to pass the Cisco Voice over Frame Relay, ATM, and IP exam (640-447).

➤ *SNA/IP Integration*—Requires you to pass the SNA Configuration for Multiprotocol Administrators (640-445) and the SNA Foundation (640-456) exams.

➤ *Network Management*—Requires you to pass either the Managing Cisco Routed Internetworks (MCRI [640-443]) or the Managing Cisco Switched Internetworks (MCSI [640-444])) exam.

➤ *Cisco Certified Design Professional (CCDP)*—The CCDP is another advanced certification. It's aimed at high-level internetwork designers who must understand the intricate facets of putting together a well-laid-out network. The first step in the certification process is to obtain the CCDA and CCNA certifications (yes, both). As with the CCNP, you must pass the Foundation exam or pass the Routing, Switching, and Remote Access exams individually. Once you meet those objectives, you must pass the Cisco Internetwork Design exam (640-025) to complete the certification.

➤ *Cisco Certified Internetwork Expert (CCIE)*—The CCIE is possibly the most influential certification in the internetworking industry today. It is famous (or infamous) for its difficulty and for how easily it holds its seekers at bay. The certification requires only one written exam (350-001); passing that exam qualifies you to schedule time at a Cisco campus to demonstrate your knowledge in a two-day practical laboratory setting. You must pass the lab with a score of at least 80 percent to become a CCIE. Recent statistics have put the passing rates at roughly 20 percent for first attempts and 35 to 50 percent overall. Once you achieve CCIE certification, you must recertify every two years by passing a written exam administered by Cisco.

➤ *Certified Cisco Systems Instructor (CCSI)*—To obtain status as a CCSI, you must be employed (either permanently or by contract) by a Cisco Training Partner in good standing, such as the Mentor Technologies (formerly Chesapeake Network Solutions). That training partner must sponsor you through Cisco's Instructor Certification Program, and you must pass the two-day program that Cisco administers at a Cisco campus. You can build on CCSI certification on a class-by-class basis. Instructors must demonstrate competency with each class they are to teach by completing the written exam that goes with each class. Cisco also requires that instructors maintain a high customer satisfaction rating, or they will face decertification.

Taking a Certification Exam

Alas, testing is not free. Each computer-based exam costs between $100 and $200, and the CCIE laboratory exam costs $1,000. If you do not pass, you must pay the testing fee each time you retake the test. In the United States and Canada, computerized tests are administered by Prometric. Prometric can be reached at (800) 755-3926 or (800) 204-EXAM, any time from 7:00 A.M. to 6:00 P.M., Central Time, Monday through Friday. You can also try (612) 896-7000 or (612) 820-5707. CCIE laboratory exams are administered by Cisco Systems and can be scheduled by calling the CCIE lab exam administrator for the appropriate location.

To schedule a computer-based exam, call at least one day in advance. To cancel or reschedule an exam, you must call at least 24 hours before the scheduled test time (or you may be charged regardless). When calling Prometric, have the following information ready for the telesales staffer who handles your call:

➤ Your name, organization, and mailing address.

➤ Your Cisco Test ID. (For most U.S. citizens, this is your Social Security number. Citizens of other nations can use their taxpayer IDs or make other arrangements with the order taker.)

➤ The name and number of the exam you wish to take. For this book, the exam name is "Routing 2.0," and the exam number is 640-503.

➤ A method of payment. The most convenient approach is to supply a valid credit card number with sufficient available credit. Otherwise, Prometric must receive check, money order, or purchase order payments before you can schedule a test. (If you're not paying by credit card, ask your order taker for more details.)

When you show up to take a test, try to arrive at least 15 minutes before the scheduled time slot. You must supply two forms of identification, one of which must be a photo ID.

All exams are completely closed book. In fact, you will not be permitted to take anything with you into the testing area. However, you are furnished with a blank sheet of paper and a pen. We suggest that you immediately write down on that sheet of paper all the information you've memorized for the test. Although the amount of time you have to actually take the exam is limited, the time period does not start until you're ready, so you can spend as much time as necessary writing notes on the provided paper. If you think you will need more paper than what is provided, ask the test center administrator before entering the exam room. You must return all pages prior to exiting the testing center.

In *Exam Cram* books, the information that we suggest you write down appears on the Cram Sheet inside the front cover of each book. You will have some time to compose yourself, to record this information, and even to take a sample orientation exam before you begin the real thing. We suggest you take the orientation test before taking your first exam, but because they're all more or less identical in layout, behavior, and controls, you probably won't need to do this more than once.

When you complete a Cisco certification exam, the software will tell you whether you've passed or failed. All tests are scored on a basis of 100 percent, and results are broken into several topic areas. Even if you fail, we suggest you ask for—and keep—the detailed report that the test administrator should print for you. You can use this report to help you prepare for another go-round, if needed. Once you see your score, you have the option of printing additional copies of the score report. It is a good idea to have it print twice.

If you need to retake an exam, you'll have to call Prometric, schedule a new test date, and pay another testing fee. The first time you fail a test, you can retake the test the next day. However, if you fail a second time, you must wait 14 days before retaking that test. The 14-day waiting period is in effect for all tests after the failure.

Tracking Cisco Certification Status

As soon as you pass any Cisco exam (congratulations!), you must complete a certification agreement. You can do so online at the Certification Tracking Web site (**www.galton.com/~cisco/**), or you can mail a hard copy of the agreement to Cisco's certification authority. You will not be certified until you complete a certification agreement and Cisco receives it in one of these forms.

The Certification Tracking Web site also allows you to view your certification information. Cisco will contact you via email and explain it and its use. Once you are registered into one of the career certification tracks, you will be given a login on this site, which is administered by Galton, a third-party company that has no in-depth affiliation with Cisco or its products. Galton's information comes directly from Prometric, the exam-administration company for much of the computing industry.

Once you pass the necessary exam(s) for a particular certification and complete the certification agreement, you'll be certified. Official certification normally takes anywhere from four to six weeks, so don't expect to get your credentials overnight. When the package arrives, it will include a Welcome Kit that contains a number of elements, including:

➤ A Cisco certificate, suitable for framing, stating that you have completed the certification requirements, along with a laminated Cisco Career Certifications identification card with your certification number on it

➤ Promotional items, which vary based on the certification

Many people believe that the benefits of the Cisco career certifications go well beyond the perks that Cisco provides to newly anointed members of this elite group. There seem to be more and more job listings that request or require applicants to have a CCNA, CCDA, CCNP, CCDP, and so on, and many individuals who complete the program can qualify for increases in pay or responsibility. In fact, Cisco has started to implement requirements for its Value Added Resellers: To attain and keep silver, gold, or higher status, they must maintain a certain number of CCNA, CCDA, CCNP, CCDP, and CCIE employees on staff. There's a very high demand and low supply of Cisco talent in the industry overall. As an official recognition of hard work and broad knowledge, a Cisco career certification credential is a badge of honor in many IT organizations.

How to Prepare for an Exam

Preparing for any Cisco test (including Routing 2.0) requires that you obtain and study materials designed to provide comprehensive information about Cisco router operation and the specific exam for which you are preparing. The following list of materials will help you study and prepare:

➤ *Instructor-led training*—There's no substitute for expert instruction and hands-on practice under professional supervision. Cisco Training Partners, such as Mentor Technologies, offer instructor-led training courses for all of the Cisco career certification requirements. These companies aim to help prepare network administrators to run Cisco routed and switched internetworks and pass the Cisco tests. Although such training runs upwards of $350 per day in class, most of the individuals lucky enough to partake find them to be quite worthwhile.

➤ *Cisco Connection Online*—This is the name of Cisco's Web site (**www.cisco.com**), the most current and up-to-date source of Cisco information.

➤ *The CCPrep Web site*—This is the most well-known Cisco certification Web site in the world. You can find it at **www.ccprep.com** (formerly known as **www.CCIEprep.com**). Here, you can find exam preparation materials, practice tests, self-assessment exams, and numerous certification questions and scenarios. In addition, professional staff is available to answer questions that you can post on the answer board.

➤ *Cisco training kits*—These are available only if you attend a Cisco class at a certified training facility, or if a Cisco Training Partner in good standing gives you one.

➤ *Study guides*—Several publishers—including Certification Insider Press—offer study guides. The Certification Insider Press series includes:

  ➤ *The* Exam Cram *series*—These books give you information about the material you need to know to pass the tests.

  ➤ *The* Exam Prep *series*—These books provide a greater level of detail than the *Exam Cram* books and are designed to teach you everything you need to know from an exam perspective.

Together, the two series make a perfect pair.

➤ *Multimedia*—These Coriolis Group materials are designed to support learners of all types—whether you learn best by reading or doing:

  ➤ *The* Exam Cram Personal Trainer—Offers a unique, personalized self-paced training course based on the exam.

➤ *The* Exam Cram Personal Test Center—Features multiple test options that simulate the actual exam, including Fixed-Length, Random, Review, and Test All. Explanations of correct and incorrect answers reinforce concepts learned.

➤ *Other publications*—You'll find direct references to other publications and resources in this text. There's no shortage of materials available about Cisco routers and their configuration. To help you sift through some of the publications out there, we end each chapter with a "Need to Know More?" section that provides pointers to more complete and exhaustive resources covering the chapter's information. This should give you an idea of where we think you should look for further discussion.

By far, this set of required and recommended materials represents an unparalleled collection of sources and resources for Cisco router configuration guidelines. We anticipate that you'll find that this book belongs in this company. In the next section, we explain how this book works, and give you some good reasons why this book counts as a member of the required and recommended materials list.

About this Book

Each topical *Exam Cram* chapter follows a regular structure, along with graphical cues about important or useful information. Here's the structure of a typical chapter:

➤ *Opening hotlists*—Each chapter begins with a list of the terms, tools, and techniques that you must learn and understand before you can be fully conversant with that chapter's subject matter. The hotlists are followed by one or two introductory paragraphs to set the stage for the rest of the chapter.

➤ *Topical coverage*—After the opening hotlists, each chapter covers a series of at least four topics related to the chapter's subject. Throughout this section, topics or concepts likely to appear on a test are highlighted using a special Exam Alert layout, like this:

 This is what an Exam Alert looks like. Normally, an Exam Alert stresses concepts, terms, software, or activities that are likely to relate to one or more certification test questions. For that reason, any information found offset in Exam Alert format is worthy of unusual attentiveness on your part. Indeed, most of the information that appears on the Cram Sheet appears as Exam Alerts within the text.

You'll find what appears in the meat of each chapter to be worth knowing, too, when preparing for the test. Because this book's material is very condensed, we recommend that you use this book along with other resources to achieve the maximum benefit.

In addition to the Exam Alerts, we have provided tips that will help build a better foundation for routing knowledge. Although the information may not be on the exam, it is certainly related and will help you become a better test taker.

This is how tips are formatted. Keep your eyes open for these, and you'll become a Cisco internetworking expert in no time!

➤ *Practice questions*—Although we talk about test questions and topics throughout the book, a section at the end of each chapter presents a series of mock test questions and explanations of both correct and incorrect answers. We also try to point out especially tricky questions by using a special icon, like this:

Ordinarily, this icon flags the presence of a particularly devious inquiry, if not an outright trick question. Trick questions are calculated to be answered incorrectly if not read more than once, and carefully, at that. Although they're not ubiquitous, such questions make regular appearances on the Cisco exams. That's why we say exam questions are as much about reading comprehension as they are about knowing your material inside out and backwards.

➤ *Details and resources*—Every chapter ends with a section titled "Need to Know More?" It provides direct pointers to Cisco and third-party resources offering more details on the chapter's subject. In addition, this section tries to rank or at least rate the quality and thoroughness of the topic's coverage by each resource. If you find a resource in this collection that you like, use it, but don't feel compelled to use all the resources. On the other hand, we recommend only resources we use regularly, so none of our recommendations will be a waste of your time or money (but purchasing them all at once probably represents an expense that many network administrators and would-be CCNPs might find hard to justify).

The bulk of the book follows this chapter structure slavishly, but there are a few other elements that we'd like to point out. Chapter 14 is a sample test that provides a good review of the material presented throughout the book to ensure you're ready for the exam. Chapter 15 is the answer key. In addition, you'll find a handy glossary and an index.

Finally, the tear-out Cram Sheet attached next to the inside front cover of this *Exam Cram* book represents a condensed and compiled collection of facts, figures, and tips that we think you should memorize before taking the test. Because you can dump this information out of your head onto a piece of paper before answering any exam questions, you can master this information by brute force—you need to remember it only long enough to write it down when you walk into the test room. You might even want to look at it in the car (not while driving) or in the lobby of the testing center just before you walk in to take the test.

How to Use this Book

If you're prepping for a first-time test, we've structured the topics in this book to build on one another. Therefore, some topics in later chapters make more sense after you've read earlier chapters. That's why we suggest you read this book from front to back for your initial test preparation. If you need to brush up on a topic or you have to bone up for a second try, use the index or table of contents to go straight to the topics and questions that you need to study. Beyond the tests, we think you'll find this book useful as a tightly focused reference to some of the most important aspects of routing.

Given all the book's elements and its specialized focus, we've tried to create a tool that will help you prepare for—and pass—Cisco Career Certification Exam 640-503, "Routing 2.0". Please share your feedback on the book with us, especially if you have ideas about how we can improve it for future test-takers. We'll consider everything you say carefully, and we'll respond to all suggestions.

Please send your questions or comments to us at **learn@examcram.com**. Please remember to include the title of the book in your message; otherwise, we'll be forced to guess which book you're writing about. Also, be sure to check out the Web pages at **www.examcram.com**, where you'll find information updates, commentary, and clarifications on documents for each book that you can either read online or download for use later on.

Thanks, and enjoy the book!

Self-Assessment

The reason we included a Self-Assessment in this *Exam Cram* is to help you evaluate your readiness to tackle CCNP certification. It should also help you understand what you need to master the topic of this book—namely, Exam 640-503, "Routing 2.0." But before you tackle this Self-Assessment, let's talk about concerns you may face when pursuing a CCNP, and what an ideal CCNP candidate might look like.

CCNPs in the Real World

In the next section, we describe an ideal CCNP candidate, knowing full well that only a few real candidates will meet this ideal. In fact, the description of that ideal candidate might seem downright scary. But take heart: Although the requirements to obtain a CCNP may seem pretty formidable, they are by no means impossible to meet. However, you should be keenly aware that it does take time and requires some expense and substantial effort to get through the process.

The first thing to understand is that the CCNP is an attainable goal. You can get all the real-world motivation you need from knowing that many others have gone before, so you will be able to follow in their footsteps. If you're willing to tackle the process seriously and do what it takes to obtain the necessary experience and knowledge, you can take—and pass—all the certification tests involved in obtaining an CCNP. In fact, we've designed these *Exam Crams*, *Exam Preps*, *Exam Cram Personal Trainers*, and *Exam Cram Personal Test Centers* to make it as easy on you as possible to prepare for these exams. But prepare you must!

The same, of course, is true for other Cisco career certifications, including:

➤ CCNA, which is the first step on the road to the CCNP certification. It is a single exam that covers information from Cisco's Interconnecting Cisco Network Devices (ICND) class. Cisco also had developed a class that was geared to CCNA certification, known as Cisco Routing and LAN Switching (CRLS; however, since ICND covers the necessary concepts, CRLS is no longer offered by most training partners.

➤ CCDA, which is the first step on the road to the CCDP certification. It is a single exam that covers the basics of design theory. To prepare for it, you should attend the Designing Cisco Networks (DCN) class and/or the Cisco Internetwork Design (CID) class. However, the CID material is covered on the CCDP Design Exam.

➤ CCDP, which is an advanced certification regarding internetwork design. It consists of multiple exams. There are two ways to go about attaining the CCDP. You could pass the individual exams for Routing, Switching, Remote Access, and Support. However, if you're not one for taking a lot of exams, you can take the Foundation Routing/Switching (FRS) exam and the Support exam. Either combination will complete the requirements.

➤ CCIE, which is commonly referred to as the "black belt" of internetworking. It is considered the single most difficult certification to attain in the internetworking industry. First you must take a written qualification exam. Once you pass the exam, the real fun begins. You will need to schedule a two-day practical lab exam to be held at a Cisco campus, where you will undergo a "trial by fire" of sorts. Your ability to configure, document, and troubleshoot Cisco equipment will be tested to its limits. Do not underestimate this lab exam.

The Ideal CCNP Candidate

Just to give you some idea of what an ideal CCNP candidate is like, here are some relevant statistics about the background and experience such an individual might have. Don't worry if you don't meet these qualifications, or don't come that close—this is a far from ideal world, and where you fall short is simply where you'll have more work to do.

➤ Academic or professional training in network theory, concepts, and operations. This includes everything from networking media and transmission techniques through network operating systems, services, and applications.

➤ Three-plus years of professional networking experience, including experience with Ethernet, token rings, modems, and other networking media. This must include installation, configuration, upgrade, and troubleshooting experience.

➤ Two-plus years in a networked environment that includes hands-on experience with Cisco routers, switches, and other related equipment. A solid understanding of each system's architecture, installation, configuration, maintenance, and troubleshooting is also essential.

➤ A thorough understanding of key networking protocols, addressing, and name resolution, including TCP/IP, IPX/SPX, and AppleTalk.

➤ Familiarity with key TCP/IP-based services, including ARP, BOOTP, DNS, FTP, SNMP, SMTP, Telnet, TFTP, and other relevant services for your internetwork deployment.

Fundamentally, this boils down to a bachelor's degree in computer science, plus three years of work experience in a technical position involving network design, installation, configuration, and maintenance. We believe that well under half of all certification candidates meet these requirements; in fact, most meet less than half of these requirements—at least, when they begin the certification process. But because thousands of people have survived this ordeal, you can survive it too—especially if you heed what our Self-Assessment can tell you about what you already know and what you need to learn.

Put Yourself to the Test

The following series of questions and observations is designed to help you figure out how much work you must do to pursue Cisco career certification and what kinds of resources you should consult on your quest. Be absolutely honest in your answers, or you'll end up wasting money on exams you're not yet ready to take. There are no right or wrong answers, only steps along the path to certification. Only you can decide where you really belong in the broad spectrum of aspiring candidates.

Two things should be clear from the outset, however:

➤ Even a modest background in computer science will be helpful.

➤ Extensive hands-on experience with Cisco products and technologies is an essential ingredient to certification success.

1. Have you ever taken any computer-related classes? [Yes or No]

   If Yes, proceed to question 2; if No, proceed to question 4.

2. Have you taken any classes included in Cisco's curriculum? [Yes or No]

   If Yes, you will probably be able to handle Cisco's architecture and system component discussions. If you're rusty, brush up on basic router operating system concepts, such as RAM, NVRAM, and flash memory. You'll also want to brush up on the basics of internetworking, especially IP subnetting and routing protocols.

   If No, consider some extensive reading in this area. We strongly recommend instructor-led training offered by a Cisco Training Partner. However, you may want to check out a good general advanced routing technology book, such as *Cisco CCIE Fundamentals: Network Design and Cast Studies* by Andrea Cheek, H. Kim Lew, and Kathleen Wallace (Cisco Press, Indianapolis, IN, 1998, ISBN: 1-57870-066-3). If this title doesn't appeal to you, check out reviews for other, similar titles at your favorite online bookstore.

3. Have you taken any networking concepts or technologies classes? [Yes or No]

If Yes, you will probably be able to handle Cisco's internetworking terminology, concepts, and technologies. If you're rusty, brush up on basic internetworking concepts and terminology, especially networking media, transmission types, the OSI Reference model, and routing technologies such as OSPF, EIGRP, and BGP.

If No, you might want to read one or two books in this topic area. Check out the "Need To Know More?" section at the end of each chapter for a selection of resources that will give you additional background on the topics covered in this book.

4. Have you done any reading on routing protocols (RIP, OSPF, EIGRP, BGP, etc.) and/or routed protocols (IP, IPX, AppleTalk, etc.)? [Yes or No]

If Yes, review the requirements stated in the first paragraphs after Questions 2 and 3. If you meet those requirements, move on to the next question.

If No, consult the recommended reading for both topics. A strong background will help you prepare for the Cisco exams better than just about anything else.

The most important key to success on all of the Cisco tests is hands-on experience with Cisco routers and related equipment. If we leave you with only one realization after taking this Self-Assessment, it should be that there's no substitute for time spent installing, configuring, and using the various Cisco products upon which you'll be tested repeatedly and in depth. It cannot be stressed enough that quality instructor-led training will benefit you greatly and give you additional hands-on configuration experience with the technologies upon which you are to be tested.

5. Have you installed, configured, and worked with Cisco routers? [Yes or No]

If Yes, make sure you understand basic concepts as covered in the classes Interconnecting Cisco Network Devices (ICND) and Building Scalable Cisco Networks (BSCN) before progressing into the materials covered here, because this book expands on the basic topics taught there.

 You can download an exam outline and other information about Cisco exams from the company's Training and Certification page on the Web at **www.cisco.com/training**.

If No, you will need to find a way to get a good amount of instruction on the intricacies of configuring Cisco equipment. You need a broad background to get through any of Cisco's career certification. You will also need to have hands-on experience with the equipment and technologies on which you'll be tested.

If you have the funds, or your employer will pay your way, consider taking a class at a Cisco Training Partner (preferably one with "distinguished" status for the highest quality possible). In addition to classroom exposure to the topic of your choice, you get a good view of the technologies being widely deployed and will be able to take part in hands-on lab scenarios with those technologies.

Before you even think about taking any Cisco exam, make sure you've spent enough time with the related software to understand how it may be installed and configured, how to maintain such an installation, and how to troubleshoot that software when things go wrong. This will help you in the exam, and in real life!

Whether you attend a formal class on a specific topic to get ready for an exam or use written materials to study on your own, some preparation for the Cisco career certification exams is essential. At $100 to $200 (depending on the exam) a try, pass or fail, you want to do everything you can to pass on your first try. That's where studying comes in.

6. Have you taken a practice exam on your chosen test subject? [Yes or No]

If Yes, and you scored 70 percent or better, you're probably ready to tackle the real thing. If your score isn't above that crucial threshold, keep at it until you break that barrier.

If No, obtain all the free and low-budget practice tests you can find and get to work. Keep at it until you can break the passing threshold comfortably.

We have included a practice exam in this book, so you can test yourself on the information and techniques you've learned. If you don't hit a score of at least 70 percent after this test, you'll want to investigate the other practice test resources we mention in this section. We also have exams that you can take online through the **ExamCram.com** Web site at **www.examcram.com**.

For any given subject, consider taking a class if you've tackled self-study materials, taken the test, and failed anyway. The opportunity to interact with an instructor and fellow students can make all the difference in the world, if you can afford that privilege. For information about Cisco classes, visit the Training and Certification page at **www.cisco.com/training** or **www.mentortech.com**.

If you can't afford to take a class, visit the Training and Certification page anyway, because it also includes pointers to additional resources and self-study tools. And even if you can't afford to spend much at all, you should still invest in some low-cost practice exams from commercial vendors, because they can help you assess your readiness to pass a test better than any other tool. The following Web sites offer some practice exams online:

➤ CCPrep.com at **www.ccprep.com** (requires membership)

➤ Network Study Guides at **www.networkstudyguides.com** (pay as you go)

When it comes to assessing your test readiness, there is no better way than to take a good-quality practice exam and pass with a score of 70 percent or better. When we're preparing ourselves, we shoot for 80-plus percent, just to leave room for the "weirdness factor" that sometimes shows up on Cisco exams.

Assessing Readiness for Exam 640-503

In addition to the general exam-readiness information in the previous section, there are several things you can do to prepare for the Routing 2.0 exam. You will find a great source of questions and related information at the CCprep Web site at **www.ccprep.com**. This is a good place to ask questions and get good answers, or simply to watch the questions that others ask (along with the answers, of course).

You should also cruise the Web looking for "braindumps" (recollections of test topics and experiences recorded by others) to help you anticipate topics you're likely to encounter on the test.

You can't be sure that a braindump's author will also be able to provide correct answers. Thus, use the questions to guide your studies, but don't rely on the answers in a braindump to lead you to the truth. Double-check everything you find in any braindump.

For Routing 2.0 preparation in particular, we'd also like to recommend that you check out one or more of these resources as you prepare to take Exam 640-503:

➤ Cisco Connection Online (CCO) Documentation (**www.cisco.com/univercd/home/home.htm**). From the CCO Documentation home page you can select a variety of topics, including but not limited to Router Configuration Tools and Cisco IOS Software Configuration, as well as Internetwork Technologies Overviews and Design Guides.

➤ Doyle, Jeff. CCIE Professional Development: *Routing TCP/IP, Volume 1,* Cisco Press, Indianapolis, IN, 1998. ISBN: 1-57870-041-8.

➤ Comer, Douglas. *Internetworking with TCP/IP, Volume 1: Principles, Protocols, and Architecture,* Prentice Hall, Englewood Cliffs, NJ, 1995. ISBN: 0-13-216987-8.

➤ Perlman, Radia. *Interconnections: Bridges and Routers,* Addison-Wesley, Reading, MA, 1992. ISBN: 0-201-56332-0.

➤ Oppenheimer, Priscilla. *Top Down Network Design,* Cisco Press, Indianapolis, IN, 1999. ISBN: 1-57870-069-8.

Stop by the Cisco home page, your favorite bookstore, or an online bookseller to check out one or more of these resources. We believe CCO Documentation provides a wealth of great material, the first two books are the best general all-around references on TCP/IP, and the final two books cover general routing and bridging conventions, as well as providing a broad coverage of network design issues.

One last note: Hopefully, it makes sense to stress the importance of hands-on experience in the context of the Routing exam. As you review the material for that exam, you'll realize that hands-on experience with the Cisco IOS with various technologies and configurations is invaluable.

Onward, through the Fog!

Once you've assessed your readiness, undertaken the right background studies, obtained the hands-on experience that will help you understand the products and technologies at work, and reviewed the many sources of information to help you prepare for a test, you'll be ready to take a round of practice tests. When your scores come back positive enough to get you through the exam, you're ready to go after the real thing. If you follow our assessment regime, you'll not only know what you need to study, but when you're ready to make a test date at Prometric. Good luck!

Cisco Certification Exams

Terms you'll need to understand:

✓ Radio button
✓ Checkbox
✓ Exhibit
✓ Multiple-choice question formats
✓ Careful reading
✓ Process of elimination

Techniques you'll need to master:

✓ Assessing your exam-readiness
✓ Preparing to take a certification exam
✓ Practicing (to make perfect)
✓ Making the best use of the testing software
✓ Budgeting your time
✓ Guessing (as a last resort)

Exam taking is not something that most people anticipate eagerly, no matter how well prepared they may be. In most cases, familiarity helps ameliorate test anxiety. In plain English, this means you probably will not be as nervous when you take your fourth or fifth Cisco certification exam, as you will be when you take your first one.

Whether it is your first exam or your tenth, understanding the details of exam taking (how much time to spend on questions, the environment you'll be in, and so on) and the exam software will help you concentrate on the material rather than on the setting. Likewise, mastering a few basic exam-taking skills should help you recognize—and perhaps even outfox—some of the tricks and gotchas you're bound to find in some of the exam questions.

This chapter, besides explaining the exam environment and software, describes some proven exam-taking strategies that you should be able to use to your advantage.

Assessing Exam-Readiness

Before you take any Cisco exam, I strongly recommend that you read through and take the Self-Assessment included with this book (it appears just before this chapter, in fact). This will help you compare your knowledge base to the requirements for obtaining a CCNP, and it will also help you identify parts of your background or experience that may be in need of improvement, enhancement, or further learning. If you get the right set of basics under your belt, obtaining Cisco certification will be that much easier.

Once you've gone through the Self-Assessment, you can remedy those topical areas where your background or experience may not measure up to an ideal certification candidate. But you can also tackle subject matter for individual tests at the same time, so you can continue making progress while you're catching up in some areas.

Once you've worked through an *Exam Cram*, have read the supplementary materials, and have taken the practice test at the end of the book, you'll have a pretty clear idea of when you should be ready to take the real exam. Although I strongly recommend that you keep practicing until your scores top the 75 percent mark, 80 percent would be a good goal to give yourself some margin for error in a real exam situation (where stress will play more of a role than when you practice). Once you hit that point, you should be ready to go. But if you get through the practice exam in this book without attaining that score, you should keep taking practice tests and studying the materials until you get there. You'll find more information about other practice test vendors in the Self-Assessment, along with even more pointers on how to study and prepare. But now, on to the exam itself!

The Exam Situation

When you arrive at the testing center where you scheduled your exam, you will need to sign in with an exam coordinator. He or she will ask you to show two forms of identification, one of which must be a photo ID. After you have signed in and your time slot arrives, you will be asked to deposit any books, bags, or other items you brought with you. Then, you will be escorted into a closed room. Typically, the room will be furnished with anywhere from one to half a dozen computers, and each workstation will be separated from the others by dividers designed to keep you from seeing what is happening on someone else's computer.

You will be furnished with a pen or pencil and a blank sheet of paper, or, in some cases, an erasable plastic sheet and an erasable felt-tip pen. You are allowed to write down any information you want on both sides of this sheet. Before the exam, you should memorize as much of the material that appears on The Cram Sheet (inside the front cover of this book) as you can so you can write that information on the blank sheet as soon as you are seated in front of the computer. You can refer to your rendition of The Cram Sheet anytime you like during the test, but you will have to surrender the sheet when you leave the room.

Most test rooms feature a wall with a large picture window. This permits the exam coordinator standing behind it to monitor the room, to prevent exam takers from talking to one another, and to observe anything out of the ordinary that might go on. The exam coordinator will have preloaded the appropriate Cisco certification exam—for this book, that's Exam 640-503—and you will be permitted to start as soon as you are seated in front of the computer.

All Cisco certification exams allow a certain maximum amount of time in which to complete your work (this time is indicated on the exam by an onscreen counter/ clock, so you can check the time remaining whenever you like). Exam 640-503 consists of between 60 to 70 randomly selected questions. You may take up to 75 minutes to complete the exam and need a score of about 69 percent to pass, although the passing score will vary slightly depending on which specific questions are generated for your particular exam.

All Cisco certification exams are computer generated and use a multiple-choice format. Although this may sound quite simple, the questions are constructed not only to check your mastery of basic facts and figures about Cisco router configuration, but they also require you to evaluate one or more sets of circumstances or requirements. Often, you will be asked to give more than one answer to a question. Likewise, you might be asked to select the best or most effective solution to a problem from a range of choices, all of which technically are correct. Taking the exam is quite an adventure, and it involves real thinking. This book shows you what to expect and how to deal with the potential problems, puzzles, and predicaments.

Exam Layout and Design

Some exam questions require you to select a single answer, whereas others ask you to select multiple correct answers, select the correct IOS command from a listing of command options, and drag and drop type questions. The following multiple-choice question requires you to select a single correct answer. Following the question is a brief summary of each potential answer and why it is either right or wrong.

Question 1

What is the key piece of information on which routing decisions are based?

○ a. Source network-layer address

○ b. Destination network-layer address

○ c. Source MAC address

○ d. Destination MAC address

Answer b is correct. The destination network layer (or layer 3) address is the protocol-specific address to which this piece of data is to be delivered. The source network-layer address is the originating host and plays no role in getting the information to the destination. Therefore, answer a is incorrect. The source and destination MAC addresses are necessary for getting the data to the router or the next hop address. However, they are not used in pathing decisions. Therefore, answers c and d are incorrect.

This sample question format corresponds closely to the Cisco certification exam format—the only difference on the exam is that questions are not followed by answer keys. To select an answer, position the cursor over the radio button next to the answer. Then, click the mouse button to select the answer.

Let's examine a question that requires choosing one or more answers. This type of question provides checkboxes rather than radio buttons for marking all appropriate selections.

Question 2

> Which routing protocols are based on standards? [Choose all that apply.]
>
> ❑ a. Open Shortest Path First (OSPF)
>
> ❑ b. Enhanced Interior Gateway Routing Protocol (EIGRP)
>
> ❑ c. Interior Gateway Routing Protocol (IGRP)
>
> ❑ d. Routing Information Protocol (RIP)
>
> ❑ e. Intermediate System to Intermediate System (IS-IS)

Answers a, d, and e are correct. OSPF, RIP, and IS-IS are all based on standards that have been established and supported by all vendors. Answers b and c are incorrect because they are Cisco proprietary protocols that are supported only by Cisco equipment.

For this type of question, more than one answer is required. Cisco does not give partial credit for partially correct answers when the test is scored. For Question 2, you have to check the boxes next to items a, d, and e to obtain credit for a correct answer. Notice that picking the right answers also means knowing why the other answers are wrong!

Although these two basic types of questions can appear in many forms, they constitute the foundation on which all the Cisco certification exam questions rest. More complex questions include so-called exhibits, which are usually network scenarios, screenshots of output from the router or even pictures from the course materials. For some of these questions, you will be asked to make a selection by clicking on a checkbox or radio button on the screenshot itself. For others, you will be expected to use the information displayed therein to guide your answer to the question. Familiarity with the underlying utility is your key to choosing the correct answer(s).

Other questions involving exhibits use charts or network diagrams to help document a workplace scenario that you will be asked to troubleshoot or configure. Careful attention to such exhibits is the key to success. Be prepared to toggle frequently between the exhibit and the question as you work.

Using Cisco's Exam Software Effectively

One principle applies when taking this exam: Get it right the first time. You cannot elect to skip a question and move on to the next one. The testing software forces you to go on to the next question, with no opportunity to skip ahead or turn back. If you encounter a question that you can't answer, you must guess an answer immediately. Not answering a question guarantees you won't receive credit for it, but a guess has at least a chance of being correct.

 You are better off guessing than leaving questions unanswered.

Exam-Taking Basics

The most important advice about taking any exam is this: Read each question carefully. Some questions are deliberately ambiguous, some use double negatives, and others use terminology in incredibly precise ways. The authors have taken numerous exams—both practice and live—and in nearly every one have missed at least one question because they did not read it closely or carefully enough.

Here are some suggestions on how to deal with the tendency to jump to an answer too quickly:

➤ Make sure you read every word in the question. If you find yourself jumping ahead impatiently, go back and start over.

➤ As you read, try to restate the question in your own terms. If you can do this, you should be able to pick the correct answer(s) much more easily.

Above all, try to deal with each question by thinking through what you know about Cisco routers and their configuration—the characteristics, behaviors, facts, and figures involved. By reviewing what you know (and what you have written down on your information sheet), you will often recall or understand things sufficiently to determine the answer to the question.

Question-Handling Strategies

Based on exams the authors have taken, some interesting trends have become apparent. For those questions that take only a single answer, usually two or three of the answers will be obviously incorrect, and two of the answers will be plausible—of course, only one can be correct. Unless the answer leaps out at you (if it does, reread the question to look for a trick; sometimes those are the ones you are most likely to get wrong), begin the process of answering by eliminating those answers that are most obviously wrong.

Things to look for in obviously wrong answers include spurious menu choices or utility names, nonexistent software options, and terminology you have never seen. If you have done your homework for an exam, no valid information should be completely new to you. In that case, unfamiliar or bizarre terminology probably indicates a totally bogus answer.

Numerous questions assume that the default behavior of a particular utility is in effect. If you know the defaults and understand what they mean, this knowledge will help you cut through many Gordian knots.

As you work your way through the exam, a counter that Cisco thankfully provides will come in handy—the number of questions completed and questions outstanding. Budget your time by making sure that you have completed one-quarter of the questions one-quarter of the way through the exam period.

If you are not finished when 70 minutes have elapsed, use the last 5 minutes to guess your way through the remaining questions. Remember, guessing is potentially more valuable than not answering, because blank answers are always wrong, but a guess may turn out to be right. If you do not have a clue about any of the remaining questions, pick answers at random, or choose all a's, b's, and so on. The important thing is to submit an exam for scoring that has an answer for every question.

Mastering the Inner Game

In the final analysis, knowledge breeds confidence, and confidence breeds success. If you study the materials in this book carefully and review all the practice questions at the end of each chapter, you should become aware of those areas where additional learning and study are required.

Next, follow up by reading some or all of the materials recommended in the "Need to Know More?" section at the end of each chapter. The idea is to become familiar enough with the concepts and situations you find in the sample questions that you can reason your way through similar situations on a real exam. If you know the material, you have every right to be confident that you can pass the exam.

After you have worked your way through the book, take the practice exam in Chapter 14. This will provide a reality check and help you identify areas you need to study further. Make sure you follow up and review materials related to the questions you miss on the practice exam before scheduling a real exam. Only when you have covered all the ground and feel comfortable with the whole scope of the practice exam should you take a real one.

TIP If you take the practice exam and do not score at least 75 percent correct, you will want to practice further.

Armed with the information in this book and with the determination to augment your knowledge, you should be able to pass the certification exam. However, you need to work at it; otherwise, you'll spend the exam fee more than once before you finally pass. If you prepare seriously, you should do well. Good luck!

Additional Resources

A good source of information about Cisco certification exams comes from Cisco itself. Because its products and technologies—and the exams that go with them— change frequently, the best place to go for exam-related information is online.

If you haven't already visited the Cisco Certified Professional site, do so right now. The Cisco Career Certifications home page (shown in Figure 1.1) resides at **www.cisco.com/warp/public/10/wwtraining/certprog/index.html**.

Note: This page might not be there by the time you read this, or it might have been replaced by something new and different, because things change regularly on the Cisco site. Should this happen, please read the sidebar titled "Coping with Change on the Web."

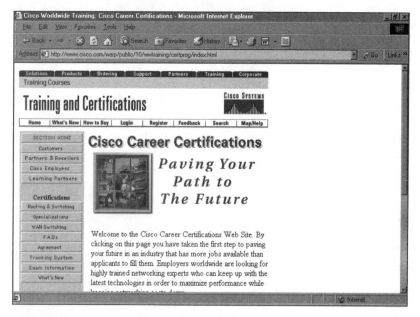

Figure 1.1   The Cisco Career Certifications home page.

The menu options in the left column of the home page point to the most important sources of information in the Career Certification pages. Here's what to check out:

➤ *Routing & Switching*—Use this entry to explore the CCIE certification track for routing and switching.

➤ *Specializations*—Use this entry to explore different CCNP specialization options.

➤ *WAN Switching*—Use this entry to explore the CCIE certification track for WAN Switching.

➤ *FAQs*—Use this entry to access the most commonly asked questions regarding any Cisco Career Certification.

➤ *Agreement*—Prior to certification, all candidates must complete the certification agreement or Cisco will not recognize them as certified professionals.

➤ *Tracking System*—Once you have registered with Sylvan Prometric, and taken any Cisco exam, you will automatically be added to a living certification tracking system so that you can keep up with your progress.

➤ *Exam Information*—This entry actually points to a class locator. It should be noted that no book is an adequate replacement for instructor-led, Cisco-authorized training. This entry will assist your efforts to find a class that meets your scheduling needs.

These are just the high points of what's available in the Cisco Certified Professional pages. As you browse through them—and we strongly recommend that you do—you will probably find other informational tidbits mentioned that are every bit as interesting and compelling.

Coping with Change on the Web

Sooner or later, all the information we have shared with you about the Cisco Certified Professional pages and the other Web-based resources mentioned throughout the rest of this book will go stale or be replaced by newer information. In some cases, the URLs you find here might lead you to their replacements; in other cases, the URLs will go nowhere, leaving you with the dreaded "404 File not found" error message. When that happens, do not give up.

There's always a way to find what you want on the Web if you are willing to invest some time and energy. Most large or complex Web sites—and Cisco's qualifies on both counts—offer a search engine. As long as you can get to Cisco's site (it should stay at **www.cisco.com** for a long while yet), you can use this tool to help you find what you need.

The more focused you can make a search request, the more likely the results will include information you can use. For example, you can search for the string "training and certification" to produce a lot of data about the subject in general, but if you are looking for the preparation guide for Exam 640-503, "Routing 2.0," you will be more likely to get there quickly if you use a search string similar to the following:

```
"Exam 640-503" AND "preparation guide"
```

Finally, feel free to use general search tools—such as **www.search.com**, **www.mamma.com**, **www.altavista.com**, and **www.excite.com**—to search for related information. The bottom line is this: If you can't find something where the book says it lives, start looking around. If worst comes to worst, you can always email us. We just might have a clue.

Internetwork Overview

Terms you'll need to understand:

✓ Scalable internetworks
✓ Hierarchical infrastructure
✓ Core router
✓ Distribution router
✓ Access router
✓ Hierarchical routing
✓ Traffic prioritization
✓ Route redundancy
✓ Network accessibility

Techniques you'll need to master:

✓ Designing scalable networks
✓ Creating a hierarchical structure
✓ Provisioning appropriate hardware
✓ Implementing route redundancy
✓ Creating an accessible, secure network

This chapter serves simply as an overview of the technologies that are covered in the remainder of the book. It addresses a number of topics that relate to the basic design of your internetwork. In doing so, some of the issues that arise in the design of any network are also addressed. The topics described in this chapter are discussed from a very high-level viewpoint. The goals of any network can fall into any or all of the guidelines discussed.

Routing Hierarchy

Any network design has goals, including deploying internetworking devices appropriately to create a logical structure for the internetwork. Cisco has developed routers and other devices that fulfill many of these goals. Figure 2.1, which serves as an example for the discussions throughout this chapter, shows a basic internetwork deployment.

Scalability

In order to be scalable, your network must meet the predefined objectives of its existence. For your network to work for you, you must first design it properly.

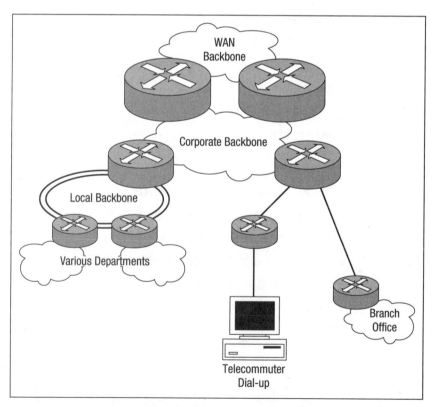

Figure 2.1 An example of a scalable network.

Before you can consider the design aspect you must define some roles that routers can play in your internetwork. A hierarchical design utilizes a distinct three-layer structure to provide complete functionality. Routers that are placed within these layers provide a unique functionality to an internetwork. The three layers of this concept are known as the *core, distribution,* and *access* layers. Referring to Figure 2.1, you can see the role each type of router plays in the network. The largest, most powerful devices exist at the highest level of the hierarchy.

The core routers carry the highest load of your internetwork traffic from site to site. The core routers are typically attached to the internetwork backbone and provide robust and redundant connectivity to other sites and networks. Appropriately, these devices are known as *core routers*.

The next level down in the hierarchy is comprised of somewhat powerful routers as well. These routers pass traffic to the core from the lower levels and back again. This means that these routers need to be capable of providing certain Quality of Service (QoS) functionality for protocols or services to optimize bandwidth utilization. This functionality identifies these devices as *distribution routers*.

At the lowest level of the hierarchy, the mission-specific routers are deployed—the routers that provide users with access to the internetwork infrastructure. They can provide users based in home offices with access to the network via dial-up services. These routers can also provide access from a satellite office to a larger centralized office network. These devices have been identified as *access routers*.

Each type of router has its appropriate place in the overall network. Obviously, an outage would have some effect at any level in the hierarchy. If a core router fails, significantly more users would be affected than if you lose an access router, but if proper fault tolerance measures are taken, these outages can be less severe.

You need to understand the different roles of the various routers in your internetwork. It is important for you to understand the position of core, distribution, and access routers, their individual responsibilities, and how they all work together.

Scalable Network Requirements

One of the key elements in designing an internetwork is defining what you want to get out of the network once it is complete. To be successful, a network should be:

➤ Reliable and available

➤ Responsive

➤ Efficient

➤ Adaptable

➤ Accessible

➤ Secure

Reliability and Availability

These two topics are mentioned together because they go hand in hand. If the network is not reliable, its availability could be compromised. Obviously, if a network is not available, it is not reliable.

What factors come to mind when you think about network reliability? The first answer is usually *redundancy*. If one piece of the network goes down, you would rather the end users not notice it. Providing redundancy requires additional hardware, multiple data pathways, software, or any number of other factors.

When you're planning any redundancy in the network, you should be careful not to create what is commonly known as a *single point of failure*—one device on which the operation of the entire network (or large portions thereof) depends. Should this single device fail in any way, a catastrophic outage would occur. You should plan carefully so that single points of failure do not exist.

Hardware Redundancy

Notice in Figure 2.1 that there's not simply one very large router functioning as the core router. Why not? What issues (a better word is *nightmares*) come to mind when you imagine a single router providing your core services? The core router is many times the most heavily loaded router, and the one you can least afford to lose. How do you avoid losing it?

One of your options is to ensure that the larger routers operate in the network by providing redundant hardware in the same chassis where possible. Many of the high-end routers, such as the 7500 and 12000 series routers, utilize dual power supplies. Other hardware options provide some level of additional protection from various failures that can occur within the device itself.

Another choice may be to implement multiple devices to do the job of the one. The purpose here is not to replace the single device, just to augment it. For instance, in Figure 2.1, you can see two core routers. Is it conceivable that one router could provide the core function? Yes, that is possible, depending on the nature of the network and the amount of traffic going across it. Implementing additional core routers—although not absolutely necessary to get the traffic across the network adequately—can provide peace of mind for the administrator. As far as the routers are concerned, the benefit of having two devices is a lower traffic load because much of the traffic has been distributed between them, thus increasing the network's functionality, reliability, and capacity, which will assist in meeting your customer's business and technical goals.

Route Redundancy

If the hardware is functioning properly but routing information is lost, the result is basically the same as the hardware failure: no data flow. Actually, the loss of routing information is many times more difficult to troubleshoot than hardware issues. With hardware issues, sometimes physical manifestations, good or bad, exist: red or amber light-emitting diodes (LEDs), Simple Network Management Protocol (SNMP) events, pops, sparks, smoke, or—in extreme cases—fires. Physical manifestations are quite straightforward (usually), whereas with routing inconsistencies, it's not so easy to find the causes.

A way to provide route redundancy is to run multiple dynamic routing protocols simultaneously. Obviously, doing so to some degree impacts the amount of system resources used; however, route redundancy is often a benefit in such scenarios. Should one protocol experience problems, such as lost routes, the other routing protocol may still be able to reach specific networks. Of course, that's the case only if the cause of the issue is not physical.

In the case of physical outages, it may be prudent to install multiple redundant pathways between points of extreme importance. Dynamic routing protocols automatically seek out equal-metric pathways to a particular destination and load-balance traffic across those pathways. Should one pathway fail, the other pathway is present to pick up the slack.

It's also a good idea to use a dynamic routing protocol that can intelligently adapt to routing changes. You may want to implement a protocol that allows you to create a hierarchical routing structure. Advanced routing protocols can minimize the impact of a topology change by localizing the impact and decreasing convergence time. By logically dividing the internetwork into separate areas, you can localize the routing change to one specific area. Convergence simply occurs within that area.

One implementation of redundancy in pathways is known as *dial backup*. Dial backup places into service a secondary pathway that's used only when the primary pathway is overloaded or down.

 You should know the basic information regarding hardware and route redundancy. You need to understand that convergence issues, routing loops, and lost reachability can occur. This means specific technologies (including dial backup) are available to deal with these losses.

Responsiveness

Responsiveness refers to how fast the network responds to topology changes, delivers requested resources, or provides any other function that it should. If the network can't perform these tasks promptly, it lacks responsiveness.

In some cases, the transport of multiple protocols can become an issue. The timing issues involved with protocols, such as IBM's System Network Architecture (SNA) protocol, can create the need for traffic prioritization. SNA does not tolerate delay well. Should congestion—or any other condition that causes additional delay—occur in the network, SNA could cease to function properly, which becomes a problem very quickly. Traffic prioritization allows the high-priority traffic to be processed before the lower-priority traffic types, thereby ensuring less delay through the network.

Queuing is a feature that will allow traffic to be reordered, allowing desirable, defined levels of traffic priority. Three forms of queuing are *weighted fair, priority,* and *custom* queuing.

Weighted fair queuing is on automatically for low-speed WAN links. This method provides equal access to all traffic across a WAN connection for all traffic by ensuring that high-bandwidth applications do not monopolize the network connection.

Priority queuing is where a certain type of traffic has been given high priority over all other types of traffic. This guarantees that the priority traffic will get processed, but other types of traffic may not be allowed to pass, which results in these types of traffic not arriving to their destination in a timely manner.

Custom queuing is where each type of traffic is allocated a certain percentage of the bandwidth across a connection. This allows applications that do not tolerate delay a larger piece of bandwidth, whereas other traffic that's not as sensitive to latency can be given a smaller allocation of bandwidth.

Efficiency

Efficiency is heavily intermeshed with responsiveness. If the network lacks responsiveness, efficiency is reduced. Efficiency can refer to bandwidth utilization, hardware deployment, or any number of other issues.

One way to make your network efficient is to implement access lists to filter traffic. Doing so keeps traffic from areas of the network where it is not wanted or needed. Access lists are meant to provide basic security, not to replace firewall implementations. If you have a Fiber Distributed Data Interface (FDDI) backbone in which no NetWare servers exist, you can use access lists to filter out unnecessary Service Advertising Protocol (SAP) broadcast traffic.

You can improve efficiency in many different ways. Using compression on slower-speed links allows you to increase the efficiency of your WAN links. However, you should take care not to overload the router. If the router's CPU utilization is already high, compression increases it, which could cause a failure. On higher-speed links, compression may actually slow down the transfer of data. There comes a point where it is faster to send the data than it would be to compress, send, and decompress it.

You can take advantage of snapshot routing to increase efficiency in dial-on-demand routing (DDR) situations, where routing updates are not desirable on Integrated Services Digital Network (ISDN) links. Snapshot routing was designed to freeze the routing tables on each side of the link when distance-vector protocols are in use. Snapshot routing stops the normal periodic updates of Routing Information Protocol (RIP) or Interior Gateway Routing Protocol (IGRP) and freezes the routing table for a number of hours (known as a *quiet period*). Once the quiet period expires, the routers exchange updates for a few minutes, and then they resume the quiet state.

You can make routing tables more efficient in several ways. *Route summarization*, for instance, reduces the overall size of the routing table. A smaller routing table means faster routing table lookups as well as lower memory and CPU utilization overall. Route summarization greatly increases the efficiency of the network's operations.

Adaptability

The network must be able to handle multiple protocols. In a multiprotocol environment, the network must be able to react to network topology changes quickly as well as to deal with the possibility of nonroutable protocols. *Nonroutable protocols* are those that do not contain a network-layer address. These protocols must be bridged or switched. Bridging protocols should not be taken lightly. Once layer 2 support has been enabled on the router, the router becomes a simple bridge. Unlike routers, bridges forward broadcasts by default.

Should you decide not to bridge the nonroutable protocols, you can deal with them in another way: by encapsulating nonroutable protocols inside Internet Protocol (IP) packets. Protocol encapsulation adds a significant amount of overhead. It is common to encapsulate NetBIOS and/or SNA or other layer 2 nonroutable protocols inside of IP so that those protocols may be transported across an internetwork.

Accessibility

The network should be accessible when needed. Whether your users are local or remote, you need to make some accommodations for them. If some of your users are remote or mobile users, you must consider some special issues.

How will they connect to the network? Will routers be placed at their homes for home office access? What technology will be used to allow connectivity to these users? If ISDN is to be used, you may need to implement DDR. If you are going to use some type of serial technology, such as High-Level Data Link Control (HDLC), you must make special provisions in the network to receive these remote users' data.

Will users be provided with mobile electronics such as laptops for access to the network? How many dial-up accounts will be necessary? What kind of dial-capable hardware will be put in place to accommodate these users? If many dial-up users will be using your network, you will need specific hardware to accomplish this somewhat large task.

Security

All the network issues discussed so far are extremely important. However, an intruder out to exploit your network can undo all of your security measures in a short time. It is unfortunate that some individuals make it their lifework to maliciously exploit network infrastructure. Without some security measures in place, the network is in danger.

Cisco has implemented many features that assist in meeting a customer's security needs for its network. The features that support network security are as follows:

➤ *Access lists*—Cisco does not promote access lists as a security measure but as an enhancement to make your network more secure.

➤ *Authentication protocols*—Password Authentication Protocol (PAP) and Challenge Handshake Authentication Protocol (CHAP) authenticate users before giving them access to the network.

➤ *Lock and key security*—This is a dynamic access list that when used in conjunction with TACACS+ server (Terminal Access Controller Access Control System) provides a central validation point for users to gain access to the network.

➤ *Network layer encryption*—This allows two peer routers to protect their network traffic by implementing the Diffie-Hellman encryption algorithm. The two routers create a key for encryption and decryption purposes across their particular connections.

Security can come in the form of a firewall placed between your network and the public data network. Firewall products are widely available and come in many implementations. There are many Unix and Windows NT software-based firewall solutions; some hardware-based firewall solutions, such as Cisco's PIX Firewall product, are also available. However, the topic of firewalls is beyond the scope of the Building Scalable Cisco Networks (BSCN) course and exam as well as this book.

Practice Questions

Question 1

What are the routers at the top of the internetwork hierarchy known as?

○ a. Core routers

○ b. Distribution routers

○ c. Access routers

○ d. None of the above

Answer a is correct. Core routers make up the very backbone of your internetwork and are generally the highest-horsepower routers in the internetwork. These routers are the cornerstones of your infrastructure. Answer b is incorrect because distribution routers provide a pathway between the lower-level routers and the core routers at the top. Answer c is incorrect because access routers actually provide the end-user network facilities. Answer d is incorrect because a correct answer is given.

Question 2

Which items are goals of the internetwork? [Choose the two best answers.]

❑ a. Accessibility

❑ b. Dial-on-demand routing

❑ c. Firewall implementation

❑ d. Efficiency

Answers a and d are correct. Accessibility and efficiency are a couple of small pieces in the overall big picture of internetwork design. Answer b is incorrect because DDR is not one of the goals; rather, it is an implementation of an internetwork goal. It is one method of making the network efficient. Answer c is incorrect because it is one method of making the network secure. Security is the goal, not just a firewall implementation.

Question 3

> Redundancy in the network is not a useful tool and should not be implemented.
>
> ○ a. True
>
> ○ b. False

Answer b is correct. Redundancy has become one of the most—if not *the* most—important aspects of network planning.

Question 4

> Which types of protocols determine the degree of adaptability needed for internetwork design and implementation? [Choose the two best answers.]
>
> ❑ a. Routing protocols
>
> ❑ b. Routable protocols
>
> ❑ c. Nonroutable protocols
>
> ❑ d. None of the above

Answers b and c are correct. Routable and nonroutable protocols that exist in your network require the network to be adaptable to handle both types. You must be able to deal with the various traffic types on your network. Answer a is incorrect because routing protocols provide path determination and reachability for routed protocols only. They do not necessarily have anything to do with the network's adaptability where multiple protocol types are concerned. Answer d is incorrect because a correct answer is given. The trick in this question lies in the fact that you may have not read all the answers adequately. If you find the basic word forms you're looking for, you'll usually pick the corresponding answer(s). Hopefully, you thoroughly read the answers and noticed that answer a (routing protocols) is incorrect and that answer b (routable protocols) is correct.

Question 5

> Where is compression best utilized?
>
> ○ a. Low-speed serial links
>
> ○ b. High-speed serial links
>
> ○ c. Ethernet interfaces
>
> ○ d. Token ring interfaces

Answer a is correct. Low-speed serial links are much easier to push into a congestion condition. Compression on these links provides additional overhead for the router but reduces the size of the data transmitted over the link. Answer b is incorrect because high-speed serial links can transmit traffic in less time than it takes to compress, send, and decompress the data. Answers c and d are incorrect because Ethernet and token ring interfaces are high-bandwidth interfaces that do not require the use of compression algorithms.

Need to Know More?

 Cheek, Andrea, Kim H. Lew, and Kathleen Wallace. *Cisco CCIE Fundamentals: Network Design and Cast Studies*. Cisco Press. Indianapolis, IN, 1998. ISBN 1-57870-066-3. Part I of this book deals with internetwork design concepts.

 Huitema, Christian. *Routing in the Internet*. Prentice Hall. Upper Saddle River, NJ, 1995. ISBN 0-13-132192-7. This book is a great resource for finding information regarding IP internetwork design and routing operations.

 Larson, Bob, Corwin Low, and Michael Simon. *CCNP Routing Exam Prep*. The Coriolis Group. Scottsdale, AZ, Fall 2000. ISBN 1-57610-778-2. This book an Exam Prep for the CCNP exam, that covers each related subject in great detail.

 Oppenheimer, Priscilla. *Top Down Network Design*. Cisco Press. Indianapolis, IN, 1999. ISBN 1-57870-069-8. This book describes hierarchical design and scalability issues, which will provide the reader with a full understanding of network design concepts.

 Visit Cisco's Web site at **www.cisco.com** and perform a search on any of the concepts discussed here (such as scalable internetworks and the core, distribution, and access layers).

Routing Protocol Overview

Terms you'll need to understand:

✓ Layer 3 forwarding (routing)

✓ Distance-vector routing protocol

✓ Link-state routing protocol

✓ Hybrid routing protocol

✓ Static routing

✓ Metric

✓ Administrative distance

Techniques you'll need to master:

✓ Configuring distance-vector protocols

✓ Configuring link-state protocols

✓ Configuring static routes

✓ Manipulating administrative distance

This chapter presents an overview of routing as a process. To make intelligent forwarding decisions, the router must list all the possible destination networks and metrics to reach those networks as well as decide through which interface to depart from to reach a specific destination network. This list is also known as the *routing table*. In this chapter, you'll look at how routers build routing tables by sharing information, focusing on the methods that routers use to share this routing information and how a packet makes its way through the router. You'll also look at all the details that must be in place for a router to make a proper decision.

Routing as a Process

Routing is routing is routing is routing. In other words, the router does not care what protocol happens to be moving across it. It treats all protocols basically the same. The routing process occurs at layer 3 (the network layer) of the Open Standards Interconnect (OSI) model. Figure 3.1 illustrates the OSI model and the names of the specific entity that exists at each layer. This is a networking book, so the OSI model has to show up somewhere, right? You are probably already familiar with it, so only a small amount of time will be spent explaining it.

The network layer's primary job is to determine the routing path. Data must go through the physical layer (layer 1) and the data link layer (layer 2) to get to the network layer.

At the physical layer, the transmission is simply binary ones and zeros. At the data link layer, the bit stream is interpreted by the network interface card (NIC) and constructed into a frame. Once the frame is constructed, a cyclic redundancy check (CRC) is performed. At that point, the device finds the destination Media Access Control (MAC) address, which is part of the frame header. If the device determines that the destination MAC address belongs to it, then it begins

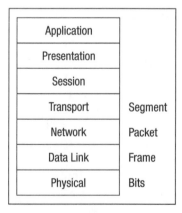

Figure 3.1 The OSI model.

processing the frame. To continue processing the frame, the frame must be passed to a higher layer (in this case the network layer). The data link framing is stripped away. The piece that's left is passed up to the network layer.

Once at the network layer, the device can look at the network specific protocol. At the network layer, this entity is known as a *packet*. The packet consists of, among other things, a destination address and source address.

The router examines the destination address and compares it to the entries in the routing table. The router is looking for the entry in the routing table that matches the most contiguous bits. For example, an Internet Protocol (IP) address is a 32-bit address. If an IP packet arrives with a destination IP address of 1.1.1.8, the router looks in the routing table for the longest (nearest) match. Table 3.1 shows an example of the routing table.

The packet with address 1.1.1.8 should be dispatched via interface Ethernet 0. In Table 3.1, all the entries partially match this packet. In other words, all the routing table entries match at least 16 bits of the destination address (2 octets). However, only the route via interface Ethernet 0 provides a longer match—24 bits are the same. This is the longest match, so it is deemed the dispatch interface. The packet is framed according to the encapsulation of the outbound interface (in this case, it is placed into an Ethernet frame) and dispatched.

Other routed protocols function in a similar fashion to the scenario just described. The longest match principle is discussed in more detail in Chapter 4. In the end, the routing process revolves around the network portion of the protocol address. If there is an entry in the routing table on which a forwarding decision can be based, the packets are forwarded accordingly. Should the router not find a match in the routing table, a "destination unreachable" message is returned to the source address.

The router must have a method of learning these routes, maintaining them, and keeping track of which routes are no longer valid. This is the function of the routing protocol. Routing protocols have evolved over recent years. Initial attempts at the creation of intelligent routing protocols have been greatly improved upon. Today there are a number of different protocols based on differing methodologies for route calculation.

Table 3.1 A sample routing table.

Destination Network	Interface Address	Outbound Interface
1.1.1.0	1.1.1.1	Ethernet 0
1.1.2.0	1.1.2.1	Ethernet 1
1.1.3.0	1.1.3.1	Ethernet 2
1.1.4.0	1.1.4.1	Ethernet 3

Routing Protocols

Now that you have an idea of how the router makes decisions, it is time to figure out how the router gets the information about each destination network in the first place. Routers learn routes through two methods: static routing and dynamic routing. Static routing is fairly straightforward and simple, whereas dynamic routing can be derived in a number of ways. This section covers the various ways the router can learn the necessary information.

Based on the method of calculating the best route for a given protocol, it stands to reason that one protocol may be more believable than another when it comes to the perception of what the best route should be. For example, would you trust a route based solely on hop count (with no regard for bandwidth, or lack thereof) over a route that does take aggregate bandwidth into account? For example, if a route from Network A to Network B is two hops away over a Frame Relay circuit but six hops away via another pathway consisting of Asynchronous Transfer Mode (ATM), which would you prefer? Which route would Routing Information Protocol (RIP) consider to be better? Which route would Open Shortest Path First (OSPF) consider to be better? It is a matter of perception in how the protocol calculates the overall route. The topic of metrics is covered in more detail later in this chapter.

Static Routing

Static routes are entries made in the routing table manually. A router administrator can use static routes to override any dynamic route(s) by configuring the destination network and specifying next hop or outbound interface information.

Static routes have a number of uses. Administrators can use them simply to override what a dynamic routing protocol may have placed into the table or to provide redundancy for dynamic routes. Static routes are commonly used in dial-on-demand routing (DDR) environments to keep dynamic routing updates from causing a dialer interface from staying active and wasting financial resources.

Use caution with static routes. Static routes, by default, have the distinction of being the most trusted routes the router can have in a routing table. A static route is believed over any other route that the router derives dynamically as long as the default administrative distance has not been altered. Although static routes are trusted routes, they do have their downfalls. The largest drawback is that they do not adapt to topology changes (that is, any changes in the network that affect the routing table entry). Administrators define static routes, so such routes are somewhat error prone. A single route can cause a significant routing loop or other unpredictable results.

Administrators should take care when implementing static routes in any form. The static route configuration should be entered at the global configuration prompt; it consists of the following command structure:

```
ip route <dest. network><dest. mask> <next hop | out interface>
```

The command includes information about the destination network and subnet mask associated with that destination network, as well as either the next hop address or the outbound interface through which to leave the router. Optionally, an administrative distance value can be specified after the next hop or outbound interface. If left unaltered, the administrative distance of a static route for which a next hop address is specified will be 1. If an outbound interface is specified, the administrative distance will be 0 and treated as a directly connected network.

Dynamic Routing

Dynamic routing protocols are those that have some mechanism of learning, maintaining, and monitoring route and routing table status. If the route to a specific network is lost, the protocol should be able to make intelligent decisions that allow it to route around the outage and then adapt again once the route to that network has returned. Obviously, redundancy will require significant planning in the initial stages of the network design. Redundancy is one of the most important issues that you may face in any internetwork design.

Dynamic routing protocols have evolved significantly since the creation of routable protocols. There are two well-known types of dynamic routing protocols and one type that is not quite as well known. The well-known types are the distance-vector and link-state routing protocols. The newer—and lesser known—type of dynamic routing protocol is the *advanced distance-vector* routing protocol.

Route Calculation

Routes are measured by metrics. The metric for different routing protocols varies according to the algorithm used to derive the route. Each routing protocol uses a different metric calculation to derive what it thinks is the best possible route to a specific destination. For example, RIP uses a hop count (that is, how many routers it must cross between source and destination hosts), OSPF uses cost based on bandwidth, and Enhanced Interior Gateway Routing Protocol (EIGRP) uses a composite metric comprised of bandwidth, delay, reliability, load, and maximum transmittable unit (MTU). Each protocol's calculation algorithm differs based on how, and why, it was created.

Distance-Vector Protocols

Distance-vector protocols were the first in the family of dynamic routing protocols. They function on the premise of metric addition. This algorithm is known as the *Bellman-Ford algorithm*.

Consider a ticket line in front of a theater. You are third in the line. What if you could not see the ticket window due to an obstruction such as a wall? Now, you know that you are third in the line only because the person ahead of you told you he is second in line. How does he know he is second in line? He knows only because the person ahead of him claims to be first. What is the ultimate destination? The destination is the ticket window. You can only know for certain that there is a person ahead of you and a person behind you. That's the principle behind distance-vector technology. A router knows its position in the network only because its neighbors told it their positions in the network. The function of this type of protocol is commonly referred to as *routing by rumor*.

Distance-vector protocols generally use periodic updates. A *periodic update* is one that's on a timed interval. Once the interval timer reaches zero, a routing update is broadcast out of every active interface, whether there have been changes or not. Because distance-vector protocols use these periodic timers, they tend to be slow to react to topological changes in the internetwork. To that end, convergence tends to be somewhat slow. In some cases, several of these protocols have implemented triggered updates to compensate for a loss of signal on the wire. The following is a list of various types of distance-vector routing protocols:

➤ IP Routing Information Protocol (IP RIP)

➤ IPX Routing Information Protocol (IPX RIP)

➤ Interior Gateway Routing Protocol (IGRP)

➤ AppleTalk Routing Table Management Protocol (RTMP)

Convergence is the process of distributing routing information throughout the network, giving all routers in the internetwork a common perspective of the topology. In other words, convergence is the process of disseminating, to every router, reachability information about every network in the internetwork. This process takes time, and the amount of time required depends on each protocol's attributes and abilities.

When a router first powers up, it performs a power-on self-test (POST) and figures out who it is. It then reads a configuration from nonvolatile RAM in order to find out how it should function on the network. Part of this information involves addressing on various interfaces. Based on those addresses, the router knows to which networks it is directly connected. Until it receives a routing update from a neighbor that's running a common routing protocol, it only knows the networks to which it is directly connected.

Once the distance-vector routing protocol has been initiated, it broadcasts all the information it knows (at this point, directly connected networks only) out of every active interface. It does not receive routing information until the neighbor routers' periodic timers expire. Once that occurs, the neighbor router(s) broadcast. Once this router receives the update(s), it alters its routing table accordingly. For the purposes of this discussion, RIP will be used as an example. RIP uses a hop count as the metric for determining the best pathway to a specific destination. The premise for any given destination is this: The fewer the number of routers it has to cross, the better the route should be to get there. Figure 3.2 shows this process from the view of the distance-vector protocol RIP.

Table 3.2 shows the initial routing table of each route. The routing table at this point consists of only the directly connected networks of each router and their interface designations.

Table 3.2	Initial routing tables.							
R1	Out Interface	Metric	R2	Out Interface	Metric	R3	Out Interface	Metric
10.1.0.0	E0	0	10.2.0.0	S1	0	10.4.0.0	E0	0
10.2.0.0	S0	0	10.3.0.0	S0	0	10.3.0.0	S1	0

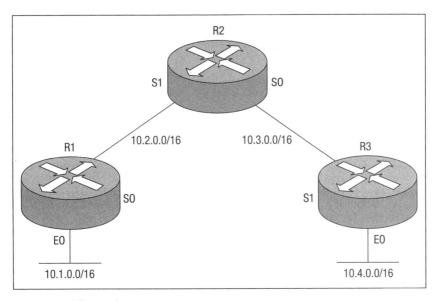

Figure 3.2 RIP operation.

As you can see, the information is limited at this point. Reachability consists only of what is directly connected to the router. Once routing updates begin to flow, the routing tables begin to converge. Table 3.3 shows each router's routing table after the first update has been received and processed. Notice that the directly connected information has not changed, but the new entries are added.

As you can see, the initial information was broadcast out of every interface. The process consisted of the expiration of the update timer, the broadcast of the update, and the processing of the update. You can also see that full convergence has not yet been reached. Also notice the metrics for each route. R1 has a new route to network 10.3.0.0 that it learned from R2 out of interface Serial 0. R2 advertised that it was zero hops from network 10.3.0.0. R1 must go through R2 to get to 10.3.0.0, so it added one hop to the metric advertised by R2 to arrive at its metric for this particular route. The process must repeat itself in order to reach convergence. Table 3.4 shows the routing table after the next update has been received and processed. Convergence has been accomplished because all routers know about all networks.

Again, the metrics reflect the fact that to get to a particular destination, each packet must traverse one additional hop.

It is apparent that the view of the internetwork from any router's perspective is the view of its neighbors. Distance-vector protocols tend to be slow to converge because they broadcast their entire routing table, which can utilize valuable bandwidth. Distance-vector protocols also tend to use less memory and CPU power

Table 3.3   Routing tables after one update.

R1	Out Interface	Metric	R2	Out Interface	Metric	R3	Out Interface	Metric
10.1.0.0	e0	0	10.2.0.0	s1	0	10.4.0.0	e0	0
10.2.0.0	s0	0	10.3.0.0	s0	0	10.3.0.0	s0	0
10.3.0.0	s0	1	10.1.0.0	s1	1	10.2.0.0	s0	1
			10.4.0.0	s0	1			

Table 3.4   Converged routing table.

R1	Out Interface	Metric	R2	Out Interface	Metric	R3	Out Interface	Metric
10.1.0.0	e0	0	10.2.0.0	s1	0	10.4.0.0	e0	0
10.2.0.0	s0	0	10.3.0.0	s0	0	10.3.0.0	s0	0
10.3.0.0	s0	1	10.1.0.0	s1	1	10.2.0.0	s0	1
10.4.0.0	s0	2	10.4.0.0	s0	1	10.1.0.0	s0	2

than their link-state counterparts. Although distance-vector protocols are less intelligent, they are less intensive than link-state protocols on system resources.

Based on what has been discussed to this point, it is easy to see what happens if a topological change occurs. Should network 10.1.0.0 disappear for some reason, the update would not be immediately apparent to R2 and R3. Changes are only sent out after three consecutive updates have been missed. It would take some time before R3 knew that network 10.1.0.0 had disappeared.

The routing updates themselves are broadcasts. When broadcasts go out, all nodes on the network are affected. It makes no difference to distance-vector protocols that an update may not be necessary (because nothing has changed in the network). Therefore, another consideration is unnecessary bandwidth utilization. It is a tradeoff. Do you want to use more system resources in the router, or do you want to use more bandwidth on the links between the routers?

Link-State Protocols

Link-state protocols were developed specifically to overcome the limitations of distance-vector protocols. Whereas distance-vector protocols simply broadcast updates out of each active interface when the update timer expires, link-state protocols send an update only when there is an update to send, and even then only the precise change goes out. Link-state protocols actually enter into a conversational state with their directly connected neighbors. This ongoing conversation consists of routing updates as well as paranoid updates, which occur usually every thirty minutes if there are no other routing changes. A *paranoid update* is simply one router asking its neighbors whether they are still there. The following is a list of link-state routing protocols:

➤ NetWare Link State Protocol (NLSP)

➤ Intermediate System to Intermediate System (IS-IS)

➤ Open Shortest Path First (OSPF)

Link-state protocols actually keep a map of the entire internetwork topology in the routing database. This map is a combination of a topological database and a Shortest Path First (SPF) tree derived from it. As you might expect, the map uses significant resources in the router.

Returning to the previous analogy, the movie-ticket line, suppose you can remove any obstructions in the way of your view of the destination (the ticket window). You can now see that you are third in the line because you see the entire line start to finish. You can see your position in the line as well as that of everyone else. You actually know the position of everyone in the line. You know who is 10th in line, and you know who is 35th in line. You know every aspect of the line. You can even see whether there is a shorter line that you could be in to speed your progress to the ticket window. Why do you know all this information? If you are a link-state protocol, you know it because each individual in line told you everything it knew about its position in the line and how it would get to the ticket window.

The algorithm that link-state routing protocols follow is known as the *Dijkstra algorithm.* This algorithm consists of the following steps:

1. Constructing a topological database
2. Running the SPF algorithm
3. Constructing an SPF tree diagram of the network
4. Constructing a routing table based on the tree

This process consumes quite a few resources. Each time a routing update arrives, the process starts over. If an interface in the internetwork is *bouncing* or *flapping* (such as changing back and forth from an up state to a down state), a large number of updates could cause an undue load on the resources of a large number of routers.

Refer back to Figure 3.2, the distance-vector example in which you saw where the routing tables evolved their way into convergence. A link-state protocol, in the same situation, would know almost instantly about all the networks in the example. Within a few seconds, the routing tables of all routers would resemble those shown earlier in Table 3.4.

When a new router comes up on the network, it begins to issue hello messages out of all active interfaces and awaits an answer. Once an answer is received, a conversation begins. This conversation basically consists of the new router introducing itself and the existing router(s) dumping everything they know onto the link to the new router. Almost instantly, the new router knows the entire network and has shared what it knows with the network.

The router will form an *adjacency* with neighboring routers. This is basically an information exchange and the initiation of an ongoing conversation. In the case of OSPF, the information that is exchanged here consists of the router ID, hello/dead interval, neighbor routers, area ID, router priority, designated router address, backup designated router address, authentication password (if any), and stub area flag. OSPF is covered in detail in Chapters 6 and 7.

Routing updates are known as *link-state advertisements (LSAs).* LSAs are sent only when there is a change to report, and they contain only the change that's being reported. LSAs propagate in a *flooding* fashion (that is, every router on the network sees them and passes them on).

When an LSA comes in, the router examines it for a timestamp and sequence numbering to ensure that this update has not been duplicated or outdated. If the update is one that should be processed, the router makes an entry in its link-state database and forwards the LSA out of every active interface (except the one through which it entered the router). It then continues to process the update according to the Dijkstra algorithm.

Hybrid Routing Protocols

Enhanced IGRP is a proprietary routing protocol developed by Cisco Systems in the 1990s. This protocol utilizes the benefits of both the distance-vector and link-state routing protocols. EIGRP is discussed in greater detail in Chapter 8.

Which Is Best?

Obviously, trade-offs are involved in using link-state routing protocols versus distance-vector routing protocols. Link-state protocols are much more intensive on system resources, and they require higher-horsepower CPUs and additional RAM resources for proper operation. However, they shine when it comes to convergence and intelligent route calculation. Convergence is completed within the internetwork almost instantly rather than the minutes—or sometimes hours—it takes with distance-vector protocols.

Link-state protocols tend to support advanced addressing functions that distance-vector protocols do not support. These include route summarization and variable-length subnet masks (VLSMs), which are discussed in Chapter 4. As you can see, the benefits of link-state protocols do seem to outweigh their disadvantages. However, that's a matter of perception. The size and function of your network will weigh heavily in the decision as well.

Believability

As mentioned, routing protocols have differing methods of computing the "best" route. These computations are based on a *metric*, which is simply a unit of measure to allow the router to compare pathways to a specific destination network.

The question "How do I tell the router what the best route should be?" arises. The answer to that question is simple if you are running only a single routing protocol. In that case, the best route is whatever the routing protocol thinks it should be. However, it is possible to run multiple routing protocols simultaneously in any given router.

The router uses a believability measurement known as *administrative distance*. Administrative distance is simply a number between 0 and 255 that gives the router an idea of which protocols to believe if two or more routing protocols come up with routing information for the same network(s). Table 3.5 lists Cisco's default administrative distances for each protocol.

Table 3.5 Administrative distance defaults.	
Protocol	**Administrative Distance**
Connected interface	0
Static route	1
EIGRP summary route	5
External Border Gateway Protocol (EBGP)	20
Internal Enhanced IGRP	90
IGRP	100
OSPF	110
RIP	120
Exterior Gateway Protocol (EGP)	140
External Enhanced IGRP	170
Internal Border Gateway Protocol (IBGP)	200
Unknown	255

 Manipulation of administrative distance is not always necessary. However, the administrative distances will allow you to understand why routes from specific protocols show up in the routing table rather than the routes of other active routing protocols.

The lower the administrative distance, the more believable the route. If you have RIP and EIGRP running at the same time, you will see only EIGRP routes in your routing table. Even though both protocols are functioning as if they were running alone, only the most believable routes appear in the routing table. However, if EIGRP does not have a route to a particular destination and RIP can provide that route, the RIP route will show up in the routing table (this type of scenario is quite rare, but not impossible).

You can configure administrative distance for a particular protocol. To change the administrative distance from the default setting, you must use the **distance** command. For example, if you want to set the administrative distance for RIP to 80 (so that RIP routes override EIGRP routes), enter the following commands:

```
Router#>Configure terminal
Router(Config)#>Router rip
Router(Config)#>Network 10.0.0.0
Router(Config-router)#>Distance 80
```

*Note: The steps to configure the administrative distance of other protocols are identical to those of this command example. Under the appropriate routing protocol configuration, you can use the **distance** command as shown here.*

You should note that directly connected networks are the most believable, followed by static routes. You can configure an administrative distance value in two ways. The first involves adding a command parameter at the end of the static route command entry, as follows:

```
ip route <dest. network><dest. mask><next hop | out int><distance>
```

 Static routes play an integral part in many technologies, such as dial-on-demand routing. Ensure that you understand the proper command parameters and variables necessary to configure static routes on a router.

After you enter the static route command but before you press Enter, you need to enter the last parameter available: **distance**. You can enter a number between 0 and 255 to specify the administrative distance for this particular route. If you do not enter a distance, the parameter defaults to 0 if you specified an outbound interface and 1 if you specified a next hop address in the command.

The second way is through manipulation of administrative distance for a specific dynamic route. Under the routing protocol configuration, you can specify distance for all routes derived by that protocol or just a single route. To configure distance for specific routes, you need to create an access list to define the networks for which the administrative distance is to be changed. Listing 3.1 shows a configuration example that defines the administrative distance for network 10.2.0.0 as 130 rather than the RIP default of 120.

Listing 3.1   Specific manipulation of administrative distance.

```
!define the access-list at global configuration mode
access-list 1 permit 10.2.0.0 0.0.255.255

!configure the distance under the protocol configuration
router rip
network 10.0.0.0
distance 130 0.0.0.0 255.255.255.255 1
```

Practice Questions

Question 1

What is the key piece of information on which routing decisions are based?

○ a. Source network-layer address

○ b. Destination network-layer address

○ c. Source MAC address

○ d. Destination MAC address

Answer b is correct. The destination network-layer address, or layer 3, is the protocol-specific address to which a piece of data is to be delivered. The source network-layer address is the originating host and plays no role in getting the information to the destination. Therefore, answer a is incorrect. The source and destination MAC addresses are necessary for getting the data to the router or the next hop address. However, they are not used in pathing decisions. Therefore, answers c and d are incorrect.

Question 2

In the following figure, what are the missing layers of the OSI model and the names of the entities that exist at those layers? [Choose the two best answers.]

❑ a. Physical, data link, network, and transport

❑ b. Source address and destination address

❑ c. Segment, packet, frame, and bits

❑ d. Application, presentation, and session

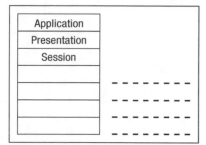

Refer back to Figure 3.1, and you'll see that the correct answers are a and c. Answer b is incorrect because source and destination addresses are specific parts of the entities that exist at the data link and network layers. Answer d is incorrect because those layers are listed in the figure and do not need to be added in.

Question 3

What is the measurement information used in calculating routes from source to destination for any single protocol known as?

○ a. Longest match

○ b. Distance-vector

○ c. Link-state

○ d. Metric

Answer d is correct. The metric is a unit of measure used to derive the best route to a particular destination. Answer a is incorrect because the longest match principle is applied after the routing table is completed. The longest match is the route that most closely resembles the destination protocol address. Answers b and c are incorrect because they are specific types of routing protocols, not measurements of routes.

Question 4

Distance-vector protocols are faster to converge than link-state protocols.

○ a. True

○ b. False

Answer b is correct. Distance-vector protocols tend to be slower to converge because they are governed by periodic updates that go out only when the timer reaches zero.

Question 5

> What is the algorithm run by link-state protocols known as?
>
> ○ a. Longest match
>
> ○ b. Dijkstra
>
> ○ c. Convergence
>
> ○ d. None of the above

Answer b is correct. The Dijkstra algorithm defines the operation of link-state protocols and how they respond to routing changes. Answer a is incorrect because longest match is the method of route selection. It is a function that runs based on the information the routing protocol collects. Answer c is incorrect because convergence is the process of all routers exchanging information to the point where they share a common perspective on the internetwork. Answer d is incorrect because a correct answer is given.

Question 6

> The believability of a route derived from one routing protocol over routes derived by another is determined by the administrative distance.
>
> ○ a. True
>
> ○ b. False

Answer a is correct. You can manipulate administrative distance protocol by protocol, or you can leave it to the default value for a particular protocol.

Question 7

> When running RIP and EIGRP, why would you see RIP routes in the IP routing table? [Choose the two best answers.]
>
> ❑ a. RIP has a better administrative distance by default than EIGRP.
>
> ❑ b. The distance has been configured manually.
>
> ❑ c. EIGRP has a higher administrative distance by default than RIP.
>
> ❑ d. EIGRP does not have a route to that destination.

Answers b and d are correct. By default, EIGRP has an administrative distance of 90, which makes it more believable than RIP at 120. If distance has been manually configured to where RIP has a distance lower than 90, or if EIGRP has been set to a distance higher than 120, the RIP route will show up. For some reason, should the situation occur where RIP has a route to a specific destination that EIGRP does not have, the RIP route will show up. Therefore, answers a and c are incorrect.

Need to Know More?

Huitema, Christian. *Routing in the Internet*. Prentice Hall. Upper Saddle River, NJ, 1995. ISBN 0-13132-192-7. This book is packed full of great information on routing in the Internet.

Larson, Bob, Corwin Low, and Michael Simon. *CCNP Routing Exam Prep*. The Coriolis Group. Scottsdale, AZ, Fall 2000. ISBN 1-56710-778-2. This book an Exam Prep for the CCNP exam, that covers each related subject in great detail.

Perlman, Radia. *Interconnections: Routers and Bridges*. Addison-Wesley. Reading, MA, 1992. ISBN 0-201-56332-0. This book is a great resource for quality information on routers and bridges.

For more information on routing protocols, visit **www.cisco.com** and perform a search for "routing protocol".

4

IP Addressing
Using VLSMs

Terms you'll need to understand:

✓ IP address

✓ Private IP address

✓ Public IP address

✓ Subnet mask

✓ Prefix

✓ Classful routing

✓ Classless routing

✓ Variable-length subnet mask (VLSM)

✓ Longest match

✓ Route summarization

✓ Network Address Translation (NAT)

Techniques you'll need to master:

✓ Planning and deploying IP addresses

✓ Calculating subnet masks

✓ Using private IP addressing space

✓ Calculating variable-length subnet masks

✓ Deploying VLSM address space properly

✓ Configuring route summarization

This chapter covers address deployment and memory utilization. In the past, network administrators deployed Internet Protocol (IP) addresses without thinking about addresses becoming depleted, which is happening today. The number of addresses on the Internet has been increasing exponentially in a very small amount of time. This chapter will also discuss some memory utilization methods of deploying scarce IP address space more efficiently as well as how to reduce the size of the routing table.

IP Addressing Basics

If you could pick any single issue in networking and call it the most misunderstood, what would you pick? Many votes would land squarely in the realm of IP address deployment. As has been the case throughout this book, it is assumed that you are at least somewhat familiar with the subject matter. This book does not aim to teach the subnetting procedure, but you must understand it before delving into the rest of this chapter's subject matter. Here's a short review.

TCP/IP Address Structure

An IP address consists of a 32-bit string of ones (1) and zeros (0). In order to make it simpler to work with, this 32-bit string has been divided into four equal pieces. Each of these pieces, known as an *octet*, consists of eight bits. These octets are converted from binary to decimal to create what's know as an address in dotted decimal notation. In other words, an IP address is simply four decimal numerals separated by periods.

As with any Network layer protocol, an IP address consists of two parts: the network portion and the host portion. The network portion designates a common domain or logical division. For example, an area code is a location-specific identifier that many physical devices in a geographic area share.

The host portion is an identifier that when coupled with the network portion creates a globally unique identifier (GUID) for a specific end host. For example, your phone number is a unique identifier for your specific phone. Is it possible for someone in another area code to have an identical phone number? Absolutely, it is possible (and common). What makes the phone number unique to you? The coupling of the phone number with the area code makes it yours alone.

When you assign an IP address to a host, you are giving it a globally unique identifier. The question that arises is "Well, how is the device supposed to know where the network portion ends and the host portion begins?" An additional piece of information, known as a *mask*, must be present in order to tell the device where the division between network and host exists.

The mask is simply a 32-bit string very similar to an IP address. The mask is a contiguous string of ones followed by a contiguous string of zeros. The point where the ones stop and zeros start in the mask is the division between the network and host portions of the address with which this mask is associated.

IP Addressing with Class

IP addresses are viewed in terms of class. The *class* of an address makes certain assumptions about the natural network and host portions of any given address based on the decimal or binary value of the first octet. These different classes have been divided based on the value of the high-order bits (the bits furthest to the left in a binary value). If the first bit value (the leftmost bit) is a zero, the address is a class A address. If the first two bits are one and zero, in that order, the address is class B. If the first three bits of the address are one, one, and zero, in that order, the address is class C. The value of each octet is computed by converting each 8-bit string from binary to decimal format. Table 4.1 illustrates the natural (or *classful*) division of IP addressing.

As you can see, some numeric values have been omitted. Specifically, these are 0, 127, and any value from 224 to 255. The distinction of designating network addresses goes to 0, and 127 is set aside to allow the use of a diagnostic loopback address. The address 127.0.0.1 is known as an *internal loopback address*. In other words, administrators can use this address to test the configuration of an individual host's IP configuration. Pinging (the process of testing reachability to an end host) this address would result in a response from the local device (basically, you are pinging yourself). The range of 224 through 239 is known as class D. class D addresses have been set aside for various multicast-related functions. For instance, the address 224.0.0.5 is an Open Shortest Path First (OSPF) multicast address used in disseminating routing information in an OSPF network. Class E includes the range 240 through 247 and is used only for research purposes. The remaining address space is allocated for future use. The value 255 is seen as a broadcast entity.

A common issue that arises is in simply knowing where to get the address space you need to deploy your internetwork addressing scheme efficiently. You can obtain registered IP address space from your Internet Service Provider (ISP) and

Table 4.1   IP Address classes.

Class	First Octet Range
A	1 through 126
B	128 through 191
C	192 through 223

deploy that address space into your internetwork. Alternatively, if your company is not planning to connect to the public Internet, you can use an address space that the internetworking industry has set aside specifically for private internetworks. Address space from each class has been set aside for private use. Anyone can use these addresses. Table 4.2 specifies this private internetwork address space, which was originally defined in RFC 1597 but revised in RFC 1918.

 It is important that you understand the private internetwork space and know the address ranges that have been set aside and how to use Network Address Translation (NAT) to access the public Internet. NAT is discussed later in this chapter.

Subnet Mask Manipulation

By manipulating the value of the mask, you can manipulate the number of hosts per network. In its natural state, each class of address has a specific number of hosts per network. Table 4.3 illustrates examples of the natural network and host divisions for IP addresses in each class.

These addresses in their natural form cover the spectrum from a ridiculously high number of hosts (a single logical network with 16,777,214 hosts) down to what may be too few hosts. To put this in perspective, imagine a single network—not an internetwork, just a single network—as shown in Figure 4.1.

Figure 4.1 shows a single network that has been assigned to a class B address. Sixteen bits are available for hosts on that single network, for a total host capacity of 65,534 hosts. That number is many times what a single Ethernet segment is capable of supporting. A single network obviously does not allow for scalability or growth.

Table 4.2 Private internetwork space.	
Class	**Range**
A	10.0.0.0 through 10.255.255.255
B	172.16.0.0 through 172.31.255.255
C	192.168.0.0 through 192.168.255.255

Table 4.3 Natural network and host divisions.				
Class	**Network Address**	**Mask**	**Number of Networks**	**Hosts**
A	10.0.0.0	255.0.0.0	1	16,777,214
B	172.16.0.0	255.255.0.0	1	65,534
C	192.168.1.0	255.255.255.0	1	254

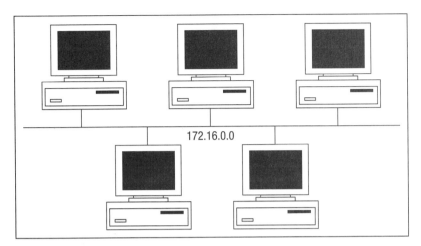

Figure 4.1 An imaginary network.

Efficiency Is the Key

A current issue involving address deployment is *address depletion*. It is our responsibility, as responsible members of the internetworking community, to efficiently deploy the address space we have. Should you run out of address space, you may be required to justify your use of that space in order to be granted additional space. If you obtain space correctly from the beginning, you will find it much easier to obtain additional space.

To deploy address space, the first step is to plan the internetwork hierarchy and figure out how many separate subnetworks you will have and how many hosts each subnetwork will require. With that information, you can create a suitable subnet mask for your subnetwork. Referring back to Figure 4.1, should you wish to deploy additional subnetworks, you would need to segment the single network address into multiple subnetwork addresses. You accomplish this task by manipulating the subnet mask. In doing so, you change the natural mask for your class B network to give you additional networks. Whereas the mask was 255.255.0.0, it is now 255.255.255.0. In effect, you have informed the router that you would like for it to look deeper into the address to make network routing decisions.

As mentioned earlier, a *mask* is a contiguous string of ones followed by a contiguous string of zeros, in binary form of course. When converted to binary, the natural mask appears, as noted in Table 4.4.

Router Logic

When distinguishing between logical networks with the same address, the router has to have a way to tell where the network portion of the address ends. It does so

Table 4.4 A mask in binary format.	
Decimal Value	**Binary Value**
255.255.0.0	11111111.11111111.00000000.00000000

by using ones in the subnet mask. When the subnet mask is put together with the actual IP address in question, a function known as a *logical AND* is performed on the two 32-bit strings. Table 4.5 illustrates this process.

When the bit positions are lined up, the function is to simply follow the rules of engagement for logical AND:

➤ 1 and 1 result in a 1

➤ 1 and 0 result in a 0

➤ 0 and 1 result in a 0

➤ 0 and 0 result in a 0

Look at the first bit position on the far left. Both values have a 1 for the first bit, so the resulting product of the logical AND is a 1. The next bit position has a 0 on the top line and a 1 on the bottom. The resulting value is 0. Apply the principle to all bit positions and you will arrive at a third 32-bit string. This string, when converted back to decimal, will yield the subnet address. Simply convert each 8-bit value into decimal to arrive at your address.

What if you were to give the router something more to look at? Assume that you would like to tell the router that it should look at the normal number of ones for a class B address. However, you would like it to look at some additional bits—in this case eight additional bits. Table 4.6 illustrates this premise.

Table 4.5 Logical AND.	
Decimal	**Binary Value Equivalent**
172.16.0.0	10101100.00010000.00000000.00000000
255.255.0.0	11111111.11111111.00000000.00000000
Subnet address	10101100.00010000.00000000.00000000

Table 4.6 Logical AND with subnetting.	
Decimal	**Binary Equivalent**
172.16.0.0	10101100.00010000.00000000.00000000
255.255.255.0	11111111.11111111.11111111.00000000
Subnet address	10101100.00010000.00000000.00000000

Up to this point, you couldn't change the value of the assigned address (172.16.0.0) because you had only a single network and the first two octets were set aside for network designation. You have now made it clear that the third octet should also be used for network designation. Whereas before you had a single network, you now have many more. To be exact, 254 networks are now available for your use. However, rather than 65,534 hosts, you now have only 254 hosts per network. At this point, your network can evolve from what it was in Figure 4.1 to what it is now in Figure 4.2.

You are still using the assigned address space, but you are simply making better use of the available space by manipulating the subnet mask. It is easy to see where you may be somewhat confused about various address values. The IP address itself is a useless piece of information if there is no subnet mask. Without the mask, it is impossible to tell where the division between network and host lies. Without that information, you can assume only the natural division.

You should determine where the boundary between network and host needs to exist during predeployment planning. You must know how many subnets you

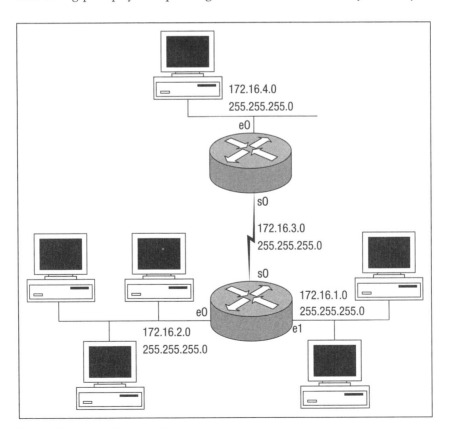

Figure 4.2 A subnetted network topology.

will need as well as how many hosts each of those subnets will need to support. Table 4.7 illustrates the subnet mask, the number of networks, and number of hosts per network that you will create when you manipulate the bit boundary between ones and zeros in the mask. The example in the table is following the sample address 172.16.0.0, first shown in Figure 4.1. The Number of Bits column in the table is the number of bits beyond those specified by the natural mask. The formula for calculating the number of hosts and/or subnets is $2^n - 2$, where n=number of bits in the host and/or subnet portion. In other words, if you want the router to pay attention to five bits beyond what it normally would for this class of address, the number of hosts would be $2^5 - 2$, for a total of 30 subnets. If you have taken five bits from an octet, three are left for the host. If you apply the same formula, $2^3 - 2$, you will get six hosts.

What's in a Name?

The natural mask, subnet mask, or any other type of mask you can associate with an IP address has another name—a *prefix*. The prefix is simply another way of specifying the mask. For example, the address 172.16.0.0 has been used with the mask 255.255.255.0. The prefix is an abbreviation. You can find out what the

Table 4.7	Subnet planning example.		
Number of Bits	Mask	Number of Subnets	Number of Hosts
0	255.255.0.0	1	65,534
1	255.255.128.0	0	32,766
2	255.255.192.0	2	16,382
3	255.255.224.0	6	8,190
4	255.255.240.0	14	4,094
5	255.255.248.0	30	2,046
6	255.255.252.0	62	1,022
7	255.255.254.0	126	510
8	255.255.255.0	254	254
9	255.255.255.128	510	126
10	255.255.255.192	1,024	62
11	255.255.255.224	2,048	30
12	255.255.255.240	4,096	14
13	255.255.255.248	8,190	6
14	255.255.255.252	16,382	2
15	255.255.255.254	32,766	0
16	255.255.255.255	N/A	N/A

abbreviated prefix is by simply counting the number of ones in the mask. In this case, 24 ones are followed by 8 zeros. As stated earlier, the router cares only about the ones, not the zeros. So the abbreviated address is 172.16.0.0/24. This address is said to have a 24-bit prefix. Eventually, most people get to where they prefer to use the abbreviation to note the address and mask together.

So, why have another name for the same entity? A *subnet mask* is a piece of information that tells you how address space has been segmented into smaller pieces. According to what's been discussed to this point, the rules state that you cannot change your assigned address. That remains true. However, what if you were assigned a block of addresses that consisted of multiple class B addresses? So far, the examples have shown only the assignment of a single address. The rules discussed up to this point are known as *classful* rules. When working with multiple network addresses that can be divided into smaller or larger host networks this function is called *classless* routing, which will be discussed next.

Classless Routing

The time has come to rise to the next level of IP address deployment and discuss what happens when the classful rules do not apply. At this point, the discussion moves partially into the realm of address assignment. Also, another method of increasing the efficiency of address deployment is discussed.

Classless routing is known as *classless interdomain routing (CIDR)*. CIDR is a method of assigning address space based on need. Assume that your company needs 2,000 host addresses. A class C address is not adequate for your needs, so you automatically assume you need a class B address. However, if you were assigned a class B address, a very large number of addresses would be wasted: You need 2,000 addresses, but a class B provides for over 65,000 addresses. In effect, that wastes over 63,000 addresses. So, what is the solution? A single class C is not enough, and a class B is too much. What if you were issued eight class C addresses? That would give you a total of 254 times 8 addresses, or 2,032. That's closer to your needs without wasting space. To that end, you could be assigned the address 222.201.40.0/21. The first reaction is that this is not a legal representation of a class C address. It should have a 24-bit prefix by default. But this is why it's called *classless*. The rules of class do not apply. Table 4.8 breaks this address into binary to illustrate what you have been given in this address.

Notice that all eight addresses have the first two octets (16 bits) in common. After that, the third octet changes. However, when you view them in binary, you can see that they all have the first five bits of the third octet in common. You can see that with 16 bits from the two octets and the five bits of the third octet all in common, the address you were given (222.201.40.0/21) is actually a single address that represents a block of addresses. Specifically, it represents eight class C addresses.

Table 4.8 Classless address example.	
Address	**Third Octet Binary Value**
222.201.40.0	00101000
222.201.41.0	00101001
222.201.42.0	00101010
222.201.43.0	00101011
222.201.44.0	00101100
222.201.45.0	00101101
222.201.46.0	00101110
222.201.47.0	00101111

A common question that arises is "How do I know when my block ends?" When the first five bits of the third octet are no longer identical to the rest of your address, your block ends. Look at the binary form of 48, the next address in the line. It is 00110000. It no longer matches the 5-bit pattern 00101. In this case, it is not a part of your block of address space.

Note: You will be given the address block in the form noted (222.201.40.0/21). You now know that this single address represents eight class C addresses. Once the space is assigned, it is your job to efficiently deploy these eight class C addresses in your internetwork, just as if each one had been assigned separately. You will need to plan, subnet, and deploy each of the eight addresses.

Variable-Length Subnet Masks (VLSMs)

Variable-length subnet masks (VLSMs), defined in RFC 1009, have been around the internetworking industry for a number of years. It is far from a new technology. Instead, it is a methodology for reducing the amount of wasted IP address space on small networks, specifically point-to-point serial links.

The first point to stress is that not all routing protocols support the use of VLSM. In order for VLSM to be supported, the routing protocol must be able to pass the prefix in routing updates. Protocols such as Routing Information Protocol (RIP) and Interior Gateway Routing Protocol (IGRP) do not include the prefix (such as subnet mask—remember?) in their routing updates. Therefore, they cannot advertise varied-length masks. Figure 4.3 shows two routers connected via a point-to-point serial link.

As you can see, the address space has been deployed according to the mask from earlier. However, on a point-to-point serial link, only two of those addresses are used. You lose a net of 252 addresses, which is wasted space. Wasting space is not

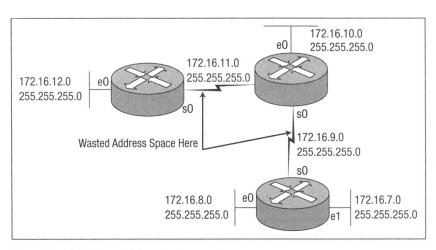

Figure 4.3   A VLSM candidate network example.

efficient deployment of scarce resources. Therefore, VLSM is the answer to the problem.

As mentioned earlier, the routing protocol must include the prefix in routing updates in order to support VLSM. If your routing protocol does not support passing the prefix, you cannot use VLSM. OSPF, Enhanced Interior Gateway Routing Protocol (EIGRP), and IS-IS are a few examples of protocols that can include prefix information in routing updates.

VLSM Methodology

To use VLSM, you must already have an internetwork design and address space allocation plan in place. Once you have decided on the subnet mask to use—in this case, 255.255.255.0—you should pick a single subnet and remove it from any plans of deployment. You are going to further subdivide this address. With the wide range of address space available in this example, singling one out should not be a problem. You will use 172.16.30.0 255.255.255.0 as the lucky subnet.

At this point, 172.16.30.0 255.255.255.0 is a single network that happens to be a piece of a larger hierarchy. You will treat this address as if it were the natural form of the address, even though you know it is not.

The procedure is simply to reapply the same rules of engagement that you used when choosing a subnet mask for the overall internetwork. Ask the same questions. How many hosts do I need on each network? In this case (a point-to-point link), you need only two. How many additional bits do I need the router to look at in order to render two hosts? The current mask (255.255.255.0) should be able to give two hosts if you change it to the value 255.255.255.252—that is, 30 consecutive ones followed by 2 zeros.

How many new subnets did I get from further subdividing the one? You gave it six additional bits, so apply the formula $2^6 - 2 = 62$ subnets. Table 4.9 shows the subnets just created.

Note: You cannot use the address that was set aside for VLSM anywhere else in the network unless it is a deployment of one of the subnets derived from applying the new mask. In this example, you may not use the network 172.16.30.0 255.255.255.0 anywhere else in the internetwork. Doing so would cause unpredictable results.

You now have 62 new networks for use on point-to-point links; you are no longer wasting space by deploying too many addresses for a single network. Figure 4.4 shows the new address deployment with VLSM in place.

VLSM was designed to work according to the rules set forth here, using address space removed from deployment for the specific use on serial links. However, the question "Can't I simply alter the mask anywhere I want?" arises. Yes, technically you can, but it's not recommended. If you are running multiple routing protocols

Table 4.9 VLSM subnets.	
VLSM Calculation	**Subnets**
Original address	172.16.30.0 255.255.255.0
New address	172.16.30.0 255.255.255.252
New subnets	172.16.30.0 to 172.16.30.3
	172.16.30.4 to 172.16.30.7
	172.16.30.8 to 172.16.30.11
	172.16.30.252 to 172.16.30.255

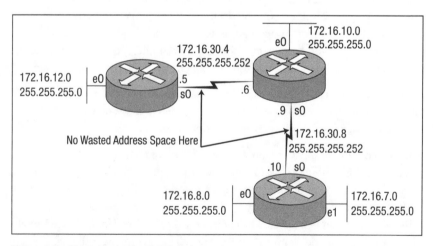

Figure 4.4 The network after VLSM deployment.

(one that supports VLSM, one that does not), VLSM can cause reachability issues. Assume you are running RIP and OSPF in a single internetwork and you are using VLSM for serial links as discussed previously. The issue is that the VLSM-capable protocol is passing specific network and mask information in the updates. Because the non-VLSM-capable protocol does not understand the mask information in the updates, it ignores this information. Now the RIP router might be able to see the same network through two interfaces, which could be in opposite directions. The routing protocol cannot distinguish between the two networks. That limitation causes an attempt to forward data to either of the two VLSM networks to be ineffective.

 It is important to know when and when not to use VLSM as well as the appropriate use for VLSM networks on serial links or other low-volume subnets.

Longest Match

Routers function on the principle of *longest match*, which means that the router, in making path-determination decisions, is simply looking at the 32-bit string in the destination IP address field of the packet to attempt to find a routing table match. It may not always have an exact match, so it will base the routing decision on the entry in the routing table that provides the closest to an exact match. This is known as the *longest match* in the routing table. Knowing this nifty piece of information gives you some very versatile functionality in the router.

Intelligent forwarding abilities focus in on a single key element—the prefix—which was discussed earlier in this chapter. At that point, it was simply an abbreviation of the subnet mask. However, if you could manipulate the prefix in a way that allows you to give reachability to the same number of networks using fewer entries in a routing table, that would be a useful tool.

Consider this analogy: Your phone number is unique. Only you have it. What makes it unique was already discussed earlier in this chapter, right? The combination of the area code, prefix, and exchange creates a globally unique identifier. Think of placing a long distance call. You are going to call the (fictitious) phone number (817) 555-4444 in Fort Worth, Texas. The call is being placed from Palo Alto, California. Do the telephone switches in Palo Alto have to know exact information about every phone number in the nation? Do they have an entry for (817) 555-4444? No. Think about what the switches need to know to make a decision. They only need to know 817. That's enough information to tell them that the destination is somewhere other than local. The switches can decide where to route the call based on the area code; they route the call to a central office (CO) in Fort Worth, Texas.

Once they have routed the call to Fort Worth, the switches see that 817 is just not enough information, so they have entries that are more specific. The 817 switch (assuming it is not the final-destination switch) needs only to know (817) 555 to decide where to forward the call. Once the call arrives at the destination switch, it needs port-specific information, (817) 555-4444, to know where to send a ring to make the phone alert the person on the receiving end of an incoming call.

Routing data works on the same basic principle. All you need to keep in a routing table is enough information to allow you to make an accurate decision. You need a longest match. However, the longest match does not necessarily have to be long.

In order to avoid maintaining unnecessary information in the routing table, routes to similar destinations can be summarized at various points. This process is known as *route summarization*. Summary routes keep the routing table smaller than it would be otherwise, thus increasing the speed of the routing table lookup process. Summarization also decreases overall memory utilization because there is a smaller amount of information overall in the router. Do not let the router keep information it does not need to keep. If you can give it an area code, why give it the full phone number?

Route Summarization

You can manipulate routers to cause an overall reduction in the size of the routing table. It takes some careful planning, but it is well worth the work for the benefits. Many of the benefits have already been discussed, such as lower processor and memory utilization. Figure 4.5 represents a network that's a candidate for route summarization.

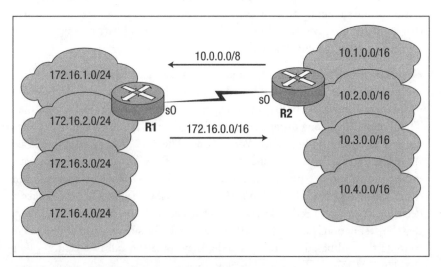

Figure 4.5 Route summarization in the internetwork.

In this example, R1 is attached directly or indirectly to many 172.16.X.0 networks. R1 can represent 254 networks. However, R1 only needs to pass a single route entry to its neighbor, R2. That single route is the pathway to 172.16.0.0 255.255.0.0. In fact, in this example, no other networks begin with 172.X.X.X. Therefore, you can send into R2 a single summary that specifies 172.0.0.0 255.0.0.0. You may be saying to yourself, "Hey, that's not a legal address; it's a class B." Actually, it is perfectly legal. Remember that all the router needs is a match in the routing table long enough to make the routing decision. If none of the other entries in the table is 172, it will be the longest match. Table 4.10 illustrates an example of the entries in R1's routing table as well as R2's routing table with the summary routes that have been advertised to both.

In the same manner, R2 can advertise a single route to network 10.0.0.0 255.0.0.0, no matter how many 10.X.X.X networks happen to be out there.

Note: For summarization to work, you must exercise caution when deploying IP addresses. If even a single 172.X.X.X network is attached to R2, the summary address will lead to a routing inconsistency.

Summarization Methodology

Route summarization focuses on reducing the routing tables of all routers in the network. It is generally performed at the edge routers at the border between two address domains, as shown in Table 4.10. Otherwise, all routers would have to keep all the networks in Figure 4.2 in their routing tables, thus increasing CPU and memory utilization. Summarization is based on finding a bit boundary where multiple addresses share a common bit pattern. Table 4.11 shows an example of how to find a bit boundary.

You can summarize these routing table entries into a single statement. To create a summary address, simply find a point in one or more of the addresses where there are bits in common. Notice that all the binary representations of the third octet begin with 10101. They all have the first five bits in common. Actually, when you look at the entire address, you can see that all the addresses have 21 bits

Table 4.10 Routing tables with summarization.	
R1 Routing Table	**R2 Routing Table**
172.16.1.0/24	10.1.0.0/16
172.16.2.0/24	10.2.0.0/16
172.16.3.0/24	10.3.0.0/16
172.16.4.0/24	10.4.0.0/16
10.0.0.0/8	172.16.0.0/16

Table 4.11 Summarizing addresses.		
Routing Table	**Third Octet Binary Value**	**Summary Address**
172.16.168.0	168 = 10101000	
172.16.169.0	169 = 10101001	
172.16.170.0	170 = 10101010	
172.16.171.0	171 = 10101011	172.16.168.0/21
172.16.172.0	172 = 10101100	
172.16.173.0	173 = 10101101	
172.16.174.0	174 = 10101110	
172.16.175.0	175 = 10101111	

in common. The differences lie in the last three bits of the third octet. Using the last three bits as the only variable bits in the address, you can create a single address to represent all eight networks with a single routing table entry: 172.16.168.0 255.255.248.0.

 As with VLSM, the routing protocol must be capable of passing the prefix along with routing updates in order to support route summarization. It is important that you understand summary addresses and where to place them.

Network Address Translation

As noted earlier in the chapter, you can acquire registered address space for your internetwork, or you can simply use the space defined by RFC 1918 for private internetwork use. Should you decide to use the private space, does that mean you cannot connect to the public Internet? No. You can still connect to the public Internet using a technology known as *Network Address Translation* (NAT).

Two of the key problems facing the Internet are depletion of IP address space and scaling in routing. NAT is a feature that allows an organization's IP network to appear from the outside to use different IP address space than what it is actually using. Therefore, NAT allows an organization with private addresses to connect to the Internet by translating those addresses into public address space. NAT also allows a more graceful renumbering strategy for organizations that are changing service providers or voluntarily renumbering into CIDR blocks. NAT is described in RFC 1631.

NAT has several applications that can be used for the following purposes:

➤ You want to connect to the Internet, but not all your hosts have unique IP addresses. NAT enables private IP internetworks that use nonregistered IP addresses to connect to the Internet. NAT is configured on the router at the border of a network (referred to as the *inside network*) and a public network such as the Internet (referred to as the *outside network*). NAT translates the internal local addresses to globally unique IP addresses before sending packets to the outside network.

➤ You must change your internal addresses. Instead of changing them, which can be a considerable amount of work, you can translate them by using NAT.

➤ You want to perform basic load sharing of TCP traffic. You can map a single global IP address to many local IP addresses by using the TCP load-distribution feature.

As a solution to the connectivity problem, NAT is practical only when relatively few hosts in a network communicate outside of the network at the same time. When this is the case, only a small subset of the IP addresses in the domain must be translated into globally unique IP addresses when outside communication is necessary, and these addresses can be reused when no longer in use. This is referred to as having an address pool where unique IP addresses are recycled between devices that require outside access.

As mentioned earlier, the term *inside* refers to those networks that are owned by an organization and that must be translated. Inside this domain, hosts will have addresses in the one address space, whereas on the outside, they will appear to have addresses in another address space when NAT is configured. The first address space is referred to as the *local address space*, and the second is referred to as the *global address space*.

Similarly, *outside* refers to those networks to which the inside network connects, and which are generally not under the organization's control. As described later, hosts in outside networks can be subject to translation, too, and can therefore have local and global addresses.

To summarize, NAT uses the following definitions:

➤ *Inside local address*—The IP address that's assigned to a host on the inside network. This address is probably a private address that's being used on the internal network.

➤ *Inside global address*—A legitimate IP address (assigned by the NIC or service provider) that represents one or more inside local IP addresses to the outside world.

➤ *Outside local address*—The IP address of an outside host as it appears to the inside network. Not necessarily a legitimate address, it was allocated from address space routable on the inside.

➤ *Outside global address*—The IP address assigned to a host on the outside network by the host's owner. The address was allocated from a globally routable address or network space.

With NAT, you simply deploy the private space within your internetwork as described throughout this chapter. The added step is that you need a device that is NAT capable. As of version 11.2, Cisco's enterprise Internetwork Operating System (IOS) software meets this requirement. Other devices that can implement NAT are Cisco's PIX Firewall and many proxy server software programs. How you do it makes no difference.

As stated earlier, when you configure NAT, you also create a pool of registered addresses. You can statically map addresses from their private values to their registered counterparts. Alternatively, you can create a dynamic registered IP address pool in which addresses are assigned on the fly.

When you are deciding how many registered addresses to obtain for NAT purposes, you need to consider a number of factors:

➤ Identifying the hosts that do not need external access. You don't want to obtain too many or too few addresses.

➤ Filtering private addresses from being advertised into the Internet.

➤ Changing IP addresses from private to public, which requires time. You will experience additional transmission delay due to processor time to perform the translation.

Practice Questions

Question 1

How many bits does an IP address consist of?

○ a. 64

○ b. 1

○ c. 32

○ d. 96

Answer c is correct. IP addresses consist of 32 bits. Answers a, b, and d are incorrect because they are not valid values for IP address lengths.

Question 2

What are the two parts of all layer 3 protocol addresses? [Choose the two best answers.]

❑ a. Network

❑ b. Host

❑ c. Range

❑ d. Boundary

Answers a and b are correct. Any layer 3 protocol address consists of network and node (or *host*) portions. In this lies their routability. Answer c is incorrect because it is not a valid piece of information for a network-layer address. Answer d is incorrect for a similar reason. Although bit boundaries (the boundary between the network and host) are discussed, the boundary is not a part of the address itself.

Question 3

> How is the class of an address determined?
>
> ○ a. Value of the first octet
>
> ○ b. Value of the second octet
>
> ○ c. Value of the third octet
>
> ○ d. Value of the fourth octet

Answer a is correct. The value of the first octet in binary, specifically the first few bits, will dictate the class. Refer back to Table 4.1 for specific address ranges. The values of the other octets have no bearing on the class of the address. Therefore, answers b, c, and d are incorrect.

Question 4

> What is the class A range?
>
> ○ a. 1 through 126
>
> ○ b. 128 through 191
>
> ○ c. 192 through 223
>
> ○ d. 224 through 239

Answer a is correct. Technically, class A is defined by the value of the most significant bit. If it is a zero, the address will be class A. The mathematical range is 0 through 127. However, you are not allowed to use 0 for address space, and 127 is reserved for diagnostic loopback addressing. Therefore, the range is 1 through 126. Because none of the other ranges begin with the proper bit pattern, answers b, c, and d are incorrect. Refer to Table 4.1 for the correct answer.

Question 5

> What is the class B range?
>
> ○ a. 224 through 239
>
> ○ b. 1 through 126
>
> ○ c. 192 through 223
>
> ○ d. 128 through 191

Answer d is correct. If the two highest-order bits are set to 1 and 0, respectively, the address will be class B. Because none of the other ranges begin with the proper bit pattern, answers a, b, and c are incorrect.

Question 6

What is the class C range?

○ a. 1 through 126

○ b. 192 through 223

○ c. 128 through 191

○ d. 224 through 239

Answer b is correct. If the three highest-order bits are 1, 1, and 0, respectively, the address will be class C. Because none of the other ranges begin with the proper bit pattern, answers a, c, and d are incorrect.

Question 7

What piece of information allows a router or other device to distinguish between network and host portions of an IP address?

○ a. Longest match

○ b. Subnet mask

○ c. VLSM

○ d. Class

Answer b is correct. The mask defines a string of ones followed by a string of zeros. The point at which the ones stop and the zeros start is the distinction between network and host. Answer a is incorrect because longest match is the principle routers use to make forwarding decisions, not for subnetting. Answer c is incorrect because VLSM is a method of address deployment once the mask has been determined and further subdivided. Answer d is incorrect because class is determined by the value of the high-order bits of the address, not the mask.

Question 8

What is the function that's performed on the IP address and mask to derive the actual subnet address?

- O a. Longest match
- O b. Prefix
- O c. Logical AND
- O d. VLSM

Answer c is correct. The AND process is performed by converting both the address and mask to binary and then comparing each bit position vertically. If both bits are 1, the result is a 1. If either bit is a 0, regardless of the value of the other bit, the result is a 0. Answer a is incorrect because longest match is the principle routers use to make forwarding decisions, not for subnetting. The trick here is that answer b is incorrect because prefix is another name for the mask itself, not the function of deriving a network address. Answer d is incorrect because VLSM is a method of address deployment once the mask has been determined and further subdivided.

Question 9

If you have an IP address with a 26-bit prefix, what is the mask?

- O a. 255.255.255.0
- O b. 255.255.224.0
- O c. 255.248.0.0
- O d. 255.255.255.192

Answer d is correct. The rest of the answers do not have enough ones in them to make up a 26-bit prefix. The prefix is simply a string of contiguous ones. If you have a /26 prefix, that means your mask should be 11111111. 11111111.11111111.11000000, which converts to 255.255.255.192. Therefore, answers a, b, and c are incorrect because they do not contain the appropriate number of contiguous ones.

Question 10

What is the process of mapping private internal addresses to registered public addresses known as?

- ○ a. Network Address Translation
- ○ b. Subnet masking
- ○ c. Address summarization
- ○ d. Classless interdomain routing

Answer a is correct. Network Address Translation (NAT) is used specifically for the purposes of allowing access to the public Internet without having to read-dress the existing network. Subnet masking is the process of dividing up the address space you have internally. Therefore, answer b is incorrect. Address summarization, otherwise known as *route summarization*, is the process of reducing the routing table through aggregating addresses based on a common bit boundary. Therefore, answer c is incorrect. Classless interdomain routing gives you the ability to conserve address space by giving you, as close as possible, the number of addresses you need, rather than wasting addresses needlessly. Therefore, answer d is incorrect.

Need to Know More?

 Huitema, Christian. *Routing in the Internet.* Prentice Hall. Upper Saddle River, NJ, 1995. ISBN 0-13132-192-7. This book focuses on basic internetwork architecture and addressing. It is a well-written book for a basic-level to an advanced-level audience.

 Larson, Bob, Corwin Low, and Michael Simon. *CCNP Routing Exam Prep.* The Coriolis Group. Scottsdale, AZ, Fall 2000. ISBN 1-57610-778-2. This book, an Exam Prep for the CCNP exam, covers each related subject in great detail.

 For more information on VLSM, CIDR, and summarization, visit **www.cisco.com** and perform searches for these keywords.

 Visit **www.cis.ohio-state.edu/htbin/rfc/rfc-index.html** to download any RFC, whether complete or in progress. Related topics to this chapter are RFC 1812 (which defines subnet masking), RFC 1009 (which defines VLSM), RFC 1918 (which defines private address space), RFC 1631 (which defines NAT), and RFCs 1517, 1518, and 1519 (which define CIDR).

Overview of Scalable Routing Protocols

Terms you'll need to understand:

✓ Distance-vector routing protocols

✓ Link-state routing protocols

✓ Classful routing protocols

✓ Classless routing protocols

✓ Protocol scalability

✓ Prefix length

✓ Variable-length subnet masks

Techniques you'll need to master:

✓ Identifying which protocols are classful

✓ Identifying which protocols are classless

✓ Assigning the proper routing protocol

Choosing the correct routing protocol when designing a network can be the most important step in the success of the network design. There are a multitude of routing protocols to choose from, and understanding each type will be a valuable tool in making your final decision. This chapter covers the different scalability issues related to routing protocols used in networking today. With this information you should be able to make informed decisions regarding each routing protocol and how it can scale in different networks and situations.

Scalable and Nonscalable Protocols

The capability to extend your internetwork is determined, in part, by the scaling characteristics of the routing protocols used and the quality of the network design.

By ensuring that you have chosen the proper routing protocol in a specific design you are increasing the overall effectiveness of a network.

Scalability Limitations

Network scalability is limited by two factors: operational issues and technical issues. Typically, operational issues are more significant than technical issues. Operational scaling concerns encourage the use of large networks or protocols that do not require hierarchical structures. When hierarchical protocols are required, technical scaling concerns promote the use of small areas. Finding the right balance is the art of network design.

Distance-vector protocols such as Routing Information Protocol (RIP), Interior Gateway Protocol (IGRP), Internetwork Packet Exchange Routing Information Protocol (IPX RIP), and Routing Table Maintenance Protocol (RTMP) do not support variable-length subnet masks (VLSM). This limits their effectiveness on a network, which hinders the overall performance of the network.

Enhanced IGRP is an advanced distance-vector protocol that has some of the properties of link-state protocols. EIGRP addresses the limitations of conventional distance-vector routing protocols. EIGRP with its support of VLSM will allow for the implementation of a scalable and effective network, but with a flat network design. Refer to Chapter 8 for further information regarding EIGRP.

Link-state routing protocols, such as Open Shortest Path First (OSPF), Intermediate System to Intermediate System (IS-IS), and Netware Link Services Protocol (NLSP), were designed to address the limitations of distance-vector routing protocols. Link-state protocol's support of VLSM will also allow for the implementation of a scalable addressing scheme on a network.

With this in mind, it is important to determine the level of scalability needed when trying to find the right balance between routing protocol functionality and customer needs.

Classful Routing Protocols

Classic classful routing protocols, such as RIP and IGRP, will not transmit any information about a network's prefix length. When routing information is received within the same *major network* (a defined network, such as a class A, B, or C address, from which you can create subnetworks), routers and hosts will assume that the prefix length is the same as the interface from which the information was received. This limitation on classful routing protocols will, therefore, not allow different prefix lengths to be used within a major network.

When IP addressing was first being implemented, devices only understood three prefix lengths in association with the different classes: class A (8-bit prefix), class B (16-bit prefix), and class C (24-bit prefix). This became a limitation as networks began to grow, so the concept of subnetting was introduced. Traditional devices were limited in their ability to understand prefix lengths and subnets. Classful routing did not transmit any information about the prefix length because it was calculated from the information about the address class that was provided in the first few bits of information.

Classful routing is a severe scalability limitation when designing a network, because it will not allow you to properly utilize valuable address space within a major network. This also leads to larger routing tables and routing traffic across a network. This limitation might not be as much of a factor if you are designing a small network that does not require all the scalability of a classless routing protocol.

Classless Routing Protocols

Classless routing protocols such as OSPF, EIGRP, IS-IS, BGP, and RIP version 2 do include prefix length information in their routing update information. This capability allows classless routing protocols to group networks into one entry and then use the prefix length to specify what networks are grouped. This means that a router that's running a classless routing protocol will not have to determine the prefix length for any given network. Different prefix length information within a major network is allowed and provides greater flexibility when you're designing a network.

Classless routing gives you the capability to have a different prefix length at different points across a network. Variable-length subnet masking supports more efficient use of address space and reduces routing tables and routing traffic through summarization.

Limitations of Routing Protocols

To maintain an optimal routing environment, it is important to determine the functionality required in selecting a routing protocol. During any network design, it is important to determine the future growth of the network and how the network will react to this growth. This is a direct impact that's associated with your choice in routing protocol, so this choice requires an overall knowledge of routing protocols that will allow you to choose the best routing protocol for your situation.

Distance-Vector Routing Protocol Limitations

There are several limitations with routing protocols that impact a protocol's overall scalability, thus impacting a network's operation. The following is a brief list of scalability limitations associated with distance-vector protocols:

➤ Convergence delay

➤ CPU utilization

➤ Bandwidth utilization

When the size of a routing table increases, so does the number of CPU cycles needed to process this information, and because distance-vector protocols such as RIP and IGRP broadcast their entire routing tables, this will increase the amount of bandwidth used. This will cause an overall snowball effect and will continue to propagate across your network, which could cause serious repercussions in your network's operation.

Link-State Routing Protocol Limitations

The limitations inherent in distance-vector protocols were addressed with link-state protocols and for the most part corrected or improved. Link-state routing protocols use Dijkstra's algorithm for route calculation, which enables the protocols to scale along with your network's growth. Link-state protocols have the advantage over distance-vector protocols in providing a better functionality on large networks. The only real limitation with link-state routing protocols is the complexity of the configuration needed by the router for operation.

Practice Questions

Question 1

> Network scalability is limited by what two factors?
>
> ○ a. Administrative issues
>
> ○ b. Equipment issues
>
> ○ c. Technical issues
>
> ○ d. Operational issues

Answers c and d are correct. Operational issues promote the use of flat areas, whereas technical issues promote the use of small areas for routing. Answers a and b are incorrect because they are not issues associated with routing protocol scalability.

Question 2

> What are the characteristics associated with using classful routing protocols? [Choose all that apply.]
>
> ❑ a. Large routing tables
>
> ❑ b. Support for VLSM
>
> ❑ c. Inability to properly utilize address space
>
> ❑ d. Lack of support for VLSM

Answers a, c, and d are correct. The limitations of classful protocols are due to the fact that they have a limited understanding of prefix length. This prohibits the protocols from supporting VLSM functionality, which causes large routing tables and an inefficient use of address space. Answer b is incorrect because classless routing protocols, *not* classful routing protocols, support VLSM.

Question 3

> Which routing protocols are classful?
>
> ○ a. RIP v.2
>
> ○ b. IGRP
>
> ○ c. IS-IS
>
> ○ d. RIP

Answers b and d are correct. RIP and IGRP are classful routing protocols because they do not send subnet prefix information in their routing updates. This limits them to using the rules of network classes. Answers a and c are incorrect because RIP v.2 and IS-IS do support prefix information being sent in their routing updates. Therefore, they are not limited to network classes.

Question 4

> What are the limitations of distance-vector routing protocols? [Choose all that apply.]
>
> ❑ a. Convergence
>
> ❑ b. Complexity
>
> ❑ c. CPU utilization
>
> ❑ d. Bandwidth utilization

Answers a, c, and d are correct. Because distance-vector routing protocols send their entire routing tables during updates, this causes an increase in bandwidth utilization across the network, especially on low-speed WAN links. This also causes an increase in network convergence time and the amount of CPU power required to calculate the routing tables. Answer b is incorrect because in general, distance-vector routing protocols are not complex to configure or maintain.

Question 5

What factors make a routing protocol "scalable"?

❍ a. VLSM support

❍ b. Fast convergence

❍ c. Hop count limitations

❍ d. Reduced routing tables

Answers a, b, and d are correct. Support for VLSM, fast convergence, and re-duced routing table size are all desired attributes for a routing protocol. Link-state routing protocols and EIGRP fit into this category and are the most scalable of all routing protocols. Hop count limitation is associated with distance-vector routing protocols and is a severe scalability limitation. Therefore, answer c is incorrect.

Need To Know More?

 Berkowitz, Howard. *Designing Routing and Switching Architectures for Enterprise Networks.* Macmillan Technical Publishing. Indianapolis, IN, 1999. ISBN 1-57870-060-4. This book is geared toward understanding the concepts of routing and switching architecture rather than analyzing everything from the manufacturer viewpoint. As a result, you get a firm understanding of the fundamentals.

 Huitema, Christian. *Routing in the Internet.* Prentice Hall. Upper Saddle River, NJ, 1995. ISBN 0-13132-192-7. This book focuses on basic internetwork architecture and addressing. It is a well-written book for all audience levels.

 Larson, Bob, Corwin Low, and Michael Simon. *CCNP Routing Exam Prep.* The Coriolis Group. Scottsdale, AZ, Fall 2000. ISBN 1-57610-778-2. This book, an Exam Prep for the CCNP exam, covers each related subject in great detail.

 For more information on classful and classless routing protocols and their limitations, visit **www.cisco.com** and perform searches using the protocols in question as keywords.

 Visit **www.cis.ohio-state.edu/htbin/rfc/rfc-index.html** to download any RFC, whether complete or in progress. Related topics to this chapter are RFC 1812 (which defines subnet masking), RFC 1009 (which defines VLSM), RFC 1918 (which defines private address space), RFCs 1517, 1518, RFC 1058 (which defines RIP v.1), RFC 1723 (which defines RIP v.2), and RFC 2178 (which defines OSPF).

Configuring OSPF in a Single Area

Terms you'll need to understand:

✓ Neighbors

✓ Adjacency

✓ Hellos

✓ Multiaccess versus non-broadcast multiaccess (NBMA) networks

✓ OSPF neighbor discovery

✓ OSPF network discovery

✓ Area types

✓ Router types

Techniques you'll need to master:

✓ Understanding why OSPF is better than Routing Information Protocol (RIP)

✓ Configuring OSPF for operation in a single-area environment

✓ Configuring route summaries

✓ Verifying configurations with **show** commands

This chapter begins the discussion of the features, use, and configuration of advanced routing protocols. Open Shortest Path First (OSPF), which was developed in the 1980s specifically to overcome the limitations of RIP, is one of the more advanced routing protocols. This chapter explores why OSPF is better than RIP and how to deploy OSPF in the network if you have determined that OSPF provides a better fit than RIP for your network. This chapter will cover how OSPF works in a single-area (small) network and will discuss detailed configurations for OSPF in both types of deployments. The chapter will also explore how OSPF locates other routers, how OSPF obtains and maintains its database, and how the routing table is generated.

OSPF vs. RIP

OSPF (a link-state protocol) was designed to improve upon RIP (a distance-vector protocol). First specified as *OSPF version 1* in RFC 1131, later as *version 2* in RFC 1247, and most recently in RFC 2328, OSPF has become a worthy standards-based replacement for RIP, which has severe limitations. OSPF's primary features include:

➤ *Fast convergence*—Because of RIP's hold-down timer, it is quite slow to converge or adapt to topology changes: It takes minutes to age and purge defunct routes. Slow convergence is a big issue in today's networks—your internetwork must be able to adapt quickly to changes in routing pathways and reachability. OSPF spreads updates quickly and is much faster at healing the network after an outage.

➤ *No hop count limits*—RIP has a maximum hop count of 15. This limitation is necessary for eliminating routing loops in distance-vector protocols. OSPF has no limit based on hops, thus allowing it to support much larger networks.

➤ *Support for variable-length subnet masks (VLSMs)*—RIP version 1 does not allow VLSMs because it does not advertise subnet masks. RIP learns the subnet mask associated with a class A, B, or C network by using an address within that network number found on one of the router's interfaces. RIP's summarization is done by another router's including only the classful A, B, or C network address, not subnets, in its updates. Summarization in RIP is limited to inclusion of the shortest hop-count path to a nonattached full class A, B, or C network address in the routing table. OSPF allows the use of VLSMs to create hierarchical routing environments. The size of the routing table can be reduced (a must considering that OSPF is used for very large networks).

➤ *Bandwidth-based path-selection metric*—RIP uses hop count as its metric, but it's blind to the link's speed. Originally, this was adequate because everything in the local area network (LAN) was very fast (for example, 10Mbps). In addition, everything in the wide area network (WAN) was fairly homogeneous at 56Kbps or so. Hop count was great when all links were considered identical because the only difference between one route and another was how many routers (hops) were in between the two networks. OSPF may use a metric related to the inverse of the bandwidth—that is, the higher the speed of the circuit, the lower the metric. Cisco's default begins with 100 million, or 10^8 divided by the bandwidth of the circuit (for example, 10Mbps Ethernet would have the metric of 10).

➤ *Update efficiency*—RIP simply copies its entire routing table (except as limited by split horizon) out of every interface periodically, whether or not changes are necessary. In a large network, this can be a burden. OSPF normally sends only changes, and then only when changes occur. In a large, stable network, the update traffic from OSPF should be negligible.

Note: Remember from your CCNA studies that split horizon occurs when routing information is prevented from exiting the router interface through which the information was received.

Overview of OSPF

Once the router is configured for OSPF, it must initiate the process of learning its environment. OSPF goes through a few phases of initialization. In the initialization of OSPF, the router goes through its process of determining its neighbors and adjacencies and compiling its routing table. This is explained in more detail later in this chapter. The following is a brief description of the initialization process:

1. The router uses hellos to determine its neighbors.

2. The router develops adjacencies with its neighbors.

3. The router starts the initial database exchange with its neighbors. This is called the ExStart phase.

4. The DR sends the router its routing information, and the new router acknowledges the receipt of this information. This is called the Exchange phase.

5. The router begins loading the routing information and compiling a routing table. This is called the Loading phase.

6. Once the router is finished calculating its routing table and is ready to become an active member of the network, it is referred to as being in its full state.

Note: OSPF is complex, and it is easy to get bogged down in the details. This overview uses OSPF terms defined later in the chapter and saves most of the explanation for later because if you've already confronted OSPF, you're ready for an overall view. If this is the first time you've heard of OSPF, you'll probably need to read this section once quickly, read the rest of the single-area part of the chapter, and then reread this section.

Identifying Neighbors with Hellos

The first step in the initialization process involves the OSPF router identifying other routers who are its neighbors—that is, other routers who share subnets with it. OSPF routers learn about neighbors using multicast hellos from their OSPF-configured interfaces.

These hellos identify neighbors and keep the OSPF router aware of the neighbors' up/down status.

OSPF hellos happen by default every 10 seconds. If a router doesn't hear its neighbor before its own dead timer fires (usually four times the hello timer), the router can assume the link (and maybe the router) is down. This fact leads to a common misconception about OSPF. OSPF does reconverge after an outage very quickly, but OSPF cannot start the reconvergence until it knows its neighbors have gone away. Either the layer 2 keepalive or the hellos could declare the link down. If the router notices the problem from the keepalives, it will take an average of 25 seconds to miss three keepalives. Then the flooding and recalculation of the routing table (described later) begins. It is usually assumed that OSPF will take 30 to 42 seconds to notice a failure and reconverge.

Developing Adjacencies

After identifying and tracking neighbors with hellos, OSPF learns network information in two distinct ways. First, the router uses the neighbor information to establish adjacencies with each other. An *adjacency* is a relationship that provides the basis for exchanging routing update information. We're willing to share our innermost secrets with adjacent neighbors. The adjacency means that I'll give you a copy of my entire routing database (not routing table) as soon as the adjacency is created. Each router adds database details it learns from its partner in the *adjacency* to its own database. On point-to-point links, adjacencies are established with all neighbors (there is only one neighbor). On multiaccess networks, OSPF has a mechanism to limit the number of adjacencies, and therefore the amount of update traffic. A designated router (DR) and a backup designated router (BDR) are elected, and all neighbors establish adjacencies with them only. The second way OSPF learns network information is by running the Shortest Path First (SPF) algorithm to produce a graph from which to extract the routing table.

Building the routing table is relatively simple. The routing table contains destination network, outbound interface, next hop address, and cost to that network. If a router has four neighbors on its attached interfaces and 1,000 destinations, all 1,000 destinations have one of the four attached routers as their next hop (except for those on connected routes).

Flooding

After the initial exchange of database information, OSPF learns of and integrates network changes by using a very different mechanism, called *flooding*. As soon as a router learns of a state change on one of its own connected links, it immediately floods an update that contains information on only the changed link—not the entire database—to all its adjacent neighbors. The neighbors change their local databases and continue flooding the change.

 The flooding should take only a couple of seconds, but that time and the SPF calculation time depend on the network's size. SPF is a computationally intense algorithm. On small routers with lower-speed processors, flooding can take a relatively long time and use a relatively large amount of memory. You'll see that one of the reasons for using a multi-area OSPF is to hold down the processing load, the memory volume, and the eventual routing table search time.

As soon as the database is changed, a new SPF update must be run. As you'll remember with distance-vector protocols, there's a problem with the freshness of the information. OSPF uses sequence numbering and reliable transfers (they must be acknowledged) to make certain the flooded information is current.

Multiple routers may report one change to a link (depending on how things are connected). If the network has slow update paths, it is possible (and even likely) that if the SPF update is run immediately upon receiving the flooded change, other changes come in during the SPF cycle, resulting in an immediate recalculation. Essentially, you might get into a continuous flurry of SPF updates (this happened in earlier versions). The solution is to dampen the update frequency or delay of the beginning of the first SPF calculation (the Cisco default is five seconds). In addition, you should delay between consecutive SPF calculations (a default of ten seconds). As a result, reconvergence is delayed, but it is usually a good trade-off.

Note: Remember that a feature of OSPF is that all routers recalculate for every change, no matter how minor (another reason for multi-area operation for larger networks).

Link-state protocols such as OSPF also flood link-state updates periodically (the default is thirty minutes) to make certain, even with all the reliability features in place, that every router's tables are correct. This periodic update is known as a *paranoid update.*

Note: Neither the BSCN class nor the test goes into every detail of OSPF operation. You may want to read the RFC 2328, all 200+ pages, and visit the Cisco Web site for more detail.

OSPF Single-Area Operation

An OSPF network consists of nodes (routers) and the links that connect them. OSPF maintains a database (not the routing table) of all neighbor routers and all active links in its universe. The total amount of information could grow without end if there weren't separate areas. *Areas* allow you to create subsets of the OSPF network. Each router in an area must maintain an identical database to that of every other router in the area. In small networks, with up to seventy routers, you can use a single area referred to as *Area 0.* Figure 6.1 illustrates the terminology used in an OSPF network.

Links connect nodes. Each link exists as a router-link in the database. Each link has a cost associated with it that the OSPF routers use as a metric (least-cost sum) to determine the best path to each destination network. Cisco has traditionally used a cost related to bandwidth (using the formula 100,000,000/BW). For example, a 56Kbps link has a cost of 1,785 associated with it, whereas a 100Mbps Fiber Distributed Data Interface (FDDI) link has a cost of 1. Link speeds have grown rapidly (for example, much faster than 100Mbps), so Cisco has added a command to allow you to increase the 100Mbps figure, thereby allowing for higher-bandwidth links to be handled correctly.

Learning Initial Database Information

The first phase of network learning starts with routers learning of each other and performing immediate, initial exchanges of their current databases. Neighbor router discovery starts with hellos. As soon as all the routers know about all other

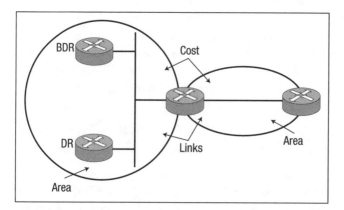

Figure 6.1 OSPF terminology.

routers, they begin the exchange protocol—the way they learn initial routing database information.

OSPF issues a number of differing packets. These packets, shown in Table 6.1, are function-specific entities, each with its own special mission.

The Hello Protocol

OSPF uses a hello protocol to discover other routers and decide how to interact with them. Once the relationships have been established, OSPF uses hellos as keepalives to learn when other routers go away. Hello messages are used to discover neighbors (routers that share links with *this* router) and are sent to the IP multicast address 224.0.0.5, an address to which all OSPF routers (and only OSPF routers) respond. Hellos contain the following fields:

➤ *Router-ID*—A 32-bit value that uniquely identifies a router. It is chosen by looking at all interfaces and choosing the IP address with the highest numeric value. If a loopback interface has been configured with an IP address, it overrides the value of any physical interface and the highest value on any loopback interface is chosen. To be selected as Router-ID, the interface does not need to be one that OSPF itself uses. Once that value is chosen, it remains even if another interface with a higher value is activated later.

➤ *Hello/Dead Intervals*—Hello intervals represent the time between Keepalive messages. If a router doesn't receive a hello from a neighbor within the dead interval, the silent router is declared down and loses status as a neighbor. The typical hello interval (40 seconds) and the dead interval are four times the hello frequency (10 seconds).

➤ *Neighbors*—Routers that share the same link. Actually, routers go through several stages before they become full partners (develop an adjacency).

➤ *Area-ID*—A numeric value shared by all routers in an area.

➤ *Router Priority*—A number that may be used to select a DR. The normal selection is done by router priority, with Router-ID being used as a tiebreaker.

Table 6.1	OSPF packet types.
Type Code	**Description**
1	Hello
2	Database description (DD or DBD or DDP)
3	Link-state request (LSR)
4	Link-state update (LSU)
5	Link-state acknowledgment (LSAck)

If no priority is chosen, the DR becomes the router with the largest Router-ID value and the BDR is the router with the second highest Router-ID value.

➤ *DR IP Address*—The router that acts as distributor of information for this multiaccess segment. Essentially, it is used to hold down the number of adjacencies on multiaccess links.

➤ *BDR IP Address*—The backup for the DR. It waits for half a second to hear DR flooding updates. If the DR doesn't do its job, the BDR preempts and passes the updates to all adjacent routers. A new BDR is then elected.

➤ *Authentication Type*—Used to provide secure updates (optional).

➤ *Authentication Password*—Authentication password (if used).

➤ *Stub Area Flag*—An area with only one point of contact with the rest of OSPF and no connections to outside routing protocols. This description is expanded later in this chapter.

A router starts out the state by saying hello to the multicast 224.0.0.5 (all OSPF routers), which lists all neighbors it has heard hellos from in the last dead interval. If things are just starting, the router is in a down state and no neighbors are in the hello message.

As soon as a router hears a hello from another router, the state machine of *this* router moves to Init, which means "I've heard from you within the last dead interval but we're not truly neighbors yet." This router's hello packets include the list of all neighbors from whom it has heard hellos within the last dead interval.

Listing 6.1 shows an EtherPeek display of a basic hello packet. The highlighted fields in the hello packet must be identical for any routers you want to be neighbors.

Note: You may change all of the timers. However, often you may not know the full impact of these changes (immediately), thus causing strange and unpredictable results.

Listing 6.1 An EtherPeek display of a basic hello packet.

```
IP Header - Internet Protocol Datagram
  Version:                4
  Header Length:          5
  Precedence:             6
  Type of Service:        %000
  Unused:                 %00
  Total Length:           64
  Identifier:             0
  Fragmentation Flags:    %000
```

```
Fragment Offset:        0
Time To Live:           1
IP Type:                0x59  OSPF
Header Checksum:        0xce9a
Source IP Address:      10.0.0.6
Dest. IP Address:       224.0.0.5
No Internet Datagram Options
OSPF - Open Shortest Path First Routing Protocol
Version:                2
Type:                   1  Hello
Packet Length:          44
Router IP Address:      172.16.64.6
Area ID:                0
Checksum:               0x1088
Authentication Type:    0  No Authentication
Authentication Data:
--------                00 00 00 00 00 00 00 00
Network Mask:           0xff000000
Hello Interval:         10  seconds
Options:                %00000010
        No AS External Link State Advertisements
Router Priority:        1
Dead Interval:          40  seconds
Designated Router:      0.0.0.0  No Desgntd Rtr
Backup Designated Router: 0.0.0.0  No Backup Desgntd Rtr
```

Neighbors

When your router sees its own router ID listed in the neighbor list of the hello packet from one of its neighbors, their relationship moves into a *two-way* state. The routers on a broadcast multiaccess network elect a DR and a BDR.

The election proceeds as follows: Each router's hello packet lists the interface address of the router that the hello-sending router believes to be the DR. Priority values start at 0 (never a DR) and go to 1 or more. The router with the numerically highest priority value wins the DR election. The router with the second highest priority is the BDR. If no priorities have been specified, the router with the largest Router-ID value wins. The router ID is defined as the numerically highest IP address on any active interface on a router. It is possible to hard-code the router's ID. To force the router's ID to be a certain address always, create a logical loopback interface and assign an IP address (no matter how high or low).

The election finishes when all the routers have settled on a DR and BDR. Now the router is ready to begin creating adjacencies, meaning the routers are ready to swap initial database information.

DR election is not necessary on point-to-point networks because both routers form an adjacency. The purpose of the DR/BDR scheme is to minimize the number of adjacencies on multiaccess networks.

Adjacencies

On point-to-point links, each router can share with its neighbor (there is only one neighbor). However, on a multiaccess network such as Ethernet, the number of connections (adjacencies) would be too large. As a result, with this initial database exchange and with the flooding of network changes later on, you would require far more bandwidth, far larger databases, and more recalculation time. Electing the DR and BDR solves the problem of many adjacencies. Figure 6.2 shows how using a BDR allows you to have fewer adjacencies.

 The number of connections between n devices is (n x (n − 1)) / 2. So, if 10 routers shared a LAN segment (a large number before LAN switching), you would need (10 × 9) / 2, or 45, adjacencies. If you establish adjacencies with only the DR and BDR, the same number of devices would need only 2 x (n − 1), or 18, adjacencies.

Listing 6.2 shows the router interface as well as some of the more interesting details of OSPF. The command used to generate this response is **show ip ospf interface Ethernet 0**.

Listing 6.2   OSPF interface parameters.

```
Ethernet0 is up, line protocol is up
  Internet Address 10.0.0.1/8, Area 0
  Process ID 1, Router ID 172.16.32.1, Network Type BROADCAST,
  Cost: 10
  Transmit Delay is 1 sec, State DROTHER, Priority 1
  Designated Router (ID) 172.16.64.8, Interface address 10.0.0.8
  Backup Designated router (ID) 172.16.64.7, Interface address
     10.0.0.7
  Timer intervals configured, Hello 10, Dead 40, Wait 40,
     Retransmit 5
    Hello due in 00:00:07
  Neighbor Count is 7, Adjacent neighbor count is 2
     Adjacent with neighbor 172.16.64.7  (Backup Designated Router)
     Adjacent with neighbor 172.16.64.8  (Designated Router)
  Suppress hello for 0 neighbor(s)
```

Some of the items of particular interest in this listing include the IP address of the router's Ethernet 0 interface, the Router-ID and Area values, the hello and dead intervals, and the Router Priority value. This is a good example of the concept of OSPF using a DR to limit the adjacencies on a multiaccess network.

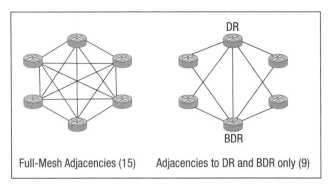

DR

BDR

Full-Mesh Adjacencies (15)   Adjacencies to DR and BDR only (9)

Figure 6.2   Adjacencies with and without the DR and BDR.

Look at the neighbor count and the adjacent neighbor count; then look below that line to see who is adjacent: only the DR and BDR. The network is a broadcast network, not a point-to-point or NBMA network configuration. Examples of NBMA networks are Frame Relay, X.25, Integrated Services Digital Network (ISDN), and Asynchronous Transfer Mode (ATM).

 NBMA versus the other types of networks is an important concept to grasp. Essentially, you select the DR and BDR with the router priority. In addition, periodic hellos are replaced with less frequently transmitted polls.

ExStart

Once the adjacencies are established, the routers move to ExStart state in order to prepare for the initial database exchange. The router over each adjacency decides a master/slave relationship. This decides which router transfers and which router listens. The master is the router with the highest interface address. At this same time, the sequence numbers that will be used to exchange the databases are decided.

Exchange

The master sends and the slave acknowledges the Database Description (DD or sometimes DBD) packets. The DD packets contain summary information of the entire master router's database. After the master finishes, the slave member of the adjacency dumps its entire database in DD packets to the master. Both routers use link-state acknowledgements (LSAcks) to verify that things have gone as expected. Otherwise, retransmissions take place.

Loading

At this time, the routers enter the Loading state and may begin sending link-state requests (LSRs) to any neighbor. They may also receive link-state updates

(LSUs) from any neighbor in the Exchange state asking about more recent information on routes learned in the summary exchange. Of course, the LSUs are carried in LSAcks.

Full

Eventually, when the databases of both routers are identical, the routers show the state between them as *full*.

Route Calculation and Cost

At this stage, all routers have identical databases. The routers run (actually have been running) the SPF calculation and build the forwarding database. OSPF uses cost as a metric, so the SPF algorithm builds a loop-free topology using the costs stored for each interface in the router-links database. To see a summary listing of the neighbors, use the command **show ip ospf neighbor**. Listing 6.3 shows a list of routers and their states summarized.

Listing 6.3 Neighbor status summary.

```
Neighbor ID  Pri  State         Dead Time   Address      Interface
172.16.32.2  1    FULL/BDR      00:00:37    172.16.32.2  ATM0.9
172.16.32.4  1    FULL/DR       00:00:30    172.16.32.4  ATM0.9
172.16.32.2  1    2WAY/DROTHER  00:00:37    10.0.0.2     Ethernet0
172.16.64.7  1    FULL/BDR      00:00:36    10.0.0.7     Ethernet0
172.16.64.6  1    2WAY/DROTHER  00:00:36    10.0.0.6     Ethernet0
172.16.64.5  1    2WAY/DROTHER  00:00:30    10.0.0.5     Ethernet0
172.16.32.4  1    2WAY/DROTHER  00:00:30    10.0.0.4     Ethernet0
172.16.64.8  1    FULL/DR       00:00:39    10.0.0.8     Ethernet0
10.0.0.3     1    2WAY/DROTHER  00:00:39    10.0.0.3     Ethernet0
```

Listing 6.3 includes nine routers. If even one of the routers had been configured with a dead timer of 39 seconds (rather than the default 40 seconds), that router could never become a neighbor (or adjacent, which is the basis for continuing the process). The routers must agree on the dead timer. The best advice is don't change anything. If you must, make certain that the parameter being changed is set to the same value in all routers that share the area.

Maintaining the Routing Table

Now that the routers have formed their adjacencies and shared their routing databases initially, it's time to move on to the normal operation of the network. The routers continue their hellos and monitor their links. As soon as the state of a link changes, the attached router needs to tell every other router as soon as possible. The technique used is referred to as *flooding*.

Flooded Updates

For the rest of the lifetime of these routers, they send LSUs, which indicate changes to a link to which they are attached. LSUs are also known as *link-state advertisements* (LSAs). In other words, phase one is over; you now have complete databases. In phase two, you use flooding to maintain the databases.

When a router notices a change in one of its links, it generates an LSU and forwards it to the DR and BDR using the 224.0.0.6 (known as "all designated routers") address. The DR then sends the LSU to every adjacent OSPF router on the link using the 224.0.0.5 (all OSPF routers) multicast address. Each router must send an LSAck back to the DR; otherwise, the LSU goes into a retransmission queue.

The BDR hears the original message to the DR and sets an internal timer (.5 seconds is the default). Should the timer fire before the DR starts sending the LSU back to everyone, the BDR takes over the update process and a new BDR election is held. If a router that had been the DR comes back up after a failure, does it become DR again? No. If the DR goes down, the BDR is promoted to DR and then an election for a new BDR is initiated. Should the original DR come back online, it does not get its job back, even though it may have a higher priority. If the new DR goes down, the new BDR is promoted into its place. Another election is forced, and the original DR gets the BDR job. At this point, it takes a DR failure for the original router to regain the DR title. Confused? In short, the DR role is not dynamically maintained. It loses its job if it cannot perform its function. It does not get it back unless the new DR fails and then the new BDR (which moves into the DR position and forces a new election for BDR) fails once it has been promoted (in that order). Only a BDR can become the DR if a DR fails.

All routers that receive the LSU flood it out of each interface to all their adjacent neighbors on other OSPF-configured interfaces. Thus, the change packet is carried to all routers in the area quickly.

Maintaining the Topology Database

Flooding essentially consists of LSUs being spread around to every router in the area. This flooding happens when a link changes state or every thirty minutes, whichever comes first. When an LSU is received, the router immediately compares it with the contents of the topology database. The resulting action depends on the state of the database as described in the following list:

➤ If the entry already exists but contains the same information, the aging timer is reset and an LSA is sent back to the DR. The router determines the information is the same by examining the sequence number.

➤ If the entry exists but the received LSU contains new information or if the entry doesn't exist, the router sends an LSR that asks for details about the entry to the original sender of the LSU. As a result, another LSU is sent back to the router asking for the update from the original sender.

➤ If the entry exists but contains older information, the router sends an LSU with the newer information back to the source of the original LSU.

Link-State Advertisement Types

There are several types of LSAs, each of which represents a different kind of information. They represent the information that will be held in the OSPF database. Be sure not to confuse them with OSPF packet types, which are not the same thing. Table 6.2 lists the LSA types.

Table 6.2	LSA types.	
Type Code	**Advertisement Name**	**Description of Advertisement**
1	Router LSA (Router link-states)	Describes the state of the router's interfaces to a collected area. This LSA is originated by all routers and is flooded in a single area only.
2	Network LSA (Net link-states)	Contains the list of routers connected to a network. This LSA is originated for multiaccess networks by the DR and is flooded in a single area only.
3	Summary LSA (Summary link-states)	Describes a route to a destination outside of the area but inside the AS. These LSAs describe routes to networks and are originated by the ABRs. They are flooded throughout the associated area.
4	ASBR Summary LSA (not shown in Listing 6.4, later in this chapter)	Describes a route to a destination outside the area but inside the AS. These LSAs describe routes to AS boundary routers and are originated by the ASBRs. They are flooded throughout the associated area.
5	AS External LSA (not shown)	Each AS external LSA describes a route to a destination in another AS. Default routes for the AS can also be described by AS external link advertisements. These advertisements are originated by the AS boundary router and are flooded throughout the AS.
6	Group-Membership LSA (not shown)	These advertisements are specific to a particular OSPF area. They are never flooded beyond their area of origination. They advertise directly attached networks.

(continued)

Table 6.2	LSA types *(continued)*.	
Type Code	**Advertisement Name**	**Description of Advertisement**
7	NSSA External LSA (not shown)	These advertisements describe routes within the Not-So-Stubby Area (NSSA). They can be summarized and converted into Type 5 LSAs by the ABRs. After conversion they will be distributed to the areas that can support Type 5 LSAs. This advertisement is originated by the ABR and flooded throughout the NSSA.
8	Link-LSA (not shown)	This LSA advertises a separate link-LSA for each link it is attached to. These LSAs are never flooded beyond the link that they are associated with.
9	Intra-Area-Prefix LSA (not shown)	This LSA advertises one or more IPv6 address prefixes that are associated with a router, attached stub network, or an attached transit network.
10	Local-Area LSA (not shown)	If the Opaque LSA is Type 10 (upon reception) and is not the same as the area associated with the target interface, the Opaque LSA must not be flooded out of the interface. Implementation should keep track of the OSPF area associated with each Opaque LSA having an area-local flooding scope.
11	External-AS LSA (not shown)	If the Opaque LSA is Type 11 (the LSA is flooded throughout the AS) and the target interface is associated with a stub area, the Opaque LSA must not be flooded out of the interface. A Type 11 Opaque LSA that's received on an interface associated with a stub area must be discarded and not acknowledged (the neighboring router has flooded the LSA in error).

For example, Router LSAs (Type 1) contain information about the links in the network. A link is identified by a combination of router ID and link identifier; both identifiers look like IP addresses. You can view these records as well as the rest of the LSAs by using the **show ip ospf database** command. Listing 6.4 shows a part of an OSPF database.

Listing 6.4   OSPF database.

```
OSPF Router with ID (172.16.32.1) (Process ID 1)

        Router Link States (Area 0)

Link ID        ADV Router     Age    Seq#         Checksum Link count
10.0.0.3       10.0.0.3       231    0x80000003 0xAF3E   1
172.16.32.1    172.16.32.1    229    0x80000003 0x3618   1
```

```
172.16.32.2    172.16.32.2    231    0x80000003 0x3417    1
172.16.32.4    172.16.32.4    226    0x80000003 0x3015    1
172.16.64.5    172.16.64.5    226    0x80000003 0xEB16    1
172.16.64.6    172.16.64.6    232    0x80000003 0xE915    1
172.16.64.7    172.16.64.7    232    0x80000003 0xE714    1
172.16.64.8    172.16.64.8    230    0x80000003 0xE513    1
```

               Net Link States (Area 0)

Link ID	ADV Router	Age	Seq#	Checksum
10.0.0.8	172.16.64.8	227	0x80000002	0xFD53

               Summary Net Link States (Area 0)

Link ID	ADV Router	Age	Seq#	Checksum
172.16.32.0	172.16.32.1	109	0x80000003	0x2F50
172.16.32.0	172.16.32.2	85	0x80000001	0x2D53
172.16.32.0	172.16.32.4	113	0x80000003	0x1D5F
172.16.64.0	172.16.64.5	70	0x80000001	0xD864
172.16.64.0	172.16.64.6	61	0x80000001	0xD269
172.16.64.0	172.16.64.7	79	0x80000003	0xC870
172.16.64.0	172.16.64.8	75	0x80000003	0xC275

               Router Link States (Area 1)

Link ID	ADV Router	Age	Seq#	Checksum	Link count
172.16.32.1	172.16.32.1	122	0x80000004	0xDCD7	1

The Router LSAs are generated by routers that describe links to which they are attached. Network LSAs are generated by DRs.

OSPF Single-Area Configuration

It's quite simple to set up OSPF for single-area operation. The OSPF configuration is almost identical to the configuration for RIP and other routing protocols. The statements to do so are shown in Listing 6.5.

Listing 6.5   Single-area OSPF configuration.

```
interface Ethernet 0
ip address 10.0.1.1 255.255.255.0
!
interface Ethernet 1
ip address 10.0.2.1 255.255.255.0
!
interface Serial 0
ip address 172.16.5.1 255.255.255.0
!
interface Serial 1
```

```
ip address 172.16.6.1 255.255.255.0
!
router ospf 1
network 10.0.0.0 0.255.255.255 area 0
network 172.16.5.1 0.0.0.0 area 0
network 172.16.6.1.0.0.0.0. area 0
```

Listing 6.5 shows that an OSPF routing process has been created. It listens and advertises routes on interfaces Ethernet 0 and 1 and Serial 0. The **network** statement in OSPF differs from that of other protocols—RIP, Interior Gateway Routing Protocol (IGRP), and Enhanced Interior Gateway Routing Protocol (EIGRP)—by using a wildcard mask (the same technique as that used with access lists) to select one or more interfaces. The statement for **network 10.0.0.0** includes any subnet and any host. If the router's interface matches the pattern, the interface belongs to OSPF.

Notice how the statements for 172.16.5.1 and 172.16.6.1 must match the interface address exactly. This specific selection of interfaces from a single IP address is unique to OSPF.

Each interface must be assigned to an area by including the area number with each **network** statement. In this example, the first area is Area 0—the backbone area to which all other areas must attach. In a single-area deployment, you have only Area 0 in your internetwork. You must therefore specify all OSPF interfaces using a **network** statement.

One final item to note: The 1 in **router ospf 1** is a process ID number. It is arbitrary and is not advertised between routers, but it can be used to allow more than one OSPF routing process running in a single router.

Verifying Proper OSPF Operation

Several common commands are used to verify that OSPF operation and router connectivity are working properly on a network. You should become very familiar with these commands to ensure that your routers are configured and operating properly on your network. The most common of these command are described in Table 6.3.

Table 6.3 OSPF commands.	
Command Syntax	**Description**
show ip route	Displays all the routes learned by the router and how they were learned.
show ip protocols	Verifies that OSPF is configured. Displays information about timers, metrics, filters, and other router information.

(continued)

Table 6.3 OSPF commands *(continued)*.	
Command Syntax	**Description**
show ip ospf interface	Displays the area ID and adjacency information. Verifies that the interfaces have been configured in the intended areas. It also displays the timer intervals, including hello intervals, and shows neighbors' adjacencies.
show ip ospf	Displays the number of times the SPF algorithm has been executed. It also shows the link-state update interval, assuming no topological changes have occurred.
show ip ospf neighbor detail	Displays a detailed list of neighbors, their states, and priorities.
show ip ospf database	Displays the contents of the topological database maintained by the router. This command also shows the router intermediate system (IS) and OSPF process ID.
clear ip route *	Clears all routes from the routing table. This allows you to verify that routes are being learned.
debug ip ospf events	Displays router interaction during the hello, exchange, and flooding processes.

Practice Questions

Question 1

What are some of the reasons OSPF is better than RIP in a large network? [Choose the three best answers.]

- ❑ a. No hop count limit
- ❑ b. Bandwidth-based metrics
- ❑ c. Lower processor utilization
- ❑ d. Faster convergence

Answers a, b, and d are correct. Lack of hop limitations, the use of cost based on bandwidth as a metric, and faster convergence make OSPF a great choice for larger internetworks. Answer c is incorrect because SPF calculation takes much more processing than does RIP.

Question 2

What is an internal router?

- ○ a. A backbone router
- ○ b. A router that connects multiple areas together
- ○ c. A router that connects to an external AS
- ○ d. A router that has all interfaces in a single OSPF area

Answer d is correct. All interfaces must be within a single area. Although an internal router can also be a backbone router, that is not the only factor. The trick is that a router can also be a backbone router without being an internal router. Therefore, answer a is incorrect. Answer b is incorrect because a router that connects multiple areas together is an ABR. Answer c is incorrect because a router that connects to an external AS is an ASBR.

Question 3

> Which OSPF initialization state is indicated when both routers' databases are the same?
>
> ❑ a. Exchange state
>
> ❑ b. ExStart state
>
> ❑ c. Loading state
>
> ❑ d. Full state

Answer d is correct. After the routers have gone through their initialization phase, their OSPF databases will become identical, and the routers are known to be in Full state. Answer a is incorrect because in the Exchange state, Database Description packets are exchanged between the master and slave routers. Answer b is incorrect because in the ExStart state, adjacencies are formed and the routers begin their exchange of database information. Answer c is incorrect because in the Loading state, the router sends link-state requests (LSRs) to its neighbors to begin building its routing table.

Question 4

> What is contained in the topology database?
>
> ○ a. Neighbors
>
> ○ b. All routes
>
> ○ c. Best routes
>
> ○ d. Address of the designated router

Answer b is correct. All possible routes to all destinations are kept in the topology database. Answer a is incorrect because neighbor information is kept in the adjacencies database. Answer c is incorrect because the best routes are kept in the routing table or forwarding database. Answer d is incorrect because the DR is used with multiaccess networks to limit the number of adjacencies and the amount of traffic.

Question 5

What are the different phases OSPF uses to learn information for its topology database? [Choose the two best answers.]

❑ a. Exchange protocol

❑ b. Hellos

❑ c. Flooding protocol

❑ d. Link-state acknowledgements

Answers a and c are correct. OSPF routers initially identify neighbors and exchange or trade their entire current databases. After this process is finished, OSPF moves on to the normal operation phase, where changes are flooded to all routers in the area. Answer b is incorrect because the hellos are simply part of both phases. Answer d is incorrect because the LSA is merely part of the flooding process.

Question 6

What command shows the router's intermediate system (IS) number?

○ a. **show ip ospf database**

○ b. **show ip ospf**

○ c. **show ip route**

○ d. **show ip ospf neighbor detail**

Answer a is correct. The command **show ip ospf database** displays information such as the contents of the topological database maintained by the router. This command also shows the router intermediate system (IS) and OSPF process ID. Answer b is incorrect because this command shows the number of times the SPF algorithm has been executed. It also shows the link-state update interval, assuming no topological changes have occurred. Answer c is incorrect because this command displays all the routes learned by the router and how they were learned. Answer d is incorrect because this command displays a detailed list of neighbors, their states, and their priorities.

Question 7

> Which command will delete OSPF routes from the routing table?
>
> ○ a. **Clear ip route**
>
> ○ b. **Clear ip route ospf**
>
> ○ c. **Clear ip route ***
>
> ○ d. **Clear ip route ospf ***

Answer c is correct. The command **clear ip route *** deletes all routes that are currently in the router's routing table. This will force the router to re-learn all of its routes. Answers a, b, and d are incorrect because they all use incorrect syntax.

Need to Know More?

 Doyle, Jeff. *CCIE Professional Development: Routing TCP/IP Volume 1*. Macmillan Technical Publishing. Indianapolis, IN 1998. ISBN 1-57870-041-8. Chapters 11 through 13 discuss related topics.

 Huitema, Christian. *Routing in the Internet*. Prentice-Hall. Upper Saddle River, NJ 1995. ISBN 0-13132-192-7. This is an excellent protocol book. Read Chapters 4 through 6 for more information on routing protocols.

 Larson, Bob, Corwin Low, and Michael Simon. *CCNP Routing Exam Prep*. The Coriolis Group. Scottsdale, AZ. ISBN 1-57610-778-2. Fall 2000. This book, an Exam Prep for the CCNP exam, covers each related subject in great detail.

 Perlman, Radia. *Interconnections: Bridges and Routers*. Addison-Wesley. Reading, PA 1992. ISBN 0-201-56332-0. Chapter 9 provides a discussion of link-state and distance-vector protocols. Chapter 10 is about OSPF, by one of the senior players in the history of protocol development.

 Stevens, W. Richard. *TCP/IP Illustrated: The Protocols*. Addison-Wesley. Reading, MA 1994. ISBN 0-20163-346-9. Chapter 10 covers the routing protocols.

 Thomas, M. Thomas II. *OSPF Network Design Solutions*. Macmillan Technical Publishing. Indianapolis, IN 1999. ISBN 1-57870-046-9. This is an excellent book on OSPF design and implementation.

 Cisco's Web site, **www.cisco.com**, includes white papers and router documentation about OSPF configuration and design.

Configuring OSPF in Multiple Areas

Terms you'll need to understand:

✓ Link-state advertisement (LSA)

✓ Link-state update (LSU)

✓ Neighbors

✓ OSPF neighbor discovery

✓ OSPF network discovery

✓ Area types

✓ Router types

✓ Virtual links

Techniques you'll need to master:

✓ Understanding why OSPF is better than Routing Information Protocol (RIP)

✓ Configuring OSPF for operation in a multi-area environment

✓ Configuring route summaries

✓ Verifying OSPF operation

Now that we have covered how OSPF operates in a single area environment, we'll discuss OSPF operation and functionality in a multi-area network. This chapter will cover the capabilities, configuration, and verification of OSPF operation in a multi-area environment. This chapter will also discuss other options associated with multi-area operation, from the different router types to the functions they perform in a network.

OSPF Multi-Area Operation

Single-area OSPF is simple to configure. If your network has fewer than 70 routers (opinions vary—some say that between 30 and 70 is a good number), don't bother creating a multi-area environment unless you have some specific issues that are mentioned later in this chapter. The concept of an *area* simply involves your ability to create a subset of the network routers to reduce processing or complexity. Areas allow for the use of variable-length subnet masks (VLSMs) to form routing hierarchies to limit detail while maintaining reachability. This can be accomplished through route summarization, which serves to create smaller routing tables overall as well as to minimize convergence time. Smaller routing tables mean faster lookups and less memory utilization. For more on route summarization, please refer to Chapter 4.

Why Multiple Areas?

Now you'll examine the reasons why multiple areas for OSPF networks might be desirable when not indicated specifically by the number of routers. Proper design of a network can make even RIP work very well for up to a fairly large number of routers. OSPF was designed for very large networks with hundreds or potentially thousands of subnetworks. Keep this concept of "large" in mind as the issues are discussed in the following sections.

Too Many Routes

The fewer the routes in the routing table, the faster the router can make its routing decisions. In addition, having fewer routes means:

➤ Less memory dedicated to routing tables

➤ Less bandwidth for passing routing updates

➤ Less processing to produce correct routes

If it were possible to summarize the information, providing a single summary address to represent a group of subnets, reachability would be maintained. However, by losing the subnet detail updates, memory usage and overall processing would be reduced.

Slow-Updating Portions of the Network

In some networks, even though the LSAs are flooded, SPF calculations can become out of synchronization with each other. For example, in parts of your internetwork where slow paths exist to remote networks, an SPF calculation in a router might run without having received all the update information.

The resulting network routing tables are broken (for example, not fully converged but unaware of that fact) because OSPF believes it has perfect knowledge of the network and calculates its tables based on the concept of its seemingly perfect information. The best-case scenario is that the routing table would be fixed by running SPF again (after a ten-second delay); the worst-case scenario is that the network might become partitioned (isolated from the rest of the internetwork).

Thrashing Due to Rapid Network Changes

Another reason to form areas is to keep network changes from thrashing all the routers. For example, a flapping interface to other OSPF routers would cause a flood of updates to all routers. This requires that the routers run the SPF calculation over and over again in a never-ending cycle to form a new routing table. Each time the link goes up or down, *every single router* in the area would go through the SPF calculation. Effectively, the routing of data comes to a halt in this type of situation.

Area Types

With multiple areas, the OSPF configuration becomes much more complex. One of the first topics of concern is the separation of areas into types and the assignment of roles to individual routers. In the multi-area model, a number of variations are possible for each area. OSPF has several types of areas, which are illustrated in Figure 7.1.

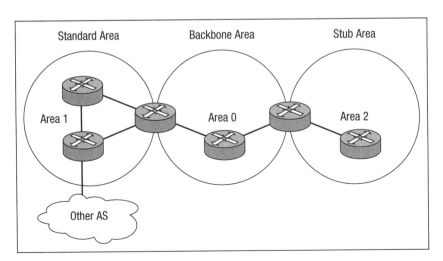

Figure 7.1 OSPF area types.

Backbone

The *backbone*, known as a *transit area*, is always area 0. As mentioned earlier, all OSPF networks must have an area 0 configured for the backbone. All traffic between other areas must flow through the backbone area. All kinds of routes (all LSA types) are present in area 0.

Address summaries collect in the backbone and are either advertised to other areas or not advertised (depending on the type of area involved). The route advertisement (or lack of route advertisement) is discussed in just a bit.

Standard Areas

Areas other than area 0 are referred to as *standard areas.* They receive all types of routing summary and external route information (unless you can fit them into one of the other area types). The other area types provide hierarchical routing because they limit the types of routes (LSAs) they'll accept.

Stub Areas

These are areas that do not accept information about routes external to the autonomous system (AS), such as routers from non-OSPF sources. If a router in a stub area needs to route to a network outside the autonomous system, the stub router would use a combination of summary routes and default routes to gain access to the Area Border Router (ABR) for processing.

Totally Stubby Areas

Cisco uses a special term for stub areas that accept only intra-area and default routes: *totally stubby areas.* In this case, even summary routes are blocked. The routers in a totally stubby area do not see external routes or summary routes; only the default route is available to reach the rest of the world. Besides the default route, these routers know only their intra-area routes.

Note: There is one more kind of area, the not-so-stubby area (NSSA). It is only supported on Cisco IOS 11.2 and later.

Router Types

To support all the differing area types, you specify specific router roles. These different router types provide different kinds of services to each area type. OSPF assigns routers roles based on where the individual routers fit into the hierarchy, both physically and logically. Figure 7.2 illustrates OSPF router types and their relationships with areas. Note that a router can fit the description of multiple roles.

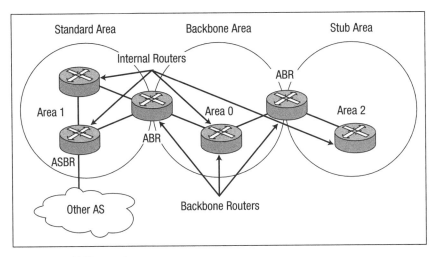

Figure 7.2   OSPF router types.

Internal Routers

An internal router has all its interfaces in a single area. Internal routers also have the same link-state database and run a single OSPF routing algorithm. The area can be a backbone, standard, stub, or totally stubby area.

Backbone Routers

A backbone router has at least one interface in area 0. It can also be an internal router, which means that all the interfaces in this router are in area 0.

Area Border Routers (ABRs)

ABRs have at least one interface in area 0 but have interfaces in one or more other areas. ABRs are the only source of OSPF inter-area routes and route summaries.

 It is important to keep the concept of a *summary* route separate from the concept of a *summarized* route. All OSPF inter-area routes are generated in ABRs and are called *summary routes*. In the ABR, you can also create a *summarized route*, which is a single route with a shorter prefix (subnet mask) to represent routes to all the included subnets. This summarized route is advertised to other standard areas and stub areas but not to totally stubby areas.

Autonomous System Border Routers (ASBRs)

An ASBR connects to other autonomous systems. An ASBR may be in the backbone or a standard area, but not in a stub or totally stubby area. An ASBR is the source of external routes and external route summaries.

The flow of routing updates between differing types of areas and differing router roles can be complex. Only specific types of LSAs can flow into and out of particular areas. Figure 7.3 specifies which types of LSAs can flow into and out of areas.

Configuring OSPF for Multiple Areas

Initially configuring multiple areas is almost identical to doing so for single areas. Listing 7.1 shows how to configure multiple areas and stub areas. Notice the entry for Serial 0 points to a standard area, the entry for Serial 1 points to a stub area, and the entry for Serial 2 points to a totally stubby area. Looking at the statements for stub area 2, you can see an example of assigning a default cost for all routes being redistributed into the area.

Listing 7.1   OSPF multiple-area and stub-area configuration.

```
interface Ethernet 0
ip address 10.0.1.1 255.255.255.0
!
interface Ethernet 1
ip address 10.0.2.1 255.255.255.0
!
interface Serial 0
ip address 172.16.5.1 255.255.255.0
!
interface Serial 1
ip address 172.16.6.1 255.255.255.0
!
interface Serial 2
ip address 172.16.7.1 255.255.255.0
!
router ospf 1
network 10.0.0.0 0.255.255.255 area 0
network 172.16.5.1 0.0.0.0 area 1
network 172.16.6.1 0.0.0.0 area 2
area 2 stub
area 2 default-cost 10
network 172.16.7.1 0.0.0.0 area 3
area 3 stub no-summary
```

Configuring Route Summarization

Figure 7.4 shows route summarization. It assumes that several subnets exist in Area 1 that use the 172.31.0.0 private class B address. Furthermore, it assumes that because the network was planned properly, the subnets are contained in the range of addresses from 172.31.32.0 to 172.31.63.0. Notice in Figure 7.4 that all

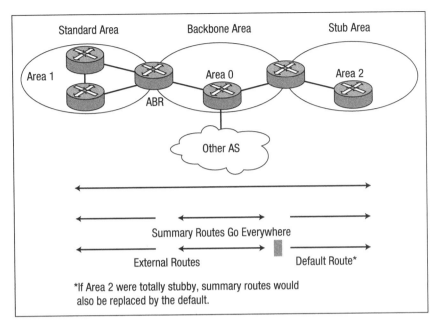

Figure 7.3 Inter-area traffic and LSA flow.

Starting Subnet:	172.31. 00100000.0
Ending Subnet:	172.31. 00111111.0
Default Prefix:	255.255.11111111.0
Summary Prefix:	255.255.11100000.0
Binary	

Figure 7.4 Route summarization.

subnets in the desired range share the high-order bits in the third octet. By shortening the prefix (subnet mask length), you can represent the whole range of subnets with a single entry. Route summarization is covered in more detail in Chapter 8.

You must keep all subnets in the same range within a single area (for example, they must be contiguous) in order to effectively deploy summarization. OSPF is a classless protocol and finds rogue subnets that are within your summary but placed in other areas. This makes it difficult to summarize. Be aware that you'll find unpredictable results. It is important to remember that one of the most influential reasons for choosing OSPF as your routing protocol in the first place is its ability to perform this summarization function. In many cases, organizations converting to OSPF readdress all or most of the internetwork before taking on the formidable task of internetwork conversion to OSPF.

It is essential to note that you must configure summarization in both directions (for example, into area 0 and into the non-area 0 areas). Listing 7.2 summarizes the routes for both area 0 and area 1. Remember also that OSPF does not automatically summarize any routes at any time. If you don't manually configure summarization, you see every possible network in each router's routing table.

In Listing 7.2, notice the summary for the class C address. The prefix is exactly the natural subnet mask for a class C address. RIP, IGRP, and EIGRP would automatically generate a class C network address and redistribute that as the route. With OSPF, you must lay out the network correctly and you must do any summarization manually. Listing 7.2 shows route summarization performed manually.

Listing 7.2   Route summarization.

```
router ospf 1
network 192.168.1.0 0.0.0.255 area 0
network 172.16.0.0 0.0.255.255 area 1
area 1 range 172.16.32.0 255.255.224.0
area 0 range 192.168.1.0 255.255.255.0
```

External Routes and Summarization

External routes are learned from another AS or another routing protocol within the same AS whose routes have been redistributed. These routes require manual redistribution (see Chapter 12), and you need to apply appropriate metrics for the redistributed routes. OSPF provides for Type 1 (E1) and Type 2 (E2) external routes—the difference being that E1 metrics include both the internal, OSPF-generated cost and the external cost from the redistribution point. The E2 metric, which is the default, uses only the external cost. The idea is that you use E1 metrics if you have multiple external contact points and you need to find the closest one.

You can choose to redistribute individual routes or route summaries from the ASBR. The summarization for an external route is shown in Listing 7.3.

Listing 7.3   OSPF external route summaries.

```
!
router ospf 1
network 10.0.0.0 0.255.255.255 area 0
redistribute rip 10 subnets
default-metric 10
address-summary 172.24.0.0 255.255.0.0
!
router rip
network 172.25.0.0
network 172.24.0.0
```

The address summary shows the command used with external routes. The area range statement shown in Listing 7.2 deals with OSPF native routes. Listing 7.3 shows a summary to some of the 172.24.0.0 subnets. The **subnets** statement for 172.25.0.0 indicates that there are probably multiple ASBRs and you need to keep track of which subnets are reached via which ASBR.

Routing Packets in a Multi-Area Environment

For a packet to make its way across a multi-area network, it must take a path that is similar to the following steps:

➤ A packet that is destined for a network that is within an area is forwarded from the internal router through the area to the destination internal router.

➤ A packet that is destined for a network outside the area must go through the following path:

1. The packet is routed from the internal router to the ABR.

2. The ABR then sends the packet through the backbone area to the ABR of the destination network in question.

All packets that are destined for a network in another area must cross the backbone area.

3. The destination ABR will then forward the packet to the internal router of the destination network.

4. The packet is then processed by the internal router for the local network.

Flooding Link-State Updates to Multiple Areas

The ABR is responsible for generating routing information about all the connected areas and flooding that information across the backbone area to all the other ABRs. This process can be broken down into a few steps that explain this process in more detail:

1. Intra-area routing processes for all areas that connect to an ABR must be synchronized before summary LSAs can be sent from the ABR.

2. The ABR reviews the link-state database and then generates summary LSAs.

3. Type 3 and 4 LSAs are placed in an LSU and distributed through all ABR interfaces.

Summary LSAs are not sent to totally stubby areas when the routers are still in the "exchange state" or below, or if the summary LSA includes a Type 5 LSA if they are connected to a stub or totally stubby area.

4. After an ABR or ASBR has received the summary LSA, it will add the LSA to the link-state database and then flood this information to its local areas. The internal routers will then update their databases with this new information.

Stub and Totally Stubby Areas

When dealing with a large network, you can experience routing tables and link-state databases that are growing too large and cannot be fixed by utilizing route summarization alone. In this case, it may be a wise idea to configure stub or totally stubby areas within your network to help alleviate this problem.

As stated earlier, a *stub area* is an area that only allows summary and intra-area routes. This means that a default route has to be used in the stub area to communicate with networks whose routes are not within its routing table, which means that when a destination address is not in the routing table, the stub area will forward the packet to its ABR, and the ABR will perform the route lookup and forward the packet through the network.

Another option may be used if the implementation of stub areas does not fix the network issues. By implementing totally stubby areas, you can achieve a smaller routing table. A totally stubby area maintains an even smaller route table because only intra-area routes are exchanged. To gain access to a network outside its directly connected area, the totally stubby area will need to utilize a default network so that the ABR can perform the proper routing of the packet through the network.

Configuring Stub and Totally Stubby Areas

Now that you are aware of the benefits that stub and totally stubby areas can provide, you should know how to configure them. The configuration of these areas is fairly simple, and the benefits can outweigh the effort. To configure a stub area, you need to perform the following steps:

1. Identify which routers will be stub or totally stubby areas.

2. Issue the following command on all routers within the area:

```
Area area id stub
```

3. To make an area totally stubby, the following command must be issued on the ABR:

```
Area area id stub no-summary
```

A router cannot be configured as a stub router if it is an ABR or if an ASBR is part of the area.

Listings 7.4 and 7.5 are examples of how a stub network would be configured on an ABR and on an internal router. Figure 7.5 illustrates how these networks would operate together to give you a better understanding of configuration.

Listing 7.4   Stub area configuration on the ABR.

```
Router ospf 10
Network 10.10.1.0 0.0.0.255 area 0
Network 10.20.1.0 0.0.0.255 area 1
Area 1 stub
```

Listing 7.5   Stub area configuration on the internal router.

```
Router ospf 20
Network 10.20.1.0 0.0.0.255 area 1
Area 1 stub
```

With this configuration, router C will only receive intra-area and summary routes.

Listings 7.6 and 7.7 are examples of how a totally stubby network would be configured on an ABR and on an internal router. Figure 7.6 illustrates how these networks would operate to give you a better understanding of configuration.

Listing 7.6   Totally stubby area configuration on the ABR.

```
Router ospf 10
Network 10.10.1.0 0.0.0.255 area 0
Network 10.20.1.0 0.0.0.255 area 1
Area 1 stub no-summary
```

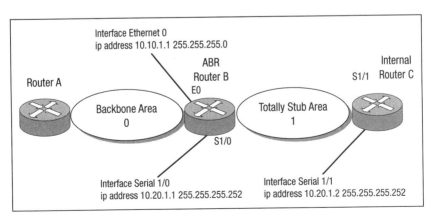

Figure 7.5   Stub area example.

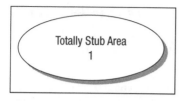

Figure 7.6 Totally stub area example.

Listing 7.7 **Totally stubby area configuration on the internal router.**

```
Router ospf 20
Network 10.20.1.0 0.0.0.255 area 1
Area 1 stub
```

With this configuration, router C will only receive intra-area and default routes. If a network needs to be reached that is not in router C's routing table, it will use the default route to the ABR.

Virtual Links

So far, the discussion has been about areas that must connect directly to area 0. However, sometimes this requirement is just not convenient. OSPF provides a *virtual link* for the purpose of extending area 0 to an attachment point across a transit area. Figure 7.7 shows a scenario in which you use virtual links. Listings 7.8 and 7.9 detail the configuration necessary for the virtual link.

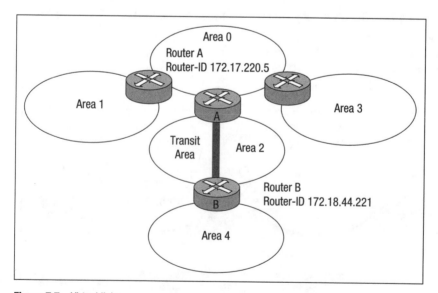

Figure 7.7 Virtual links.

Listing 7.8   Configuring router A.

```
router ospf 1
network 172.16.0.0 0.0.255.255 area 0
network 172.17.0.0 0.0.255.255 area 2
area 2 virtual-link 172.18.44.211
```

Listing 7.9   Configuring router B.

```
router ospf 1
network 172.17.0.0 0.0.255.255 area 2
network 172.18.0.0 0.0.255.255 area 4
area 2 virtual-link 172.17.220.5
```

Notice that the **virtual-link** statement connects the router IDs of the routers at the ends of the link. Also note that the area number specified in the **virtual-link** statement is the transit area (that is, the area the virtual link must traverse to reach area 0). Finally, remember that one of the routers must be connected to area 0.

Note: Virtual links should only be implemented when no other solution is available. This solution is nothing more than allowing for work arounds when an area does not have a physical connection to the backbone, or fixing discontiguous networks in area 0.

Verifying Proper OSPF Operation

Several common commands are used to verify that OSPF operation and router connectivity are working properly on a network. You should become very familiar with these commands to ensure that your routers are configured and operating properly on your network. The most common of these commands are described in Table 7.1.

Table 7.1 OSPF commands.	
Command Syntax	**Description**
show ip route	Displays all the routes learned by the router and how they were learned.
show ip protocols	Verifies that OSPF is configured. Displays information about timers, metrics, filters, and other router information.
show ip ospf interface	Displays the area ID and adjacency information. Verifies that the interfaces have been configured in the intended areas. It also displays the timer intervals, including Hello intervals, and shows neighbors' adjacencies.

(continued)

Table 7.1 OSPF commands *(continued)*.	
Command Syntax	**Description**
show ip ospf	Displays the number of times the SPF algorithm has been executed. It also shows the link-state update interval, assuming no topological changes have occurred.
show ip ospf neighbor detail	Displays a detailed list of neighbors, their states, and their priorities.
show ip ospf database	Displays the contents of the topological database maintained by the router. This command also shows the router intermediate systems (IS) and OSPF process ID.
show ip ospf border-routers	Displays the internal OSPF routing table entries to an ABR.
show ip ospf virtual-links	Displays the current parameters of OSPF virtual links.
clear ip route *	Clears all routes from the routing table. This allows you to verify that routes are being learned.
debug ip ospf events	Displays router interaction during the hello, exchange, and flooding processes. (Several additional commands can be used to give you more detail. Just use "**?**" after **OSPF** to display the options.)

Practice Questions

Question 1

What characteristics identify a totally stubby area from a stub area? [Choose two.]

❑ a. A totally stubby area contains only intra-area routes.

❑ b. A totally stubby area processes summary routes.

❑ c. A totally stubby area contains only inter-area routes.

❑ d. The ABR uses the **no-summary** command in the stub area configuration.

Answers a and d are correct. A totally stubby area contains only intra-area routes and a default route to the ABR. If any network needs to be reached that is not in the routing table, it is forwarded to the ABR for processing. The ABR uses the **no-summary** command to specify a stub area as totally stubby. By not using this command, the area is identified as a normal stub area. Answer b is incorrect because the ABR does not forward summary routes into a totally stubby area. This is identified with the **no-summary** command. Answer c is incorrect because the ABR does not inject the inter-area routes into the totally stubby area. All inter-area routing is performed by the ABR when dealing with a totally stubby area.

Question 2

What type of areas accept Type 5 LSAs?

○ a. Backbone

○ b. Stub

○ c. Totally stubby

○ d. All areas

Answer a is correct. The backbone area has to be able to accept every type of LSA to ensure proper OSPF operation. Answers b, c, and d are incorrect because stub and totally stubby areas do not accept Type 5 LSAs by default. This means that all areas cannot process Type 5 LSAs.

Question 3

Which command displays the Hello interval for the OSPF process?

○ a. **show ip ospf interface**

○ b. **show ip ospf neighbors detail**

○ c. **show ip route ospf**

○ d. **show ip ospf database**

Answer a is correct. The **show ip ospf interface** command displays time interval information to include Hello packets' intervals. Answer b is incorrect because the **show ip ospf neighbors detail** command shows specific information about the router's current OSPF neighbors' priorities and what state they are currently in. Answer c is incorrect because the **show ip route ospf** command shows specific information pertaining to the current OSPF routing table. Answer d is incorrect because the **show ip ospf database** command shows the OSPF topological database along with other information, such as the OSPF ID.

Question 4

What type of link will allow an area that is separated from area 0 to gain access to area 0?

○ a. Point-to-point link

○ b. NBMA link

○ c. Virtual link

○ d. Multi-access link

Answer c is correct. If needed, a virtual link can be configured to allow a separated area to gain access to the backbone area without having a physical connection in Area 0. Answers a, b, and d are incorrect because these types of links would all have to be physically connected to area 0.

Question 5

When are routes in OSPF marked as external routes? [Choose two.]

❑ a. When the routes are from another AS.

❑ b. When the routes are from the backbone area.

❑ c. When the routes are from another area.

❑ d. When the route are from another routing protocol.

Answers a and d are correct. An OSPF route is marked as *external* if that route is learned from a different autonomous system (AS) or from another routing protocol that's be redistributed into OSPF. Answers b and c are incorrect because routes that are from the backbone area or any other area within the OSPF AS are marked as normal OSPF routes.

Question 6

What is an internal router?

○ a. A backbone router.

○ b. A router that connects multiple areas together.

○ c. A router that connects to an external AS.

○ d. A router that has all interfaces in a single OSPF area.

Answer d is correct. All interfaces must be within a single area. Although an internal router can also be a backbone router, that is not the only factor (being a backbone router is possible without being an internal router). Therefore, answer a is incorrect. Answer b is incorrect because a router that connects multiple areas together is an ABR. Answer c is incorrect because a router that connects to an external AS is an ASBR.

Question 7

When redistributing RIP into OSPF the router is called what type of router?

○ a. Area Border Router (ABR)

○ b. Autonomous System Boundary Router (ASBR)

○ c. Internal Router

○ d. Virtual Link

Answer b is correct. A router is considered an ASBR any time that it connects to an external internetwork or a non-OSPF network. The router redistributes non-OSPF information to the OSPF network. In this case, the router is redistributing RIP into OSPF and visa versa. Answer a is incorrect because the ABR is a router that connects to multiple areas. This is kind of tricky to keep straight because the ABR has interfaces into internetworks, but they are internal internetworks, not external internetworks. Answer c is incorrect because the internal router is a router that has all of its interfaces in one area. Answer d is incorrect because a virtual link is a feature of OSPF that is used to connect a discontiguous network that has no connection to the backbone to area 0.

Need to Know More?

Doyle, Jeff. *CCIE Professional Development: Routing TCP/IP Volume 1*. Macmillan Technical Publishing. Indianapolis, IN 1998. ISBN 1-57870-041-8. Chapters 11 through 13 discuss topics related to this chapter.

Huitema, Christian. *Routing in the Internet*. Prentice-Hall, Upper Saddle River, NJ 1995. ISBN 0-13132-192-7. This is an excellent protocol book. Read Chapters 4 through 6 for more information on routing protocols.

Larson, Bob, Corwin Low, and Michael Simon. *CCNP Routing Exam Prep*. The Coriolis Group. Scottsdale, AZ, Fall 2000. This book, an Exam Prep for the CCNP exam, covers each related subject in great detail.

Perlman, Radia. *Interconnections: Bridges and Routers*. Addison-Wesley. Reading, MA 1992. ISBN 0-201-56332-0. Chapter 9 provides a discussion of link-state and distance-vector protocols, and Chapter 10 is about OSPF, by one of the senior players in the history of protocol development.

Stevens, W. Richard. *TCP/IP Illustrated: The Protocols*. Addison-Wesley. Reading, MA 1994. ISBN 0-20163-346-9. Chapter 10 covers the routing protocols.

Thomas, M. Thomas II. *OSPF Network Design Solutions*. Macmillan Technical Publishing. Indianapolis, IN 1999. ISBN 1-57870-046-9. This is an excellent book on OSPF design and implementation.

Cisco's Web site, **www.cisco.com**, includes white papers and router documentation about OSPF configuration and design.

Enhanced IGRP

....

Terms you'll need to understand:

✓ Advanced distance-vector routing protocol

✓ Autonomous system

✓ Neighbor router

✓ Neighbor table

✓ Topology table

✓ Routing table

✓ Current successor

✓ Feasible successor

✓ Route summarization

Techniques you'll need to master:

✓ Configuring Enhanced Interior Gateway Routing Protocol (EIGRP) for IP

✓ Configuring EIGRP route summarization

✓ Verifying EIGRP operation and configuration

This chapter discusses the Cisco proprietary advanced distance vector routing protocol Enhanced Interior Gateway Routing Protocol (EIGRP). EIGRP was developed to overcome many of Routing Information Protocol's (RIP) limitations, such as the 15-hop limitation and the inability to support variable-length subnet masks (VLSMs) and/or route summarization. Unlike the other routing protocols discussed at different points throughout this book, EIGRP was not designed strictly as an IP routing protocol. EIGRP can also take the place of Internetwork Packet Exchange (IPX) RIP. In many ways, EIGRP acts as a link-state routing protocol. In other ways, it resembles a distance-vector routing protocol.

EIGRP Basics

EIGRP was developed to provide a single routing protocol solution in a multiprotocol environment. You can use EIGRP, designed by Cisco as a proprietary routing protocol, to provide reachability to remote networks in IP, IPX, and AppleTalk environments. Rather than using three separate routing protocols to manage these three routed protocols, EIGRP provides a single solution to meet the network's needs.

Where Did It Come From?

The principle behind EIGRP is based on distance-vector technology. Each router does not necessarily need to know all the router/link relationships for the entire network. Individual routers advertise destinations with a corresponding distance. Every router that hears the information adjusts the distance and propagates the information to neighboring routers. The distance information in EIGRP is represented as a composite of available bandwidth, delay, load utilization, link reliability, and maximum transmittable unit (MTU). This allows fine-tuning of link characteristics to achieve optimal paths.

How Does It Work?

EIGRP uses the Diffusing Update Algorithm (DUAL) to achieve a loop-free network at every instant throughout route computation. DUAL allows all routers involved in a topology change to synchronize at the same time. Routers that are not affected by topology changes are not involved in the recomputation of updated routing information. EIGRP has been extended to be independent of layer 3 protocols, thereby allowing DUAL to support other protocol suites.

EIGRP has four main components in its operation:

➤ Neighbor discovery/recovery

➤ Reliable transport protocol

➤ DUAL finite state machine

➤ Protocol-dependent modules

Neighbor discovery is the process of instigating a hello protocol outbound on each active interface in order to discover routers that are directly connected to the same networks. It is also used to learn whether those routers have dropped off the network for whatever reason.

The *reliable transport protocol* is responsible for guaranteed and ordered delivery of EIGRP packets to all neighbors. For efficiency, reliability is provided only when necessary.

The *DUAL finite state machine* represents the intelligence of the decision process for all route computations. It tracks the routes that all neighbors advertise. DUAL uses the distance information, known as a *metric*, to select efficient loop-free paths.

The *protocol-dependent modules* are responsible for each specific network-layer protocol. For example, the IP-EIGRP module is responsible for sending and receiving EIGRP packets for IP operations. There's an additional module for IPX and one more for AppleTalk. These processes are completely independent of each other. The routing of multiple protocols in an environment where one routed protocol has no effect whatsoever on another is known as "ships in the night" routing.

Dynamic Routing Protocols

EIGRP was known as an advanced distance vector routing protocol. In other words, it doesn't fall under the descriptions of traditional routing protocols. Traditional routing protocols are either distance-vector or link-state protocols. EIGRP is neither. In creating EIGRP, Cisco has taken the benefits of both types of protocols.

Distance-Vector Protocols

Distance-vector protocols tend to be relatively slow when it comes to convergence; however, they also tend to consume a much lower amount of overall router resources (RAM, CPU, and so on). Distance-vector devices view the network from the point of view of their directly connected neighbors. They have very little first-hand information. They obtain all information (except that which deals with directly connected networks) from their neighbors, who obtained it from their neighbors, and so on. This type of information sharing is sometimes known as *routing by rumor*. Distance-vector protocols operate on update timers and triggered updates. When the update timer expires, the routing table is broadcast out of each active interface. If there are no changes in the routing table, updates are still broadcast out. The end result of this is wasted bandwidth.

Link-State Protocols

Link-state protocols tend to be extremely fast when it comes to convergence. That sounds great until you look at the amount of additional resources the link-state routing process requires in the router. Link-state protocols tend to be quite taxing on system resources because they're keeping so much information in memory. As a result, link-state protocols, such as Open Shortest Path First (OSPF), can waste memory space. Unlike distance-vector routing protocols, link-state routing protocols send updates only when necessary. When a network change is detected, a routing update is triggered and only the changes are flooded out of the interfaces. This flood of packets, known as *link-state advertisements (LSAs)*, goes to every router in the area.

Getting to the Point

EIGRP, being neither a distance-vector nor a link-state protocol, is actually a combination of the best of both types of protocols. It combines very fast convergence with lower memory requirements and less processor utilization. It gets its speed and efficiency by acting as a link-state protocol to its neighbors and a distance-vector protocol to the rest of the internetwork. Consider Figure 8.1, which shows an example of an EIGRP network. If router A found it necessary to send an update, to which routers would the update go? With a link-state protocol, all routers would receive the update and forward it to their neighbors in a flooding pattern. EIGRP is no different from a link-state protocol in that it sends the update instantly to its neighbors. However, EIGRP does not use the flooding concept. When a routing change is necessary, EIGRP simply updates the directly connected neighbors, who then update their neighbors. The result is a more well behaved update process.

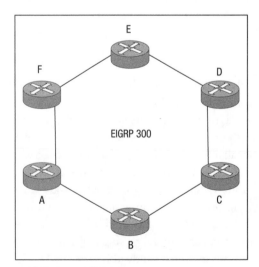

Figure 8.1   An example of an EIGRP network.

Enhanced IGRP Operation

EIGRP knows about all the routers' directly connected neighbors. It knows about all the networks in the internetwork through those neighbors. EIGRP is basically distance-vector to the rest of the internetwork. The only information it knows is the distance to get to a particular network and to which neighbor to forward packets destined for that network.

Route Calculation Considerations

As mentioned earlier, EIGRP uses the concept of distance as a metric. This distance is derived through a composite calculation. The values used in this computation are known as *k values*. The values are, in order of precedence, as follows:

➤ Bandwidth

➤ Delay

➤ Reliability

➤ Load

➤ MTU

By default, all *k* values, except bandwidth and delay, are set to zero unless they are needed. This method of calculation using a composite metric gives bandwidth the priority over all other values in route calculation. The faster the links between source and destination, the better the route.

*Note: Bandwidth is the primary metric for route determination, so it is imperative that all interfaces, especially serial interfaces, know their bandwidth. The default bandwidth of a serial interface is 1.544Mbps. In other words, if you have a 64Kbps link, you must issue the command **bandwidth 64**. Otherwise, the EIGRP route calculations will be incorrect. The **bandwidth** command is illustrated in the figures within this chapter.*

As mentioned previously, distance is the product of the route calculation. The lower the distance representation, the better the route.

In order to support these processes and keep them efficient, EIGRP keeps three tables in memory at any given time. These tables are as follows:

➤ Neighbor table

➤ Topology table

➤ Routing table

By default, the route calculation uses bandwidth and delay. It will use the remaining values when necessary to serve as tiebreakers.

Neighbor Table

The *neighbor table* is a listing of directly connected neighbors. When a router learns about new neighbors, it records each neighbor's address and interface. This information is stored in the neighbor data structure. Listing 8.1 shows output of the **show ip eigrp neighbors** command.

Listing 8.1   The **show ip eigrp neighbors** command.

```
R1#show ip eigrp neighbors
IP-EIGRP neighbors for process 100
H   Address        Interface Hold Uptime   SRTT  RTO Q  Seq
                             (sec)          (ms)    Cnt Num
1   10.0.0.2       Et0       12 00:02:45   1  200 0  1
0   144.254.100.2 AT0.1      10 00:02:46   0 4500 0  2
```

The Address column indicates the address of the directly connected neighbor. The Interface column designates the outbound interface to get to that particular neighbor. When a neighbor sends a Hello, it advertises a hold time. The *hold time* is the amount of time for which a router treats a neighbor as reachable and operational. In other words, if a Hello packet isn't heard within the hold time, the hold time expires. When the hold time expires, DUAL is informed of the topology change. Sequence numbers are employed to match acknowledgments with data packets. The receiving router records the last sequence number it received from the neighbor so that it can detect out-of-order packets.

Topology Table

The *topology table* contains all destinations that neighboring routers advertise as well as the interfaces through which to dispatch packets destined for those networks. Notice that each of the routes in Listing 8.2 (which shows the **show ip eigrp topology** command) is designated as a successor. The meaning of *successors* is discussed later in this chapter.

Listing 8.2   The **show ip eigrp topology** command output.

```
R1#sh ip eigrp topology
IP-EIGRP Topology Table for process 100

Codes: P - Passive, A - Active, U - Update, Q - Query, R - Reply,
       r - Reply status
```

```
P 144.254.100.0/24, 1 successors, FD is 18944
        via Connected, ATM0.1
P 10.0.0.0/8, 1 successors, FD is 281600
        via Connected, Ethernet0
P 192.168.1.0/24, 1 successors, FD is 146944
        via 144.254.100.2 (146944/128256), ATM0.1
        via 10.0.0.2 (409600/128256), Ethernet0
P 144.254.0.0/16, 1 successors, FD is 18944
        via Summary (18944/0), Null0
```

Associated with each entry are the destination address and a list of neighbors that have advertised the destination. For each neighbor, the advertised metric is recorded. This is the metric that the neighbor stores in its routing table. If the neighbor is advertising this destination, it must be using the route to forward packets. The output specifies the destination network followed by the number of routes the router has that can get packets to that network. Also noted in Listing 8.2 is feasible distance (FD). *Feasible distance* is the total distance from R1 (this router) to the listed destination network. Feasible distance is discussed in further detail, along with successor routes, later in this chapter.

Routing Table

The *routing table* is the listing of the calculated "best" routes to known destination networks. This routing table reads the same as any other routing table for other routing protocols. Listing 8.3 shows the **show ip route** command.

Listing 8.3   The **show ip route** command output.

```
R1#show ip route
Codes:C-connected, S-static, I-IGRP, R-RIP, M-mobile, B-BGP
      D-EIGRP, EX-EIGRP external, O-OSPF, IA-OSPF inter area
      N1-OSPF NSSA external type 1, N2-OSPF NSSA external type2
      E1-OSPF external type 1, E2-OSPF external type 2, E-EGP
      i-IS-IS,L1-IS-IS level-1,L2-IS-IS level-2,*-candidate
      default, U - per-user static route, o - ODR


Gateway of last resort is not set

C 10.0.0.0/8 is directly connected, Ethernet0
D 192.168.1.0/24 [90/146944] via 144.254.100.2, 00:22:51, ATM0.1
  144.254.0.0/16 is variably subnetted, 2 subnets, 2 masks
C    144.254.100.0/24 is directly connected, ATM0.1
D    144.254.0.0/16 is a summary, 00:22:51, Null0
  172.30.0.0/24 is subnetted, 1 subnets
C    172.30.1.0 is directly connected, Loopback0
```

Listing 8.3 shows a legend of various routing protocols and the codes that go with them. This is to illustrate how the particular route shown in the listing was derived, because it is possible and common to run multiple routing protocols on a single router. The code in the legend matches the letter in the far-left column. The codes in this table are C and D. The C code denotes a directly connected network. The D code denotes an EIGRP-derived route. If you read the table from left to right, you learn the following information:

➤ How this route was derived.

➤ The destination network address followed by the prefix (that is, subnet mask for that destination address in bit format). The designation of /24 denotes a subnet mask of 255.255.255.0 because the first 24 bits are set to 1.

➤ The administrative distance/metric distance (in brackets).

➤ The next hop address.

➤ The age of this route.

➤ The outbound interface.

The routing table is the key to the entire operation of your internetwork. You should monitor it regularly to ensure its accuracy.

EIGRP can keep up to six redundant pathways at any given time. This sounds like a typical capability of any routing protocol. However, these six paths do not have to be equal-metric pathways. If an administrator configures a variance value under the router EIGRP configuration, it is possible to configure which paths should be used. The *variance* is a multiplier for traffic sent across suboptimal routes. For example, if under the router EIGRP configuration, you set the variance to four, the router would send four times the amount of traffic over the best route as it does over the suboptimal routes. This feature allows for additional load-sharing capabilities and more granular traffic engineering potential than exists in a RIP network.

You'll need to know the exact commands to show the information included in the preceding three sections relating to the neighbor, topology, and routing tables. Review these a few times before taking the exam.

Rights of Succession

As you saw in Listing 8.3, some routes are designated as successors. A *successor route* is the best route based on available information to this point. The successor is the only route actually kept in the routing table. A secondary route may be kept in the topology table along with the current successor route. This secondary route is known as a *feasible successor*. The criteria for selecting a feasible successor are quite strenuous. Figure 8.2 shows an example of the network topology.

The router in question is router A. View this scenario from the perspective of router A as the source and the 172.16.31.0/24 network as the destination network. The distances of the links are listed. The distances listed in the figure are false and are for demonstrative purposes only.

The route with the shortest feasible distance, as noted earlier, is the best route. This route is known as the *current successor*. The current successor is listed in the routing table as the preferential pathway to the destination network.

Notice that two values are associated with each route. One is the feasible distance, and the other is the advertised distance. Recall in the discussion of hybrid routing protocols that EIGRP is a little bit of a link-state protocol and a little bit of a distance-vector protocol. A distance-vector protocol works on the assumption that router A's neighbor (router B) is a certain distance away. The distance for router A to get to a destination must be router B's distance from that destination plus the distance from router A to router B. That's precisely the premise you're dealing with when the EIGRP feasible and advertised distances are calculated.

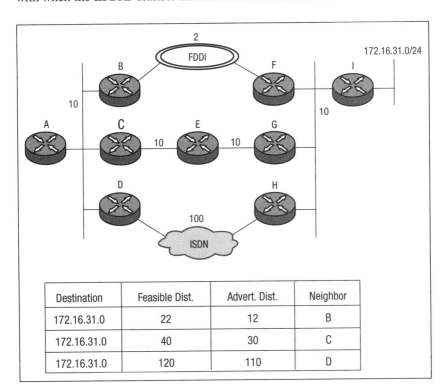

Destination	Feasible Dist.	Advert. Dist.	Neighbor
172.16.31.0	22	12	B
172.16.31.0	40	30	C
172.16.31.0	120	110	D

Figure 8.2 An EIGRP topology scenario.

What Is Distance?

Advertised distance is the distance that a router's neighbors are advertising as their own distance to get to a particular destination—in this case, 172.16.31.0. Once router A has received distance information from all neighbors, it can add the distance to each particular neighbor to those advertised distances to create the feasible distance. Therefore, feasible distance is the distance calculated for router A to reach 172.16.31.0 as a destination network.

Now that the best route has been crowned, it's time to determine whether there's a suitable route to fill the role of backup route. This backup route is known as the *feasible successor*. Even though multiple routes may lead to a single destination, as shown in Figure 8.2, a feasible successor is not always selected. In Figure 8.2, the route to network 172.16.31.0 through neighbor B is the current successor because it has the shortest feasible distance. The route through neighbor C is the next best, followed by the route through neighbor D.

Look at the advertised distance of 30 via neighbor C, the second-best route. With that in mind, look at the feasible distance of 22 via neighbor B, the best route. If the advertised distance of the second-best route is shorter than the feasible distance of the best route, the second-best route is designated as the feasible successor.

Should router B fail, the route via router C would be immediately updated to the status of current successor. It's important to mention that if the Fiber Distributed Data Interface (FDDI) network goes down, neighbor B sends out to all its neighbors a routing update concerning only that network. Now that the best route is no longer available and the feasible successor has been promoted to current successor, it's time to select a new feasible successor if possible. Figure 8.3 shows the new topology of the network.

Apply the rules for crowning a feasible successor to this scenario now. In order for a feasible successor to be selected, the advertised distance of the second-best route must be shorter than the feasible distance of the new best route. The criterion is not met in this case, so the route via neighbor D is not selected as feasible successor. Should the route via neighbor C disappear for some reason, the route via neighbor D is the only alternative. Even so, it is not a feasible successor in the eyes of the algorithm.

If the router cannot find a feasible successor, it issues a route request to its neighbors for a feasible successor route to that specific destination network. If the neighbors can provide the information, the route is installed as feasible successor. Otherwise, the router goes on without a feasible successor.

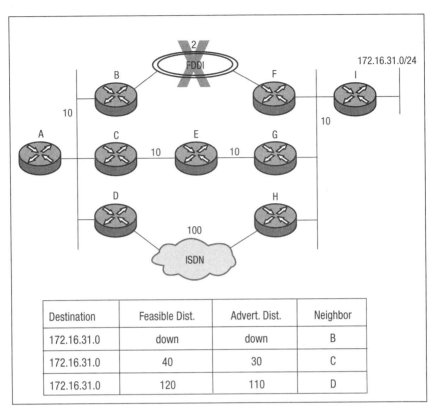

Destination	Feasible Dist.	Advert. Dist.	Neighbor
172.16.31.0	down	down	B
172.16.31.0	40	30	C
172.16.31.0	120	110	D

Figure 8.3 Promotion of the feasible successor to successor.

 Route-selection criteria for the current and feasible successors is critical to the overall topology of the network.

Enhanced IGRP Configuration

Configuring EIGRP for IP is quite simple. The procedure for basic configuration is the same procedure used in configuring IGRP and RIP. The configuration consists of selecting an autonomous system (AS) number as well as networks to send updates to. The AS simply consists of all the routers under a common administration. All the routers in your network that are exchanging route information have the same autonomous system number. In order to share route information between dissimilar AS numbers, you must configure redistribution. Figure 8.4 shows a basic EIGRP configuration example, and Listing 8.4 displays the configuration commands necessary to configure the R1 router in the figure.

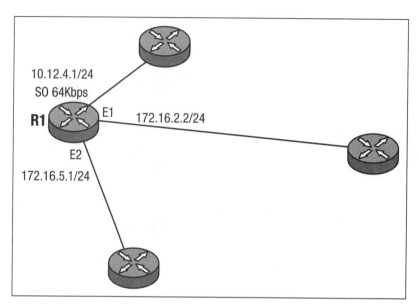

Figure 8.4 Basic EIGRP IP configuration.

Listing 8.4   Configuration commands for Figure 8.4.

```
interface ethernet 1
ip address 172.16.2.2 255.255.255.0
!
interface ethernet 2
ip address 172.16.5.1 255.255.255.0
!
interface serial 0
ip address 10.12.4.1 255.255.255.0
bandwidth 64
!
router eigrp 400
network 10.0.0.0
network 172.16.0.0
```

Even though there are three interfaces, the configuration requires only the two network statements listed. EIGRP configuration, like that for RIP and IGRP, requires that you specify only the natural network number.

The AS number must be the same on all routers in the AS. It's important to understand the network statements and their uses.

Route Redistribution

Although route redistribution is addressed in Chapter 12, it's appropriate to address it here to a degree. Redistribution is usually a manual configuration. It's automatically done for you in specific cases. EIGRP encompasses most of those instances.

In cases where EIGRP and IGRP are being run together on a single router, automatic redistribution is performed if, and only if, the autonomous system numbers for both routing protocols have been configured identically. Listing 8.5 shows an example of when automatic redistribution between EIGRP and IGRP occurs if both protocols are to be implemented on R1 in Figure 8.4.

Listing 8.5   IGRP and EIGRP together.

```
interface serial 0
ip address 10.12.4.1 255.255.255.0
bandwidth 64
!
router igrp 400
network 10.0.0.0
network 172.16.0.0
passive-interface e1
!
router eigrp 400
network 172.16.0.0
passive-interface e2
```

 If the AS numbers for EIGRP and IGRP are identical, route redistribution between the two protocols is done automatically. If the AS numbers are different, redistribution has to be manually configured.

The code in Listing 8.5 shows that passive-interfaces have been implemented. The configuration for EIGRP and IGRP uses the natural network numbers for any given network, so it's necessary to keep each protocol from sending updates out unnecessarily through interfaces where no neighbors are listening for those updates. In this case, IGRP is configured to be sent out of interfaces Ethernet 0 and Ethernet 2. There's no reason to send IGRP updates out of interface Ethernet 1 if the neighboring router is not an IGRP router. The end result of using passive interfaces is bandwidth conservation.

Route Summarization

EIGRP was designed with some scalability in mind. Route summarization is one of the key elements in scalability. EIGRP does not build a hierarchy in the same manner that Open Shortest Path First (OSPF) does (discussed in Chapters 6 and 7). However, it is capable of routing table reduction. Reducing the overall number of routes in a routing table has the following benefits:

➤ Less memory utilization

➤ Faster routing table lookups

➤ Reduction in delay through the router

When left to its default settings, EIGRP automatically summarizes to the boundaries of natural class. In other words, the summary routes are advertised at the class A, B, or C boundaries. This means that, by default, EIGRP does not support variable-length subnet masks (VLSMs). You can manually override the automatic summarization feature in the EIGRP configuration by using the **no auto-summary** command and placing a summary route. You typically perform such physical configuration of summary route information on the outbound interface on an edge router between two autonomous systems. Figure 8.5 shows an example of EIGRP route summarization. Listing 8.6 details the commands necessary for configuring a summary route.

Listing 8.6 R1 route summarization configuration.

```
router eigrp 400
network 10.0.0.0
network 172.16.0.0
no auto-summary
!
interface serial 0
ip address 10.1.27.5 255.255.255.0
bandwidth 64
ip summary-address eigrp 400 172.16.0.0 255.255.0.0
```

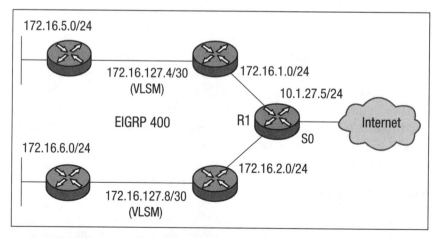

Figure 8.5 EIGRP manual route summarization.

In this example, all the 172.16.0.0 networks are advertised out as a single route to the rest of the world. Rather than keeping all its routes in the external routing tables, the router keeps only a single route that can generalize all of autonomous system 400's networks. The result is an overall reduction in the number of entries in external routing tables. The reverse scenario could be true. In autonomous system 400, it's likely that the many routes that may find their way into the internal routing tables are not welcome. Therefore, you can manually force a reduction in the overall number of routes. Route summarization is only one tool you can use to reduce the size of routing tables. You can also implement default routes and route filtering. Again, the benefits of a correctly summarized routing table tend to far outweigh the consequences.

Verifying Proper EIGRP Operation

It's recommended that some type of monitoring be in progress on any internetwork. Whether it's done through the use of traditional Simple Network Management Protocol (SNMP) implementations or through manual monitoring, management is an essential part of the internetwork. Table 8.1 lists the various commands that will assist you in the monitoring of individual routers.

Table 8.1   EIGRP's useful show commands.

Command	Description
show ip eigrp neighbors	Displays the EIGRP IP neighbor table
show ip eigrp topology	Displays the EIGRP IP topology table
show ip route eigrp	Displays the EIGRP routing table
show ip protocols	Displays a detailed listing of all active routing protocols
show ip eigrp traffic	Monitors EIGRP packets sent and received

Practice Questions

Question 1

EIGRP is which type of routing protocol?

○ a. Distance-vector

○ b. Link-state

○ c. Advanced distance vector

○ d. None of the above

Answer c is correct. EIGRP does not fall into the category of either answer a or b. However, it does have some of the characteristics of both types of protocols. It is considered to be link-state to its neighbors and distance-vector to the rest of the network. Answer d is incorrect because a correct answer is given.

Question 2

EIGRP, like OSPF, is a standardized routing protocol defined by an official RFC.

○ a. True

○ b. False

Answer b is correct. EIGRP is a Cisco proprietary routing protocol.

Question 3

Which of the following tables does EIGRP keep? [Choose the three best answers.]

❑ a. ARP table

❑ b. Routing table

❑ c. Neighbor table

❑ d. Topology table

Answers b, c, and d are correct. EIGRP keeps routing, neighbor, and topology tables for each of the protocols for which it is configured. Answer a is incorrect because although the router keeps an ARP cache in active memory, EIGRP does not maintain the table.

Question 4

The best route to any specific network is known as a *successor.*

O a. True

O b. False

Answer a is correct. The best route is known as the *successor* or *current successor.* The next-best route, if it meets specific criteria, is known as the *feasible successor.*

Question 5

When a network topology change occurs, routing updates are sent to which of the following?

O a. All routers in the internetwork

O b. All routers in the area

O c. All directly connected routers

O d. None of the above

Answer c is correct. Because EIGRP is not considered a "hierarchical" routing protocol, it creates a large flat network (such as nonhierarchical). In a flat network, all updates must be propagated to all routers. Answer a is incorrect because that type of update propagation is known as *flooding.* EIGRP does not cause link-state advertisement flooding. Answer b is incorrect because EIGRP does not use an area hierarchy as does OSPF. Answer d is incorrect because a correct answer is given.

Question 6

EIGRP uses which of the following for default route metric calculation? [Choose the two best answers.]

❑ a. Hop count

❑ b. Cost

❑ c. Delay

❑ d. Load

❑ e. Bandwidth

Answers c and e are correct. Bandwidth is the primary metric value, followed by delay. Because they are the primary metrics, they are used by default. Should additional information be necessary to calculate a tiebreaker between two routes, load, reliability, and MTU size will be added into the calculation. Answer a is incorrect because hop count is used by RIP for route calculation. EIGRP does not include hop count in its calculations. Answer b is incorrect because cost is used by OSPF, not EIGRP, in route calculation.

Question 7

Examine the following image. What are the correct configuration commands to properly configure the EIGRP process?

Build an EIGRP configuration.

The correct code command is as follows:

```
interface ethernet 0
ip address 192.168.1.1 255.255.255.0
!
interface serial 0
ip address 172.16.192.5 255.255.255.252
bandwidth 256
!
router eigrp 604
network 192.168.1.0
network 172.16.0.0
```

The EIGRP configuration requires the configuration of an AS number as well as appropriate network statements.

Question 8

Which command represents the correct use of the EIGRP summarization command for the Serial 0 interface configuration in Question 7?

○ a. **ip summary 172.16.192.0 255.255.240.0**

○ b. **ip summary-address eigrp 604 192.168.0.0 255.255.0.0**

○ c. **summary 192.168.1.0 255.0.0.0**

○ d. None of the above

Answer b is correct. This statement advertises that all networks contain 192.168 as the first two decimal values, regardless of the values of the last two. Answer a is incorrect because both the syntax and the network address being summarized are not correct. Answer c is incorrect due to syntax. Answer d is incorrect because a correct answer is given.

Need to Know More?

Cisco Systems Staff. *Cisco IOS Solutions for Network Protocols, IP Vol. 1.* Cisco Systems. Indianapolis, IN 1998. ISBN 1-578-70049-3. Covers in depth IP and routing protocol documentation.

Huitema, Christian. *Routing in the Internet.* Prentice Hall. Upper Saddle River, NJ 1995. ISBN 0-13-132192-7. This book focuses on basic internetwork architecture and addressing. It is a well-written book for a basic-level to an advanced-level audience.

Larson, Bob, Corwin Low, and Michael Simon. *CCNP Routing Exam Prep.* The Coriolis Group. Scottsdale, AZ. ISBN 1-57610-778-2. Fall 2000. This is part of a companion series of books for the CCNP exam that covers each related subject in great detail.

For more information on EIGRP, visit **www.cisco.com** and perform a search using "Enhanced IGRP" as keywords.

BGP Configuration

Terms you'll need to understand:

✓ Internet Service Provider (ISP)

✓ Autonomous system (AS)

✓ Interior Gateway Protocol (IGP)

✓ Exterior Gateway Protocol (EGP)

✓ Border Gateway Protocol (BGP) neighbor

✓ Internal Border Gateway Protocol (IBGP)

✓ External Border Gateway Protocol (EBGP)

Techniques you'll need to master:

✓ Configuring BGP neighbors

✓ Configuring Internal BGP

✓ Configuring External BGP

✓ Configuring peer groups

This chapter presents how to configure and connect a company to an Internet Service Provider (ISP) and the ordeals and issues that may arise in doing so using Border Gateway Protocol (BGP) version 4 (the current version). BGP is the protocol of choice for most ISPs, so you don't have much choice in the matter when it comes to deciding how to connect to them. ISPs have the resource you want—the Internet—so you have to agree to abide by their policies. BGP gives them the power to affect Internet Protocol (IP) routing policy throughout the networks that attach to their systems. By the same token, National Access Providers (NAPs) are implementing policy above ISPs in the grand scheme of things. ISPs must therefore adhere to policies handed down to them as well.

Connecting to an ISP

Selecting an ISP is a rather painful process at times. Many factors come into play, including the size of your company, the spectrum of user types, and the points of presence you will need. *Points of presence* refer to the geographic diversity of your Internet connection points. The placement of these points will have a profound effect on the flow of your Internet traffic. The size of your company weighs in heavily because it provides the basis for your Internet plan. Here are some questions you should ask about your own network prior to beginning your ISP quest:

➤ How many users in the company require Internet access (presumably all)?

➤ How many of these users are connected to your company's local area network (LAN)?

➤ How many of these users require mobile accounts?

➤ How much bandwidth is sufficient to support all of the above?

➤ How do you handle electronic mail?

➤ If your company is nationwide, do you require multiple points of presence on the Internet? That is, does the New York office have to go through the San Francisco office to get to the Internet, or is there a separate local connection in each location within the network?

➤ How do you connect to your ISP? Via a serial link? At what speed?

➤ Is this Internet connection mission critical? If so, you should provide some redundancy for your Internet access.

Redundant links to an ISP will require the use of BGP to affect routing policy. Without routing policy, there's a high likelihood of routing loops or other routing inconsistencies. BGP policies will flow down from the top tiers of the Internet backbone. You must also be sure to filter the IP

> network space reserved for private use on your side of the link so that those addresses do not leak out into the Internet. The potential result is routing loops and/or other inconsistencies.

These are only a few of the questions you need to answer. A small ISP, although inexpensive, may not be the answer for a nationwide company. Once you've selected an ISP that can meet your needs, it's time to start thinking of how you will be sending and receiving data. You have a number of data-forwarding alternatives. This chapter explores these differing methods.

Your Autonomous System and You

What is an autonomous system? The term alone sounds intimidating. *Autonomous system* (AS) is simply a generic term that defines all the devices under a common administration. In other words, all the routers that your company owns and operates are part of the same AS. In some routing protocols, it is necessary to define a numeric value (or name) for this AS. If you're not connecting to the public data network, you can simply make up a number for use in every router.

Be careful with autonomous system numbers. If your routing protocol requires the number to be defined as part of the configuration, it must be the same on all routers. Examples of routing protocols that require this are Interior Gateway Routing Protocol (IGRP), Enhanced Interior Gateway Routing Protocol (EIGRP), and Border Gateway Protocol (BGP). Routers that are not configured as part of the same AS do not exchange network reachability updates (such as routing updates).

Within your AS, you run a dynamic routing protocol. A routing protocol that runs within an AS is known as an *Interior Gateway Protocol* (IGP). Examples of IGPs include Routing Information Protocol (RIP), Open Shortest Path First (OSPF), IGRP, EIGRP, and a few others. It is possible to run multiple routing protocols within a single AS. If you do so, you have to redistribute the routing information between the protocols. Usually, this is a manual process that you must do on the router that borders both autonomous systems. However, if you are running IGRP and EIGRP with the same AS number, the routing process automatically does the redistribution for you. If your protocols require manual redistribution, you must accomplish that on your own before any updates can pass between the two dissimilar protocols. Route redistribution is covered in Chapter 12, so that topic will only expanded upon here except where relevant.

At times, it becomes necessary to connect your AS to another AS. This would be the case when you connect to your ISP. You must advertise reachability to the Internet's networks throughout your private network. You can accomplish this in a number of ways. The first thing you need to know is how you connect your AS to the ISP. Connecting two autonomous systems is done via an *Exterior Gateway Protocol* (EGP). The most common EGP is the Border Gateway Protocol.

BGP Basics

BGP has a relatively short history in the grand scheme of internetworking technologies. The protocol itself is connection oriented. It relies on Transmission Control Protocol (TCP) for connectivity before it begins communication with a neighboring device. Configuring BGP, RIP, and IGRP are similar processes. You simply start the process in the router and define the networks you want to advertise. Unlike with RIP and IGRP, you do not simply configure the directly connected networks on which you want to send updates. You must configure all the networks—directly connected or not—that you want BGP to advertise. Once the network statements are in the configuration, your work is not done. You must define the neighbor to which the BGP process on this router connects at the ISP side of the connection.

BGP Path Selection

The BGP process selects a single autonomous system path to use and to pass along to other BGP-speaking communication devices. The BGP implementation has a reasonable set of factory defaults that can be overridden by administrative weights. The algorithm for path selection is as follows:

➤ If the next hop is inaccessible, do not consider it.

➤ Consider larger BGP administrative weights first.

➤ If the routes have the same weight, consider the route with higher local preference.

➤ If the routes have the same local preference, prefer the route that the specified communication server originated.

➤ If no route was originated, prefer the shorter AS path.

➤ If the AS paths are of the same length, prefer external paths over internal paths.

➤ If all paths are external, prefer the lowest origin code.

➤ If origin codes are the same and all the paths are from the same AS, prefer the path with the lowest **MULTI_EXIT_DISC** metric. A missing metric is treated as zero.

➤ If IGP synchronization is disabled and only internal paths remain, prefer the path through the closest neighbor.

➤ Prefer the route with the lowest IP address value for the BGP router ID.

BGP Configuration

To enable BGP routing, you need to establish a BGP routing process on the router and specify the networks within your AS that you want to advertise. To enable the BGP routing process, follow these steps for basic initialization:

1. Enter global configuration mode by completing the following command from the privileged mode prompt:

```
configure terminal
```

2. Start the BGP routing process by completing the following command:

```
router bgp autonomous-system
```

3. Identify the networks you would like to advertise from your AS by issuing the following command:

```
network network-number mask network-mask
```

 When dealing with BGP, the **network** command only controls which networks are advertised in the BGP process. This is in direct contrast to IGP protocols such as RIP and IGRP, which use the **network** command to determine where routing updates are sent.

Listing 9.1 shows you what the basic commands look like once they're in the configuration. This configuration is necessary for router A to connect to the ISP router in Figure 9.1. Once the routers are connected and functioning properly, they are know as *peers*, and the term *peering* refers to the connection between the two.

Listing 9.1 The basic BGP configuration for router A.

```
router bgp 100
network 172.16.0.0 mask 255.255.0.0
```

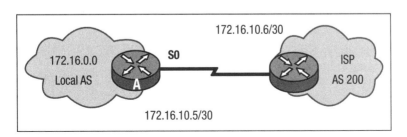

Figure 9.1 A basic BGP configuration.

External BGP Configuration

The peering of routers in dissimilar autonomous systems is an example of External BGP (EBGP) configuration. EBGP is simply a connection to a remote AS. The **neighbor** statement establishes router A as a peer to the ISP router. Would you ever want to peer two routers in your internal network? Certainly the case may arise. Configuring such a connection, known as *Internal BGP* (IBGP), is very similar to configuring the external peer connection. To configure BGP neighbors, you can perform the following command in router configuration mode:

```
neighbor ip-address remote-as number
```

Note: You can also configure neighbor statements that use a word argument rather than the neighbor's IP address. This is an advanced feature, so it's advised that you not use this feature without thoroughly understanding your network's architecture and this application.

Refer back to Figure 9.1 for an example of an EBGP configuration. Listing 9.2 shows the basic configuration commands necessary to create the external peer connection. Note that **remote-as** is the same as the AS number of the ISP network. This tells the router that the neighbor is external.

Listing 9.2 BGP neighbor configuration.

```
router bgp 100
network 172.16.0.0 mask 255.255.0.0
neighbor 172.16.10.6 remote-as 200
```

Internal BGP Configuration

IBGP is a function that's supported by BGP, where BGP routes are exchanged with routers within the same AS. Figure 9.3 shows an IBGP network in which two pathways will be utilized. Listings 9.3 and 9.4 show the basic configuration commands necessary to create the internal peer connection. Note that **remote-as** is the same as the local AS number defined by the **router bgp 100** command. This tells the router that the connection is internal.

Listing 9.3 IBGP neighbor 1 configuration.

```
router bgp 100
network 172.16.0.0 mask 255.255.0.0
neighbor 172.16.1.1 remote-as 100
```

Listing 9.4 IBGP neighbor 2 configuration.

```
router bgp 100
network 172.16.0.0 mask 255.255.0.0
neighbor 172.16.3.1 remote-as 100
```

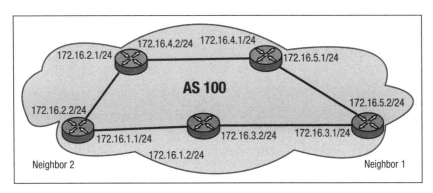

Figure 9.2 An IBGP configuration.

The neighbor address is specified as 172.16.1.1. What would happen if that particular interface were lost? The answer is that BGP would lose the connection, even in the presence of another route to that particular router. To avoid such a situation, you should create a logical loopback interface and then configure an IP address on this logical interface. In the BGP configuration, set the neighbor IP address to that of the loopback interface. Doing so forces BGP to use both available pathways to get to the logical network, as shown in Figure 9.3. Listing 9.5 shows the creation of a logical loopback interface and the change in code on the neighbor 1 router.

Listing 9.5   New neighbor 1 configuration.

```
Interface loopback 0
Ip address 10.1.1.1 255.255.255.255
!
Router bgp 100
Network 172.16.0.0
Network 10.0.0.0
Neighbor 11.1.1.1 remote-as 100
```

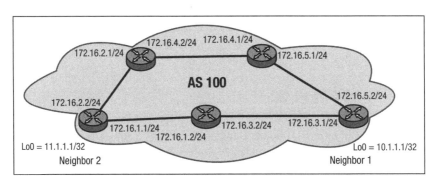

Figure 9.3   Forcing BGP to use multiple available pathways to gain access to the logical network.

Listing 9.6 shows the similar changes on the neighbor 2 router.

Listing 9.6 New neighbor 2 configuration.

```
Interface loopback 0
Ip address 11.1.1.1 255.255.255.255
!
Network 172.16.0.0
Network 11.0.0.0
Neighbor 10.1.1.1 remote-as 100
```

Resetting a BGP Connection

Once you have your BGP process initialized and your router has neighbored with the external BGP router, they will start to exchange routing information. Once this exchange has started, it should not be interrupted, but if there's a need to break this connection for any reason (such as changing the metrics or making any configuration changes), you'll need to reset the BGP connection before the configuration change will take effect. To reset the BGP connection, all you have to do is perform the following steps in privileged mode:

1. To reset a particular BGP connection, complete the following command:

```
clear ip bgp address
```

2. To reset all BGP connections, complete the following command:

```
clear ip bgp *
```

3. To automatically reset BGP sessions for directly connected external peers, complete the following command:

```
bgp fast-external-fallover
```

This information is important to remember because it's easy to forget to reset a BGP connection after any type of outage or configuration change, and you could spend many hours troubleshooting an issue that's simple to fix.

BGP Route Filtering

If you want to start restricting routing information that the router learns or advertises, you can filter BGP routing updates to and from any particular neighbor. There are different ways to filter BGP traffic, but for this chapter only the two following variations will be covered.

Route Filtering by Neighbor

When route filtering by neighbor, you must define an access list and apply it to the routing updates. After defining an access list that will filter particular BGP routes, you'll have to associate the access list with a distribute list. Remember that distribute lists are applied to network numbers and not AS paths, which will be discussed next. To configure a BGP route filter, perform the following task in configuration mode:

1. Configure an access list that will filter the BGP routing updates that you want to filter by completing the following command from global configuration mode:

```
access-list access-list-number {deny|permit} source

[source-wildcard mask]
```

2. After configuring the access list that will filter the BGP routing updates, you must apply it to the routing process by completing the following command:

```
neighbor ip-address distribute-list access-list-number {in |
out}
```

This will apply the access list that will filter the routing updates to the specific neighbor's IP address and filter the routing updates on either an inbound or outbound basis. Listing 9.7 displays the way that this configuration should look once applied to the router's configuration. Refer back to Figure 9.2 to see how the routes will be filtered and kept within AS 100.

Listing 9.7   Route filter configuration.

```
Router bgp 100
Network 172.16.0.0 mask 255.255.0.0
Neighbor 172.16.3.1 remote-as 100
Neighbor 172.16.1.1 remote-as 100 distribute-list 1 out

Access-list 1 deny 172.16.5.0 0.0.0.255
Access-list 1 permit 0.0.0.0 255.255.255.255
```

With this configuration, the use of the **distribute-list** command and **access-list 1** prevents the BGP routing updates from neighbor 1 propagating into neighbor 2's routing table. In addition to filter-routing updates based on network numbers, you can specify an access list filter on both incoming and outbound updates based on the BGP AS path.

Path Filtering by Neighbor

Filtering routes based on AS path information can become very useful when filtering is needed for all routes within the same or multiple autonomous systems. This is much more efficient than listing multiple routes based on the neighbor IP address. This function will also allow you to specify an access list on both inbound and outbound updates based on the value of the AS path. To configure a BGP path filter, perform the following task in configuration mode:

1. Configure an access list that will filter the BGP routing updates that you want to filter by completing the following command from global configuration mode:

```
access-list access-list-number {deny|permit} source
[source-wildcard mask]
```

2. Define a BGP-related access list by completing the following command:

```
ip as-path access-list access-list-number {permit|deny}
as-regular-expression
```

3. Enter router configuration mode by completing the following command:

```
router bgp as-number
```

4. Establish a BGP filter by completing the following command:

```
neighbor ip-address filter-list access-list-number
{in|out|weight weight}
```

This filter list works in conjunction with the AS path access list to filter the appropriate updates. Listing 9.8 displays the way that this configuration should look once applied to the router's configuration. Refer back to Figure 9.2 to see how the AS paths will be filtered within AS 100.

Listing 9.8   AS path filtering.

```
Router bgp 100
Network 172.16.0.0 mask 255.255.0.0
Neighbor 172.16.10.6 remote-as 200
Neighbor 172.16.1.1 remote-as 100
Neighbor 172.16.1.1 filter-list 1 out
Neighbor 172.16.3.1 remote-as 100
Neighbor 172.16.3.1 filter-list 1 out

Ip as-path access-list 1 permit ^$
```

Note: The expression ^$ indicates that an AS path is empty. The "^" symbol indicates the beginning of the AS path, and the "$" symbol indicates the end of the path.

Peer Groups

A *peer group* is a group of BGP neighbors that share the same update policies, such as distribute lists, route maps, and filter lists. Instead of identifying the policy for each individual neighbor, you can define a peer group name and assign policies to the group itself. Refer back to Figure 9.2 for an example of a BGP peer group and how the routers are connected. Listing 9.9 shows how the configuration should look once the router is configured.

Listing 9.9   Peer group configuration.

```
Router bgp 100
Network 172.16.0.0 255.255.0.0
Neighbor PEERGROUP peer-group
Neighbor PEERGROUP remote-as 100
Neighbor 172.16.2.1 peer-group PEERGROUP
Neighbor 172.16.3.1 peer-group PEERGROUP
```

All devices that are members of a peer group inherit all the configuration options of the peer group. One restriction that applies to peer groups is that a peer group should not be set using EBGP neighbors. This may lead to external neighbors being affected by a peer group configuration that might result in routes being improperly interpreted.

Redistributing IGP into BGP

Routes can be redistributed into BGP by utilizing either static or dynamic means. The choice is entirely up to you, but the number of routes and the routes' stability will play an important role in this decision. The first option covered is how to configure a router to dynamically redistribute routes into BGP.

Dynamic Redistribution

When dealing with dynamic redistribution, you are taking an IGP routing protocol such as RIP, IGRP, or OSPF and redistributing that routing information into BGP. When configuring dynamic redistribution, you'll be dealing with two new commands that will be needed in the configuration. These two commands are the **passive-interface** and **redistribute** commands. To have better control of the routing updates being redistributed from your IGP into BGP, use the **network** command. This command is a way to list each network prefix that you want to advertise in BGP individually. These commands are configured under the router configuration. The following is a brief description of each command and how it would be implemented:

➤ **Passive-interface** *type interface-number* — This command disables sending routing updates on the specified interface. This is configured in the routing process that you want to block updates from.

➤ **Redistribute** *protocol [process id]* — This command injects routes from one routing protocol into another. This is configured in the routing process on which you want the redistribution to occur.

Note: A configuration example showing how to use the network command is shown earlier in this chapter under the "Configuring BGP" section.

Static Redistribution

If a network that's listed in your BGP configuration goes down, what does this do to your routing process? Every time that a route goes down, BGP will send an update saying that the route is down. When the route comes back up, BGP will send another update saying that the route is up. If the IGP continues this network instability, it will propagate into your BGP process and make it unstable. The only way around this issue is to statically assign routes. This ensures that the routes will always remain in the routing tables and will always be advertised in the network.

The drawback of this approach is that even when a route is down it will still be advertised by BGP as being active. Compared to the possibility of network instability that may be caused by dynamic redistribution, you may find this option more effective. The main difference you'll see concerning the configuration is that instead of redistributing a routing protocol, you'll be redistributing static routes into BGP. You'll also have to establish a static route that points to a next-hop address of your ISP, or you can specify the interface.

 By specifying a static route that uses the interface option instead of a next hop, that route will be advertised as a directly connected network.

In most circumstances, you will not want to redistribute your IGP into BGP. Just list the networks in your autonomous system with **network** router-configuration commands, and your networks will be advertised. Networks that are listed this way are referred to as *local networks* and have a BGP origin attribute of "IGP." They must appear in the main IP routing table and can have any source; for example, they can be directly connected or learned via an IGP. The BGP routing process periodically scans the main IP routing table to detect the presence or absence of local networks, updating the BGP routing table as appropriate.

If you do perform redistribution into BGP, you must be very careful about the routes that can be in your IGP, especially if the routes were redistributed from BGP into the IGP elsewhere. This creates a situation where BGP is potentially injecting information into the IGP, which is then sending this information back into BGP, and vice versa.

Verifying Proper BGP Operation

You can display specific statistics, such as the contents of BGP routing tables, caches, and databases. Information provided can be used to determine resource utilization and solve network problems. You can also display information about network reachability and discover the routing path your device's packets are taking through the network. Table 9.1 displays a list of commands that can be used to verify proper BGP operation and assist in troubleshooting any problems that may arise.

Table 9.1   BGP verification commands and descriptions.

Command	Description
Show ip bgp filter-list *access-list number*	Displays routes that are matched by the specific AS path access list
Show ip bgp [*network*] [*network-mask*] [**subnets**]	Displays the contents of the BGP routing table
Show ip bgp neighbors [*address*]	Displays detailed information on the TCP and BGP connections to individual neighbors
Show ip bgp paths	Displays all BGP paths in the database
Show ip bgp peer-group [*tag*] [**summary**]	Displays information about BGP peer groups
Show ip bgp summary	Displays the status of all BGP connections

Practice Questions

Question 1

> Routing Information Protocol is an example of an Exterior Gateway Protocol.
>
> ○ a. True
>
> ○ b. False

Answer b is correct. RIP is an IGP, which is defined as any of the commonly used protocols to facilitate the dissemination of private internetwork reachability information. An EGP serves to connect dissimilar autonomous systems.

Question 2

> Which of the following items can you use to connect to your ISP?
>
> ○ a. BGP
>
> ○ b. Static routes
>
> ○ c. RIP
>
> ○ d. All of the above

Answer d is correct. You can use any method the ISP chooses to connect the two internetworks. The propagation of routes to the ISP is your responsibility within your own internetwork.

Question 3

> Using the following image, what is the correct use of the BGP neighbor command to connect your router to the ISP? (Use R1 as the edge router for your network and R2 as the edge router of the ISP.)
>
>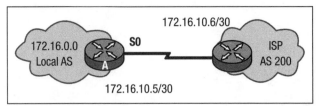

The correct answer is **Neighbor 192.168.1.6 remote-as 300**.

Question 4

Which protocol does BGP depend on for neighbor connectivity?

○ a. UDP

○ b. IPX

○ c. TCP

○ d. None of the above

Answer c is correct. BGP is TCP connection oriented. Answer a, UDP (User Datagram Protocol), is a connectionless protocol and is therefore incorrect. Internetwork Packet Exchange (IPX) is a separate Layer 3 protocol suite and has nothing to do with IP or IP routing protocols. Therefore, answer b is incorrect. Answer d is incorrect because a correct answer is given.

Question 5

Which of the following scenarios requires BGP routing? [Choose the two best answers.]

❑ a. You need to make a decision based on the source and destination of internal traffic within an AS.

❑ b. You need to make connections to different Internet Service Providers.

❑ c. Security concerns require that you must filter all but three networks from the Internet.

❑ d. The ISP you connect to uses BGP.

Answers b and c are correct. When connecting to different providers, it is necessary to configure BGP to select the appropriate pathway to the Internet. You must also filter the private internetwork addresses to keep them off the Internet. Answer a is incorrect because your internal traffic will be forwarded based on your IGP, not BGP. Answer d is incorrect because your ISP will be using BGP at some points within the network. The fact that an ISP is using BGP does not dictate that you have to use it. It's still a matter of discretion on the ISP's part.

Question 6

What command will allow you to have better control of routing updates when redistributing from your IGP into BGP?

- O a. **passive-interface**
- O b. **network**
- O c. **redistribute**
- O d. **neighbor**

Answer b is correct. By specifying the **network** command you will have better control of the routing updates being redistributed from your IGP into BGP. This command is a way to list each network prefix that you want to advertise in BGP individually. Answer a is incorrect because the **passive-interface** command disables sending routing updates on the specified interface. This is configured in the routing process that you want to block updates from. Answer c is incorrect because the **redistribute** command injects routes from one routing protocol into another. This is configured in the routing process on which you want the redistribution to occur. Answer d is incorrect because the **neighbor** command specifies a neighbor router with which you wish to establish a peer connection.

Question 7

What command displays detailed information on the TCP and BGP connections to individual neighbors?

- O a. **Show ip bgp neighbors [*address*]**
- O b. **Show ip bgp neighbors [*address*] detail**
- O c. **Show ip bgp neighbors detail**
- O d. **Show ip neighbors detail bgp**

Answer a is correct. This command will display detailed information concerning the TCP and BGP connections to individual neighbors by using the address option. Answers b, c, and d are incorrect because they are all using invalid commands or syntax. With other protocols such as OSPF you can use the **show ip bgp neighbors detail** command, but with BGP this is not a valid option.

Need to Know More?

 Halabi, Basam. *Internet Routing Architecture.* Cisco Press. Indianapolis, IN 1997. ISBN 1-56205-652-2. This book is an authoritative guide to BGP configuration.

 Larson, Bob, Corwin Low, and Michael Simon. *CCNP Routing Exam Prep.* The Coriolis Group. Scottsdale, AZ. ISBN. 1-57610-778-2. Fall 2000. This book, an Exam Prep for the CCNP exam, covers each related subject in great detail.

 Stewart, John W. *BGP4: Inter-Domain Routing in the Internet.* Addison-Wesley. New York 1998. ISBN 0-02013-7951-1. This is a must-read for more information on interdomain routing in the Internet.

 Check out **www.cisco.com** and perform a search on BGP. You'll get numerous hits on that search. There's one particular document known as the "BGP Design Guide." Check it out.

BGP Scalability

Terms you'll need to understand:

✓ Static routing

✓ Dynamic routing

✓ Interior Gateway Protocol (IGP)

✓ Exterior Gateway Protocol (EGP)

✓ Default routes

✓ Route maps

✓ Border Gateway Protocol (BGP) attributes

✓ Load balancing

✓ Route reflectors

✓ Confederations

Techniques you'll need to master:

✓ Understanding route selection

✓ Identifying when to use static routes

✓ Identifying when to use dynamic routes

✓ Identifying BGP attributes

✓ Understanding route filtering

✓ Understanding route reflectors

✓ Understanding confederations

When dealing with networks that are as complex as the Internet, network scalability can become a major issue. BGP is a path vector routing protocol that's used to carry routing information between different autonomous systems. The term *path vector* is related to the fact that BGP information carries a sequence of autonomous system (AS) numbers. These AS numbers are related to the route path that information has used to travel across the network. BGP uses TCP as the transport protocol, which ensures that the reliability is taken care of by TCP and does not need to be developed into BGP itself. This chapter will discuss many of the scalability issues associated with BGP, such as route/path selection and optimization techniques, and other varying issues associated with BGP.

Scalability Issues

Large networks such as the Internet have certain aspects that require careful thought and design. When your network is connecting to an ISP with any type of high-speed connection, the ISP is going to want to have some control over the traffic being sent to it. Two of the issues discussed in this section deal with redundancy and load balancing, which when incorporated in the proper manner can alleviate common network issues.

Route Redundancy

Route redundancy is accomplished when multiple paths are available for traffic to flow through. Route redundancy is accomplished when there are multiple entrance and exit points from your network to your service provider. Having multiple connections provides the ability to continue traffic processing in the event that one of those connections goes down due to any of the multiple reasons that exist. Many companies require a certain amount of route redundancy in a network so that production will not be affected by one of these outages. One of the downfalls of having route redundancy is that you create more route entries in the routing tables of your routers, and this can affect the processing of routing traffic. One way that you can achieve route redundancy without the overhead is by using *default routes*. A default route can provide you an alternate path if one path becomes unavailable.

Default Routes

Default routes provide the redundancy required by many networks while reducing the amount of networks that a router has to learn about and maintain in its routing tables. Cisco refers to such a default route as a *gateway of last resort*. A default route is a route that all traffic will use if a more specific route is not known in the routing table. Default routes can be advertised either statically or dynamically on a network.

With dynamic default routes, you receive your gateway-of-last-resort information from your ISP or another outside source. This dictates the route that all traffic that's not represented in the routing table will take. For redundancy purposes, you should receive a default route from each network exit point, so you'll have multiple default routes. This gives you little control over your traffic, and there's the possibility of your ISP injecting the wrong default route. This brings us to the second type of default route: the static default route.

With static default routes, you're provided the gateway-of-last-resort information and you configure this information locally on your routers. Just like in a dynamic default route, all traffic not represented in the routing table will use this route for access to external networks. Using this method gives you more control over default route configuration and ensures that your ISP doesn't inject a bad default route. There is a downside, however. This option can be administratively demanding. Every time the ISP makes a configuration change, you'll have to make the appropriate change on your end of the link. Again, for redundancy, you should utilize multiple static routes for traffic to use in the event that a route becomes unavailable.

Load Balancing

As you should know by now, *load balancing* is the capability to divide network traffic over multiple connections. Load balancing tries to achieve a diverse traffic load that will utilize multiple connections for redundancy. It's important to remember that the traffic you're dealing with is both inbound and outbound traffic.

The pattern of inbound and outbound traffic relates directly to the way you advertise your routes and how you're able to learn about advertised routes. Inbound traffic is affected by the way the AS advertises its networks to the outside. Outbound traffic is affected by the way routing updates are learned from the outside.

Load balancing with BGP only works properly when you're receiving identical updates from the same provider. Load balancing will not work when you're utilizing multiple service providers.

Route Selection

When you connect to your ISP or any other network via BGP, you have a number of options. These options are key points to consider in how you configure route reachability to the Internet itself. Who chooses the options? Well, you *are* connecting to the ISP's network. Therefore, the ISP can choose what options to implement based on your network's size. Now, you can define your network's size in two ways. First, how many nodes do you have on your internal internetwork?

Second, how spread out geographically are these nodes? The answers to these questions point to the method of connection. The options available are *static routes* between your company and the ISP, and *dynamic routes* between your company and your ISP. Static routes are route table entries that an administrator has placed into service. Dynamic routing protocols advertise and generate routing tables. The following sections look at these more closely.

Static Routing

At the ISP's discretion, you may be allowed to run static routes in order to connect to its network. If this is the case, your job can be difficult or easy, depending on how you choose to administer your static routes. In every router, you can set static routes that point back to the ISP's network. Doing so becomes cumbersome and is quite error prone. The ISP gives you the appropriate information necessary to create the static routes. Figure 10.1 shows a sample network scenario.

To specify the next-hop address to get the data traffic out to the ISP's edge router, use the following command:

```
ip route 10.0.0.0 255.0.0.0 172.16.4.6
```

To specify the interface through which the data traffic should leave the edge router to get to the ISP's edge router, use the following command:

```
ip route 10.0.0.0 255.0.0.0 Serial 0
```

Static routing can be a chore (*administrative nightmare* is possibly a more accurate term). You must inform each router in your network about the pathway to the ISP. Rather than going through the pain of making manual entries on every router, consider using a default route. You can set a default route on the edge router and force it to inject backwards into your network. Network 0.0.0.0 with the mask 0.0.0.0 is considered to be a default network. If you set this route to exit interface Serial 0, the router assumes that 172.16.10.4 (the network address of the serial link) is now the IP default network. This route is propagated along with

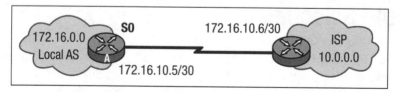

Figure 10.1 A sample network scenario.

your regular routing updates. The following code is an example of the use of a static default route, using Figure 10.1 as a reference scenario:

```
ip route 0.0.0.0 0.0.0.0 s0
```

 Set a default static route at the edge router of your AS. Be sure to give it an outbound interface, not a next-hop address. When a static route has an outbound interface, it is automatically redistributed throughout your network. All routers then have a gateway of last resort set automatically; they will therefore know how to get to your ISP's network with little configuration on your part.

Dynamic Routing

Your ISP can decide, with your input of course, to run dynamic routes across the connection between your network and its network. The choice here is what type of dynamic routing protocol to use. You can use IGPs or EGPs, as mentioned earlier.

Interior Gateway Protocols

IGPs include all the traditional routing protocols you would use in your private internetwork. These protocols include, but are not limited to, Routing Information Protocol (RIP), Open Shortest Path First (OSPF), Interior Gateway Routing Protocol (IGRP), and Enhanced Interior Gateway Routing Protocol (EIGRP). All these protocols are discussed at various points in this book. However, RIP and IGRP aren't covered in great detail because they are not part of the exam criteria. For information on OSPF, see Chapters 6 and 7. For EIGRP, see Chapter 8.

Whatever protocol you run internally, the ISP may determine that it is in your mutual best interests to use an IGP. If so, you simply configure your edge router(s) to redistribute the ISP's networks into your own. You'll probably want to filter out many of the routes that will then come pouring into your routing tables. See Chapter 12 for more information on route redistribution.

Exterior Gateway Protocols

EGPs are protocols designed with the purpose of connecting two dissimilar autonomous systems. This almost sounds much like what is being attempted here. EGPs include Exterior Gateway Protocol (EGP)—yes, that's its name—and BGP. EGP is not widely used these days, so the focus will be on BGP version 4.

BGP offers some capabilities that other dynamic routing protocols lack. One specific ability has made BGP the most popular protocol among ISPs and their big brothers, the National Access Providers (NAP): being able to affect routing policy at a high level and to have it flow down through all the connected autonomous systems. This feature allows the NAPs to set rules and regulations regarding route propagation at the highest levels of the Internet hierarchy. NAPs can also know that all autonomous systems connecting to them, however far down the chain, are subject to those rules and regulations. Figure 10.2 depicts the basic Internet hierarchy.

In Figure 10.2, you can see that there are a number of connection options. You are not limited to connecting to a single ISP. For the purposes of redundancy, you may want to connect to multiple ISPs. The geography of your company may also be a deciding factor. If your ISP does not have coast-to-coast points of presence, multiple ISPs may be your only option.

BGP Path Selection

As stated in Chapter 9, the BGP process selects a single autonomous system path to use and then passes this path along to other BGP-speaking communication devices. The BGP implementation has a reasonable set of factory defaults that can be overridden by administrative weights. The algorithm for path selection is as follows:

➤ If the next-hop is inaccessible, do not consider it.

➤ Consider larger BGP administrative weights first.

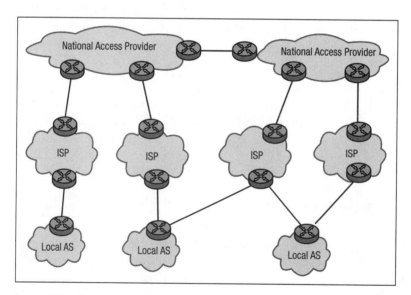

Figure 10.2   Basic internet hierarchy.

➤ If the routes have the same weight, consider the route with higher local preference.

➤ If the routes have the same local preference, prefer the route that the specified communication server originated.

➤ If no route was originated, prefer the shorter AS path.

➤ If the AS paths are of the same length, prefer external paths over internal paths.

➤ If all paths are external, prefer the lowest origin code.

➤ If origin codes are the same and all the paths are from the same AS, prefer the path with the lowest **MULTI_EXIT_DISC** metric. A missing metric is treated as zero.

➤ If IGP synchronization is disabled and only internal paths remain, prefer the path through the closest neighbor.

➤ Prefer the route with the lowest IP address value for the BGP router ID.

BGP Optimization

Traffic flows both inside and outside the AS always follow the routes that are established. Every time these routes change, the traffic and all its behaviors change with the routes it takes. This can lead to complexities in your network that can only be addressed by manipulating the traffic so that the traffic behavior can be properly managed. When you're attempting to control network routes, there are a couple of questions that need to be answered in order to properly assess the situation. The following list of questions will help you when confronted with the task of controlling routes:

➤ How do I prevent private networks from being advertised?

➤ How can I filter certain networks from my networks?

➤ How can I manipulate the traffic to take one route over the other?

BGP Attributes

BGP attributes are parameters that describe the characteristics of a certain BGP route. The decision process will use these attributes, sent via BGP routing updates, to select the best route for traffic to take to reach a certain destination. Several attributes are associated with BGP and the route selection. A brief description of each type of attribute and its function appear in the following sections.

Next-Hop Attribute

You are probably well aware of what the next-hop function of an IGP is and how it functions. With BGP, the next-hop attribute is a mandatory attribute, and it can take on one of three specific functions:

➤ In Exterior Border Gateway Protocol (EBGP) sessions, the next-hop is the IP address of the neighbor that announced the route.

➤ In Interior Border Gateway Protocol (IBGP) sessions, if the route originated inside the AS, the next-hop is the IP address of the neighbor that announced it. If the route is injected via EBGP, the next-hop is the IP address of the EBGP neighbor from which the route was originally learned.

➤ When the route is advertised on a multiaccess media, the next-hop is the IP address of the interface connected to the multiaccess media that originated the route.

AS Path Attribute

This attribute is another mandatory attribute that's a sequence of AS numbers a route travels to reach its final destination. When the journey begins, the AS that originated the route will add its own AS number and then each AS that the route travels will add its AS number to the beginning of the path list. This final list represents all the autonomous systems that the route has traveled, with the originating AS at the end of the list. This type of list is known as an *AS sequence list* because the AS numbers are in sequential order.

This attribute is utilized to ensure that there's a loop-free topology on the Internet, because each route will carry a list of all AS numbers that it has passed through. This attribute is one of the attributes that BGP uses to determine the best route that traffic should take to get to a destination. BGP will compare different routes, and the one with the shortest path is preferred if all other attributes are even.

Private AS Numbers

The American Registry for Internet Numbers (ARIN) will generally assign a private AS number for organizations whose policies are the same as their provider's. In this situation, the provider will request that the customer use a private AS number from the AS pool. This provides a bit of a problem because private AS numbers, like private IP ranges, cannot be advertised to the Internet. With this in mind, Cisco has implemented a feature that strips the private AS number from the AS path list and replaces it with the AS number of the customer provider.

 ARIN is responsible for maintaining a public trust. Among its other responsibilities, ARIN promotes the conservation of IP address space, maintains impartiality while determining the size of address blocks to be allocated or assigned, and supports efforts to keep the global routing tables to a manageable size to ensure routability of information over the Internet. Continued operation of the Internet depends, in part, upon the conservation and efficient use of IP address space. You can visit their Web site at **www.arin.net**. The private AS range is 64512 to 65535.

Route Summarization

Route summarization is the aggregation of ranges of routes into one or more routes. This will assist in reducing routing table information, processing time, and convergence, but there are drawbacks. When using summarization, you loose a certain amount of granularity in comparison to using singular routes. This means the AS path information would be lost and all paths would be combined into one path advertisement. This is where another type of attribute comes into play. The **AS SET** attribute lists the AS paths in an unordered manner. Summary routes carrying the **AS SET** information would have a complete list of AS paths that form individual routes. This alleviates the problem of multiple routes being represented by a single AS and allows the use of summarization to its full capability.

Local Preference Attribute

This attribute is a preference that's assigned to a route to compare with other routes for the same destination. This is a varying preference, where a high local preference indicates a more preferable route to take. The local preference attribute is only exchanged between IBGP peers and is never passed on to EBGP peers.

MED Attribute

The **MULTI_EXIT_DISC** (MED) attribute is an external metric of a route, where a lower MED value is preferred over a higher MED value. It can be used to let external neighbors know about the preferred route into an AS with multiple entry points. The MED attribute can be passed between autonomous systems, but once a MED enters an AS, it does not leave.

When a route is originated by the AS, the MED value is associated with the IGP metric on the route. This can be very handy when you have multiple connections to the same provider. The IGP metric reflects how close or how far a network exit point is, and the closer exit point will have a lower IGP metric. This lower IGP metric will translate to a lower MED. This means that traffic entering the AS can enter from the link closer to the destination due to the low MED. This attribute can be used to balance the traffic over multiple links between multiple autonomous systems.

Community Attribute

A *community* is a group of destinations that share a common property. A community is not restricted by network or AS; in fact, there is no boundary. Communities are used to simplify routing policies by identifying routes based on common logical property rather than an IP address or AS. This can be used in conjunction with other BGP attributes to control which routes are accepted, rejected, and preferred to pass onto other BGP neighbors.

ORIGIN Attribute

This attribute indicates the origin of routing updates in relation to the AS that originated the route. BGP will consider three types of origins: IGP, EGP, and INCOMPLETE. BGP considers the ORIGIN attribute when making its processing decisions to establish a preference ranking among multiple routes. BGP prefers the route with the lowest origin type, with IGP lower than EGP, and EGP lower than INCOMPLETE.

Route Filtering

A BGP router can determine which routes to send and which routes to receive from any of its peers. An AS can specify the inbound traffic that it is willing to accept from neighbors by specifying a list of routes that it will advertise to its neighbors. An AS can also control outbound traffic by specifying the routes that it accepts from its neighbors. Filtering is an essential step when implementing routing policies.

Route Maps

Cisco uses route maps for route filtering. Route maps are used in conjunction with BGP to control and modify routing information and define when routes are redistributed between routing domains. To configure route maps on a router, just use the following format:

```
Route-map map-tag [[permit | deny] | [sequence-number]]
```

Here, *map-tag* is the name of the route map, whereas *sequence-number* indicates the position that an instance of the route map is to have in relation to other instances of the same route map. The access list is a method for identifying routes that you may want to manipulate. You can either use a standard or extended access list with the route map. It just depends to what degree of specification you want to incorporate.

Route Reflectors

As has been stated, a BGP peer that is a member of another AS is an EBGP (External BGP) peer and in most cases will be directly connected to the local router. However, when the BGP peer is a member of the same AS, it is known as an IBGP (Internal BGP) peer and is usually a number of hops away. When constructing large IBGP networks, issues can arise as the number of peer routers increases. IBGP requires that all peers within an AS be fully meshed with one another. This results in a large number of peers (20 routers means 190 peerings) and an administratively cumbersome network. *Route reflection* was devised to help alleviate this problem. Central peers can be configured to pass routing information between their neighbors. This is known as route reflection. In route reflection, multiple IBGP peers peer with one router that is known as the *concentration* router. This concentration router acts as a focal point, allowing all the routers to peer with one router instead of multiple routers.

On the reflector clients there is no configuration. All configuration is performed on the concentration router. After the neighbor statements are added, an additional line of configuration per neighbor is inserted. The command is **neighbor** *<ip address>* **route-reflector-client**. Once this is done, it is no longer necessary for a router's IBGP neighbors to peer with each other, because the concentration router will pass BGP updates between them. Figure 10.3 illlustrates the concept of the route reflector.

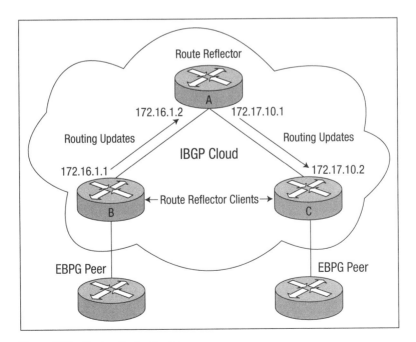

Figure 10.3   Route reflector topology.

Listing 10.1 shows the basic commands necessary to create a route reflector on a router.

Listing 10.1   Route reflector configuration.

```
router bgp 100
network 172.16.0.0 mask 255.255.0.0
neighbor 172.16.1.1 remote-as 100
neighbor 172.16.1.1 route-reflector-client
neighbor 172.17.10.2 remote-as 100
neighbor 172.17.10.2 route-reflector-client
```

Confederations

Confederations are an extension of the route reflector concept. Instead of looking at the issue from a router-specific IBGP point of view, confederations deal with entire autonomous systems. A confederation is based on the fact that you can divide an AS into multiple sub-ASes, thereby reducing the number of IBGP peers. The rules of BGP apply to all routers within this sub-AS, and since each sub-AS has its own AS number, you must run external BGP between multiple ASes. Although EBGP is being used between the sub-ASes, the confederation adheres to the rules of IBGP. The confederation is technically a number of ASes but is advertised to the outside world as a single AS. The confederation configuration is invisible to external ASes.

The drawback to working with a confederation is that migrating from a nonconfederation to a confederation design requires major reconfiguration on all the routers. In addition, routes can be learned via a nonoptimal route, which can create problems later. The only way to address this is by manually configuring the BGP policies for a particular router or path. Listings 10.2, 10.3, and 10.4 show the basic commands necessary to create a BGP confederation on the routers in Figure 10.4. Figure 10.4 illustrates the concept of the confederation topology.

Listing 10.2   Router A BGP confederation configuration.

```
router bgp 100
bgp confederation identifier 400
bgp confederation peers 200 300
neighbor 172.16.1.1 remote-as 200
neighbor 172.16.2.1 remote-as 300
```

Listing 10.3   Router B BGP confederation configuration.

```
router bgp 200
bgp confederation identifier 400
bgp confederation peers 100 300
neighbor 172.16.1.2 remote-as 100
```

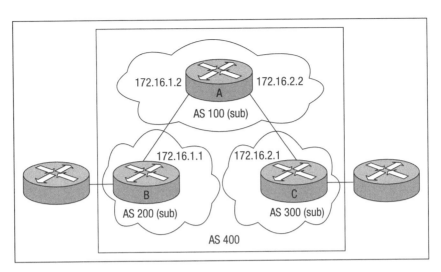

Figure 10.4 BGP confederation example.

Listing 10.4 shows the configuration of the confederation peer router C.

Listing 10.4 Router C BGP confederation configuration

```
router bgp 300
bgp confederation identifier 400
bgp confederation peers 100 200
neighbor 172.16.2.2 remote-as 100
```

The command **bgp confederation identifier** specifies which confederation this router belongs to. The command **bgp confederation peers** specifies which peers will be part of the confederation. All BGP peer routers in the same major AS will have the same bgp confederation identifier. The confederation peers statement must list all the sub-ASes

BGP Synchronization

There is a basic rule that exists in an IBGP routing environment: Do not use, or advertise to an external neighbor, a route learned by IBGP until a matching route has been learned from an IGP. IBGP routers will not place in the routing table a route that is unknown to the local IGP. For example, if you're running RIP and it is not aware of an internal network being advertised between two IBGP peers, that route will not be placed in the routing table. This ensures the consistency of information throughout the AS and avoids a phenomenon known as a black hole (that is, advertising routes that do not exist), which diminishes your routing capabilities. If you are running BGP on all routers in the AS and you are *not* a transit AS, you can disable synchronization using the **no synchronization** command. If you disable synchronization, the fact that the IGP doesn't know the route will not stop the route from populating the BGP routing table. If you are routing Internet traffic across your AS (that is, you're a transit area), *do not* turn off synchronization. It is possible to populate routes using static entries if the IGP cannot, for whatever reason, learn the route(s) on its own. In Figure 10.5 router B does not advertise network 10.10.10.0 to router A until an OSPF route for network 10.10.10.0 exists. If you specify the **no synchronization** router configuration command, router B advertises network 10.10.10.0 as soon as possible.

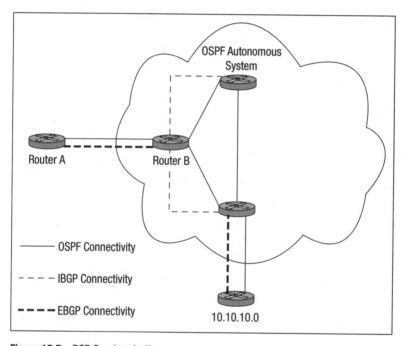

Figure 10.5 BGP Synchronization.

Practice Questions

Question 1

What routing protocols are considered exterior gateway protocols? [Choose two.]

❏ a. BGP

❏ b. EGP

❏ c. RIP

❏ d. All of the above

Answers a and b are correct. BGP (Border Gateway Protocol) and EGP (Exterior Gateway Protocol) are exterior gateway protocols that were developed by the Internet Engineering Task Force (IETF). Answer c is incorrect because RIP is considered as an IGP protocol because it was developed for use on small networks. Answer d is incorrect because answers a and b are correct.

Question 2

How can you utilize route redundancy with the least amount of router overhead?

○ a. By using dynamic routes

○ b. By using dedicated routes

○ c. By using static routes

○ d. By using default routes

Answer d is correct because a default route is a way for the router to learn of its gateway of last resort via dynamic route injection from the ISP or locally administered static routes. Answer a is incorrect because dynamic routes have a large amount of overhead associated with them. Answer b is incorrect because there is no such thing as a *dedicated route* when dealing with route selection or processing. Answer c is incorrect because static routes are a type of default route. Remember that there are two types of default routes: dynamic and static.

Question 3

> What is the range of private AS numbers?
>
> ○ a. 64000 to 65000
>
> ○ b. 1 to 255
>
> ○ c. 64512 to 65535
>
> ○ d. 64128 to 65355

Answer c is correct. The actual pool range of private AS numbers is 64512 to 65535. Answers a, b, and d are incorrect because they are numbers that have no relation to the AS private pool range.

Question 4

> What type of BGP attribute has no physical boundaries?
>
> ○ a. Community attribute
>
> ○ b. Local preference attribute
>
> ○ c. MED attribute
>
> ○ d. AS Path attribute

Answer a is correct. The community attribute has no physical boundaries and is based on a common logical property. Answer b is incorrect because the local preference attribute assigns a preference to a route to compare with other routes of the same destination. Answer c is incorrect because the MED attribute is a metric associated with an external route. Answer d is incorrect because the AS Path attribute is a list of AS numbers that a route takes to reach its final destination.

Question 5

> What feature is essential when implementing routing policies?
>
> ○ a. Static routes
>
> ○ b. Route filtering
>
> ○ c. Default routes
>
> ○ d. Dynamic routes

Answer b is correct. When you determine what type of routing policy you want to introduce, you'll need to implement a route-filtering technique. Answers a, c, and d are all incorrect because you can use any combination of these techniques in correlation to route filtering with the same outcome. Filtering has no preference in what type of route it is using or filtering.

Question 6

What BGP concept is described as dividing an AS into multiple ASes?

○ a. Attribute

○ b. Confederation

○ c. Router reflector

○ d. AS division

Answer b is correct. A confederation is an AS that is divided into multiple sub-ASes with each sub-AS having its own AS number and connecting to each other via EBGP. A confederation still looks like a single AS to devices outside the network. Answer a is incorrect because BGP attributes are used to determine BGP path selections and represent other mechanisms within the BGP routing process. Answer c is incorrect because route reflectors are where multiple BGP routers peer with a single router known as a *concentration* router. Answer d is incorrect because this is an invalid BGP concept name.

Question 7

What BGP term describes multiple BGP routers peering with a single router?

○ a. Confederation

○ b. Static route

○ c. Route reflector

○ d. None of the above

Answer c is correct. A route reflector is where multiple BGP routers peer with a single router known as a *concentration* router. These reflectors will then peer with other reflectors so that all BGP routers will seem to be peering with each other. Answer a is incorrect because a confederation is described as an AS that is divided into multiple sub-ASes with each sub-AS having its own AS number and connecting to each other via EBGP. This confederation still looks like a single AS to devices on the outside of the network. Answer b is incorrect because static routes are a way to direct traffic without using a routing protocol such as BGP.

Need to Know More?

 Halabi, Basam. *Internet Routing Architecture.* Cisco Press. Indianapolis, IN 1997. ISBN 1-56205-652-2. This book is an authoritative guide to BGP configuration.

 Larson, Bob, Corwin Low, and Michael Simon. *CCNP Routing Exam Prep.* The Coriolis Group. Scottsdale, AZ. ISBN 1-57610-778-2. Fall 2000. This book, an Exam Prep for the CCNP exam, covers each related subject in great detail.

 Stewart, John W. *BGP4: Inter-Domain Routing in the Internet.* Addison-Wesley. New York 1998. ISBN 0-02013-7951-1. This is a must-read for more information on interdomain routing in the Internet.

 Check out **www.cisco.com** and perform a search on BGP. You'll get numerous hits on that search. There's one particular document known as the "BGP Design Guide." Check it out.

Traffic Management

. . . .

Terms you'll need to understand:

✓ Standard access lists

✓ Extended access lists

✓ Wildcard masks

✓ Access class

✓ Null interfaces

✓ Helper addresses

✓ Tunnels

Techniques you'll need to master:

✓ Coding wildcard masks

✓ Configuring standard and extended IP access lists

✓ Understanding access list positioning

✓ Limiting virtual terminal access

✓ Using a static route to the null interface as an alternative to access lists

✓ Understanding helper address configuration

✓ Using tunnels to connect network islands

This chapter looks at some of the Cisco Internetwork Operating System (IOS) features used to make IP more efficient and secure. It starts by reviewing standard IP access lists, commonly called *filters*, and moves on to the more complicated extended versions. Along the way, you'll learn about issues such as the placement of access lists for correct operation and maximum efficiency in the network. Additionally, you'll examine an alternative to access lists called the *null interface*. This chapter illustrates how to use access lists to increase router security with access classes as well as examines the concept of the IP helper address.

Access lists can be used with all protocols, including IPX, AppleTalk, and DecNet. This chapter will also discuss the concept of a protocol encapsulation method known as a *tunnel*, which can connect to noncontiguous network layer protocol implementations.

Traffic Congestion

Traffic congestion can occur any time when the amount of traffic on a network exceeds the allocated bandwidth. This can still allow network traffic to traverse the network, but people will perceive the network as being "slow." Traffic congestion can be expected to occur on almost every network, but with varying degrees of impact.

There's a difference between temporary congestion and chronic traffic congestion. Temporary congestion is very common in networks today because of the "bursty" nature of many of today's user applications. This type of congestion is not as serious as chronic congestion because it's not on a continuous basis, but the causes should be identified for future reference and possibly fixed in any future upgrades. Chronic traffic congestion is much more serious and can have a detrimental effect on all traffic that's trying to cross the network. Chronic congestion is defined as any type of congestion that occurs on regular intervals or as a result of regular network use. This type of congestion should be immediately identified and fixed as soon as possible to bring the network back to acceptable user parameters.

 To determine whether you are experiencing traffic congestion, use a network analyzer to determine the amount of bandwidth being used on a network segment.

IP Network Traffic

When you're dealing with network traffic, it's important to know the many sources associated with that type of traffic. With IP traffic, the sources of data and overhead traffic can be categorized into several groups. Table 11.1 lists these categories and a gives brief description of what type of traffic fits into each category.

Table 11.1 IP traffic categories.	
Traffic Type	**Description**
Routing protocol updates	Routing protocols send updates according to the type of protocol.
User applications	Data traffic is usually generated by user applications that use FTP, Telnet, or SMTP.
Overhead traffic	This is any type of traffic that is not directly associated with user applications. Types of overhead traffic are DNS requests and broadcast requests.
Encapsulated traffic	By joining networks via tunnels, you may be creating an increased amount of traffic on the network. If the originating network has a large amount of traffic, this will result in increased traffic on the IP network.

Other types of traffic can be associated with the lower layers of the OSI model. These types of traffic include Address Resolution Protocol (ARP), keepalives, and time-to-live (TTL) updates.

Managing IP Traffic

Sorting of IP traffic with access lists for any of the uses listed earlier comes in two flavors. Standard IP access lists use only the packet's source address for comparison. Extended access lists provide for more precise packet selection based on source and destination addresses, protocols, and port numbers.

Defining Access Lists

Other than hierarchical design issues, the most common problem with efficiency in networks is that LAN protocols make heavy use of broadcasts to transfer information. In a small network with a few LAN segments, broadcasts work well and cause few problems. Unfortunately, as networks scale upward in size, broadcast traffic grows to the point where it may compromise successful network operation. This is where access lists come in.

Access lists are filters that administrators use to separate traffic of all protocols. IP access lists come in two varieties: standard and extended. Access lists provide a facility to sort traffic and are used with many IOS features, including the following:

➤ *Traffic filtering*—Allows filtering or forwarding traffic into or out of an interface based on administrative policy.

➤ *Security*—Allows or prevents Telnet access to or from router virtual terminals

➤ *Dial-on-demand routing (DDR)*—Selects interesting traffic to force dialing.

➤ *Priority and custom queuing groups*—Assigns traffic to queues with more precision than simply specifying an interface or a protocol.

➤ *Route filtering*—Restricts the contents of routing updates.

➤ *Service filtering*—Restricts Novell Service Advertising Protocol (SAP) and AppleTalk zone update filtering.

Basic Operation

When an administrator wants to select traffic for one of the purposes listed previously, he or she creates one or more rules to test against traffic packets. If the address being checked matches, the packet is selected and either permitted or denied (denied also means *dropped* or *filtered*) immediately. If a packet being tested does not match any of the rules in the access list, it is dropped at the end of the list. If the packet is filtered either explicitly (due to one of the rules) or implicitly (by not matching any rule), an Internet Control Message Protocol (ICMP) "Administratively Prohibited" message is sent. Standard access lists use only the packet's source address for comparison. In other words, IP standard access lists can make filtering decisions base solely on the source address of the packet. Extended access lists provide for selection based on source address, destination address, protocol, and port numbers. Extended access lists require more processing but provide finer tuning of the selection process.

Access list functionality is available for a large variety of protocols and is identified by the router based on the list number and the range into which it falls. Table 11.2 provides some of the ranges supported by the router.

Other access lists exist. See the Cisco Documentation CD or Web site for further information.

Table 11.2 List number ranges for access lists.	
Range	**Description**
1 through 99	Standard IP
100 through 199	Extended IP
200 through 299	Ethernet type code (transparent and source-route bridging)
300 through 399	DECnet
400 through 499	Xerox Network Services (XNS)
500 through 599	Extended XNS
600 through 699	AppleTalk
700 through 799	Vendor code (transparent and source-route bridging)

(continued)

Table 11.2 List number ranges for access lists *(continued)*.	
Range	**Description**
800 through 899	Standard Internetwork Packet Exchange (IPX)
900 through 999	Extended IPX
1000 through 1099	IPX Service Advertising Protocol (SAP)
1100 through 1199	Extended transparent bridging
1200 through 1299	NetWare Link Services Protocol (NLSP) route summary route

Standard IP Access Lists

All access lists are coded globally and then associated with an interface for traffic filtering. Once the interface for the access list has been determined, you must decide the direction for the access list. You can filter traffic inbound to the router or outbound from the router. If you filter inbound, the filtering decision is made prior to the routing table lookup. If you filter outbound, the routing decision has been made and the packet is switched to the proper outbound interface before it is tested against the access list. The lists default to the outbound direction on the interface for compatibility with older IOS versions. However, the in or out direction is part of the interface assignment statement. You may use this same list for DDR, priority and custom queuing, and traffic filtering.

Access List Processing Logic

The rules of the basic IP access lists are processed in accordance to the sequence illustrated in Figure 11.1.

As you can see in the figure, at each of the one or more rules, the source IP address is either matched or not. A match causes immediate processing of the permit or deny statement, depending on how the statement is coded. If the logic is "permit," whatever action the access list is associated with (for example, filtering/forwarding, DDR, or sorting traffic for queuing) is performed. In this case, the example shows a simple traffic filter, so the packet is forwarded out of the interface to which this filter is attached. If the action is "deny," the packet is dropped and an ICMP "Administratively Prohibited" (RFC-1812) message is returned to the source address.

 Some security administrators don't like to let someone who may be attacking the network have any detail on denied access. To avoid this situation, use an access list to deny the return "Administratively Prohibited" messages at the security domain boundary.

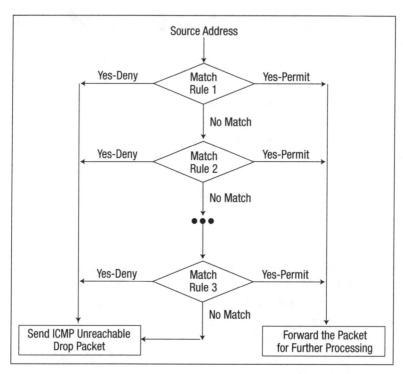

Figure 11.1 Standard access list processing.

Wildcard Masks

It is necessary, when configuring access lists, to specify the traffic you are trying to filter by address. You can be very specific regarding an address or very general. To specify the generality or specificity of a filter, access lists use a wildcard mask. The wildcard mask is a way to specify which bits must match and which bits don't matter, octet by octet, in the comparison of the packet's address to the rule. The masking process is similar to the **AND** used for subnet processing, which is discussed in the Introduction to Cisco Router Configuration (ICRC) course. The difference is that the wildcard mask uses bits that are (1s) to indicate bit positions that should be ignored in the comparison and zeros (0s) for bit positions that must match in the comparison. Sometimes, bits in the wildcard mask that are 1s are referred to as *don't care bits*. Tables 11.3 and 11.4 compare the two masking processes.

The result is that 1 bits in the mask are used to indicate don't care bits, and 0 bits in the mask are used to indicate bits that must match. Table 11.5 shows an example of a match that keeps only the 8-bit subnet on the class B address.

The Cisco IOS allows one access list per protocol, per interface, per direction. If two IP access lists that currently exist should both be applied to the same

Table 11.3 Logical AND mask processing used for subnet derivation.

Address Bit	Mask Bit	Result
1	1	1
1	0	0
0	1	0
0	0	0

Table 11.4 Wildcard mask processing for access lists.

Address Bit	Mask Bit	Result	Indication
1	1	0	Ignore (don't care)
0	1	0	Ignore (don't care)
1	0	1	Must match
0	0	0	Must match

Table 11.5 Wildcard mask example.

Component	Dotted Decimal	Binary
Source address	172.16.5.1	10101100.00010000.00000101.00000001
Wildcard mask	0.0.255.255	00000000.00000000.11111111.11111111
Result	172.16.0.0	10101100.00010000.00000000.00000000

interface and in the same direction, you must combine them into a single list and assign it to the interface instead.

Refer to the command format in Listing 11.1 in the following section. The access list number does two things. First, it tells the IOS what kind of access list is being coded (numbers between 1 and 99 indicate a standard IP access list). Second, it ties the statements of the access list together.

Notice also in Listing 11.1 that the access list does not have line numbers. The commands are executed from top to bottom. Therefore, for the access list to work correctly, it is critical that you enter the statements in the correct order. Address selections must go from more specific to more general. Essentially, individual addresses must come before subnets, subnets before networks, and networks before **permit any** or **deny any** statements. The "any" implies a match for every address. Remember that each packet is selected by the first line of the access list it matches. So, if the same packet matches as an individual address and as part of a subnet, the individual address must come first. If the subnet match occurs first, the packet never reaches the individual address statement.

Use the following tips to help ensure that you correctly place and operate an access list:

➤ First, it is usually much more reasonable to create the list on a desktop computer with a text editor of your choice and then use Trivial File Transfer Protocol (TFTP) to deliver it to the router. If you do this, remember to put the **no access-list** statement at the beginning of your file (which will remove all lines of access list). Otherwise, the new statements are added to the end of the existing list rather than replacing it.

➤ If a network-management tool such as Netsys (see the Cisco Web site or the Documentation CD for details) is available, allow it to look at your list before you install it into a production network, especially in a remote router.

Note: If you place a list in a router that accidentally blocks more traffic than desired, the list may even block Telnet access for the administrator trying to fix the problem, thereby cutting off remote access to the router.

➤ Allow a colleague or group of colleagues to review the access list and the location within the network where you will place the list.

➤ When you load the access list into the remote router, you should load it into active RAM (the running-config). Do not save it initially in case there are problems with it and you get cut off from the router due to the effects of the access list. At that point, power-cycling the router by a person who is local to the router can remove the list's effect.

Command Syntax and Examples

The basic format of the global access list command is shown in Listing 11.1.

Listing 11.1   Global access list command.

```
[no] access-list number {permit | deny } source-ip-address
    wildcard-mask [log]
```

Listings 11.2 through 11.6 show some standard IP access lists. They also illustrate the sequence-of-commands issue. The first line would make all other lines ineffective because all traffic is permitted immediately and never reaches the lines below it.

Listing 11.2   Permitting all IP source addresses because all the wildcard bits are 1s.

```
access-list 20 permit 0.0.0.0 255.255.255.255
```

Listing 11.3   Permitting all packets from the network number 172.16.0.0 (all subnet and host bits are ignored).

```
access-list 20 permit 172.16.0.0 0.0.255.255
```

Listing 11.4   Permitting traffic from subnet 172.16.1.0 (assuming a 24-bit prefix or subnet mask).

```
access-list 20 permit 172.16.1.0 0.0.0.255
```

Listing 11.5   Permitting traffic from the host 172.16.1.1 only.

```
access-list 20 permit 172.16.1.1 0.0.0.0
```

Listing 11.6   Permitting traffic from subnets 172.16.0.0 through 172.31.0.0 (assuming a subnet prefix of 24 bits).

```
access-list 20 permit 172.16.0.0 0.15.255.255
```

Listings 11.7 and 11.8 show some common access list mistakes.

Listing 11.7   An erroneous access list line example.

```
access-list 21 permit 172.16.0.0
```

This code does not function because the default mask is 0.0.0.0. No source address would ever have the address 172.16.0.0 as a host address. This address is actually the network number without a subnet or host.

Listing 11.8   Another erroneous access list line example.

```
access-list 21 deny 0.0.0.0 255.255.255.255
```

This code is referred to as a **deny any** and is not required. If a packet's address does not match an earlier statement, an implicit **deny any** occurs at the end of every access list automatically.

In IOS version 10.3, several new changes were added to make the access lists more legible and their coding less error prone. One type of change involves using code words to replace common patterns. Another type of change involves using named access lists. Listings 11.9 and 11.10 show common errors in access list coding.

Listing 11.9   These two statements are identical in operation.

```
access-list 22 permit 0.0.0.0 255.255.255.255
access-list 22 permit any
```

Listing 11.10   These two statements are also identical.

```
access-list 23 permit 172.16.1.1 0.0.0.0
access-list 23 permit host 172.16.1.1
```

Named access lists were first introduced in IOS 11.2. Named access lists are an attempt to overcome one of the major configuration issues with access lists: the inability to selectively remove lines from a list. For example, refer back to Listing 11.10. If this represented only one line of a 30-line access list, the command **no access-list 23 permit host 172.16.1.1** would completely remove all lines for access list 23. Named access lists allow the selective removal of access list lines (but it's still easier to work with text files and TFTP servers or to cut and paste from a terminal emulator). Listing 11.11 shows a named access list.

Listing 11.11   A named access list example.

```
ip access-list standard mike
permit host 10.1.1.1
deny 10.2.0.0 0.0.255.255
permit any
!
interface serial 1
ip access-group mike in
```

The access list, coded globally (for the whole router), is associated with a specific interface and direction with the command shown in Listing 11.11.

Here are some issues to remember when configuring access lists:

➤ Processing occurs line by line from top to bottom. Tests must be manually sorted from more specific addresses to the more general. Also, to boost efficiency, place more frequently accessed items before less frequently accessed ones.

➤ New lines are added only at the end of the current list (IOS 11.2 allows individual line changes with named access lists only).

➤ Undefined lists (the existence of an access-group statement on an interface but no corresponding global access list definition in the router configuration) imply a **permit any**. Watch out: Prior to IOS 10.3, the default was **deny any**. At that time, all the interface knew was that there was supposed to be an access list and the only line it could assume was the implicit deny.

➤ The last line of an access list is an implicit **deny any** (usually what you want).

Extended IP Access Lists

Extended IP access lists are similar in operation to standard IP access lists, but they provide for more extensive filtering and allow you to be more flexible when placing them within the router hierarchy. Extended IP access lists allow filtering on source address, destination address, protocol, port, and other conditions. The processing flow of an extended IP access list is shown in Figure 11.2.

As you can see from the figure, the processing logic of the extended access list is similar to, but more extensive than, the standard access list. In order for the explicit permit or deny action to apply, all conditions must match. The test sequence is as follows: source address, then destination address (both of which must have wildcard masks associated with them), then protocol field, and finally, port number or protocol options.

The extended IP access list uses the range 100 through 199. The general format for an extended access list is illustrated in Listing 11.12.

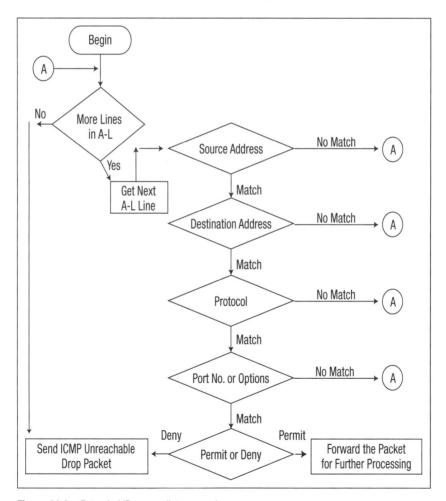

Figure 11.2 Extended IP access list processing.

Listing 11.12   Extended access list command parameters.

```
[no] access-list number {permit | deny} { protocol | protocol
      keyword }
      { source-ip-address source-wildcard-mask | any }
      { destination-ip-address destination-wildcard-mask | any}
      [ protocol-specific options ] [ log ]
```

In the access list command, you must specify the protocol to be matched. This parameter can support a number of different protocol options. The protocol keywords are **eigrp, icmp, igmp, igrp, ip, nos, ospf, tcp,** and **udp.** These can be used to filter specific traffic types beyond the simple IP realm.

You must configure source and destination addresses that must be matched. Each must contain a wildcard mask or a keyword representing the wildcard mask (such as **any, host,** and so on). The terms *address* (source or destination) and *keyword* mean the same as for the standard access lists.

The optional keyword **log** causes each packet that matches this statement to generate a log entry, which is recorded by the router. This can generate significant processing and uses bandwidth if it is logging to a remote syslog server or router memory. One strategy would be to use this feature to monitor the traffic periodically. Another approach might be to use a **show** command that displays the number of times a statement has been matched. By using the **show** command or using Simple Network Management Protocol (SNMP) to retrieve the information over a known period of time, you can track the information without constant logging, thereby saving valuable processor resources.

TCP-Specific Access Lists

You can use extended access lists to filter the transport layer protocol TCP. TCP is a connection-oriented protocol. The TCP protocol-specific format is shown in Listing 11.13.

Listing 11.13   TCP access lists syntax.

```
[no] access-list <number> {permit | deny} tcp { source-ip-address
      source-wildcard-mask| any } [ operator source-port |
      source-port ]
      { destination-ip-address  destination-wildcard-mask | any}
      [ operator destination-port | destination-port ]
      [ established ]
```

The **operator** option is used to specify application port numbers or a group of port numbers. The values for **operator** include **gt** (greater than or equal), **eq** (equal), and **lt** (less than or equal).

The port number itself, as mentioned, can be application specific. Port numbers range from 0 through 65535. In most cases, the port number can use a name rather than a number for clarity. Here's a partial list of the names in the IOS along with their port numbers:

➤ **bgp**—Border Gateway Protocol (179)

➤ **bootpc**—Boot Protocol client (68)

➤ **bootps**—Boot Protocol server (67)

➤ **discard**—Dump port (9)

➤ **domain**—Domain Name Server (53)

➤ **finger**—Finger port (79)

➤ **ftp-control**—FTP control port (21)

➤ **ftp-data**—FTP data port (20)

➤ **gopher**—Gopher port (70)

➤ **hostname**—NIC hostname port (101)

➤ **klogin**—Kerberos login port (543)

➤ **kshell**—Kerberos shell port (544)

➤ **nntp**—Network News Transfer Protocol (119)

➤ **pop3**—Post Office Protocol version 3 (110)

➤ **smtp**—Simple Mail Transfer Protocol (25)

➤ **snmp**—Simple Network Management Protocol (161)

➤ **sunrpc**—Sun Remote Procedure Call (111)

➤ **syslog**—Syslog port (514)

➤ **tacacs-ds**—TACACS Database Service (65)

➤ **telnet**—Telnet; also known as Network Virtual Terminal port (23)

➤ **tftp**—Trivial File Transfer Protocol (69)

➤ **uucp**—Unix-to-Unix Copy Path (117)

➤ **whois**—Whois port (43)

➤ **www**—World Wide Web port (80)

➤ And a few hundred more

Another very handy keyword you can use is **established,** which means this: If traffic came from within your network and had to leave your network (possibly out to the Internet), **established** will let it back into your network. This command was designed to allow outbound traffic to come back through the security of a firewall or access lists. Any TCP header that contains the ACK (Acknowledge) and/or RST (Reset) bit will match the **established** keyword and be allowed back into the network. Figure 11.3 shows the effect of the established keyword.

The ACK bit is not set (equal to 1) on the SYN message in the first packet that initiates the three-way handshake. The ACK bit is set in every other packet in the TCP connection. Placing an inbound access list using the **established** keyword (on the interface shown) allows sessions to be started from within "your" part of the network. Conversations cannot originate from outside the network. This assumes that your own people may start TCP conversations freely. This is useful, but remember that an access list is not a firewall. For more information, check the Cisco Web site (**www.cisco.com**), the Documentation CD, or the Computer Emergency Response Team (CERT) bulletins at **www.cert.org**.

Note: The CERT Coordination Center is part of the Survivable Systems Initiative at the Software Engineering Institute at Carnegie Mellon University. They were started by the Defense Applied Research Projects Agency (DARPA, part of the U.S. Department of Defense) in December 1988. Since then they have worked to help start other incident response teams, coordinate the efforts of teams when responding to large-scale incidents, provide training to incident response professionals, and research the causes of security vulnerabilities, prevention of vulnerabilities, system security improvement, and survivability of large-scale networks.

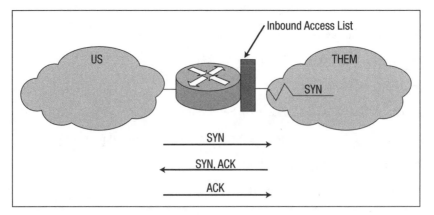

Figure 11.3   Operation of the **established** keyword for TCP conversion.

UDP Extended Access List Syntax

You can use access lists to filter protocol-specific options of User Datagram Protocol (UDP). UDP is a connectionless protocol that has much less overhead than its connection-oriented brother, TCP. The syntax of the UDP version of the extended access list command is illustrated in Listing 11.14.

Listing 11.14 UDP extended access list command syntax.

```
[no] access-list <number> {permit | deny} udp { source-ip-address
     source-wildcard-mask| any }
     [ operator source-port | source-port ]
     { destination-ip-address destination-wildcard-mask | any}
     [ operator destination-port | destination-port ]
```

Notice that no **established** keyword exists in Listing 11.14 because UDP is connectionless. The concept of connection orientation is TCP based. The words used to replace port numbers are similar to those used in the TCP format. Here are some of them:

➤ bootpc

➤ bootps

➤ discard

➤ dns

➤ dnsix

➤ echo

➤ mobile-ip

➤ nameserver

➤ netbios-dgm

➤ netbios-ns

➤ ntp

➤ rip

➤ snmp

➤ snmptrap

➤ sunrpc

➤ syslog

➤ tacasds-ds

➤ talk

➤ tftp

➤ time

➤ whois

ICMP Extended Access List Syntax

TCP and UDP are not the only protocol-specific options available for filtering traffic. You can use access lists to filter ICMP traffic. ICMP is an extremely powerful and useful protocol. However, its versatility is also its downfall. It can be used by a hacker to search out possible exploits in your network. To avoid that, you can filter any of the ICMP protocol options. Listing 11.15 shows the Internet Control Message Protocol (ICMP) format prototype.

Listing 11.15   ICMP extended access list command syntax.

```
[no] access-list <number> {permit | deny} icmp { source-ip-address
      source-wildcard-mask | any } { destination-ip-address
      destination-wildcard-mask | any} [ icmp-type [ icmp-code]
      | icmp-message ]
```

For ICMP, the protocol-specific options are message types that range from 0 through 255. Message codes, used to further subdivide message types, have the same range. Here are some protocol-specific keywords you can use instead of the numeric message types and message codes for ICMP:

➤ administratively-prohibited

➤ alternate-address

➤ conversion-error

➤ dod-host-prohibited

➤ dod-net-prohibited

➤ echo

➤ echo-reply

➤ general-parameter-problem

➤ host-isolated

➤ host-tos-redirect

➤ host-tos-unreachable

➤ host-unknown

➤ host-unreachable

➤ information reply

➤ mask-reply

➤ mask-request

➤ mobile-redirect

➤ net-redirect

➤ net-tos-redirect

➤ net-tos-unreachable

➤ net-unreachable

➤ network-unknown

➤ no-room-for-option

➤ option-missing

➤ packet-too-big

➤ parameter-problem

➤ port-unreachable

➤ reassembly-timeout

➤ redirect

➤ router-advertisement

➤ router-solicitation

➤ time-exceeded

➤ traceroute

➤ ttl-exceeded

➤ unreachable

Placing Access Lists

It's very important to effectively decide where you should place access lists. When you are using an access list as a traffic filter, you can attach it to an interface in the inbound or outbound direction. The amount of processing the router must do and which routers in the hierarchy do the processing may greatly affect the network's performance.

Remember that much access list processing is done in the process routing path. On newer versions of the IOS and on larger routers, the traffic, after the first packet is routed and has survived the access list, may take one of the fast switch paths. In other words, the first packet from a specific source to a specific destination is routed using a routing table lookup. The result of the routing decision is placed into a switching cache in the router. Subsequent packets from that source to that destination are switched based on the switching cache entry, not the routing table. The difference in placement determines whether the traffic is to be filtered before or after the routing table lookup. All packets must be examined with an inbound access list that results in a significant processor load if the packets are not dropped. This is justifiable for lists placed primarily for security. Penetration-attempt traffic (if it can be identified) would be dropped without the overhead of a routing table lookup.

It is also important to determine how many interfaces would be involved on the router. If, for example, six outbound lists could be replaced by an inbound list, the result is probably better. By default, all access lists are outbound unless otherwise specified. Figure 11.4 illustrates the difference between inbound and outbound

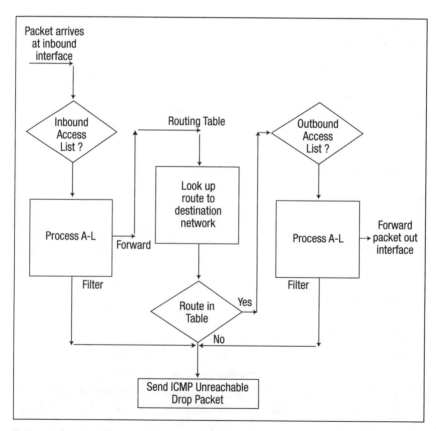

Figure 11.4 Inbound versus outbound access list processing.

processing within a single router for all access lists (standard and extended for all protocols).

Standard IP access lists use only source addresses and require fewer CPU cycles than extended access lists. However, you must place standard IP access lists as close to the destination as possible. Otherwise, traffic is blocked unnecessarily and perhaps incorrectly. Positioning the access list within the router hierarchy is shown in Figure 11.5.

Position 4 would be the location for placing a basic access list to block access from device A to device B. If you placed a standard access list at other positions, device A would be blocked from all positions beyond the access list in the hierarchy.

Extended access lists are much more flexible than standard access lists, but they add to the CPU load. You should try to place the filter as close to the source as possible. This approach keeps the undesired traffic and the ICMP messages from traversing the network backbone. In addition, administrators can choose which routers will take the CPU hit associated with the access list processing. They can put the access lists into access routers or distribution routers. The trade-off is between managing a large number of possibly identical lists in the access routers

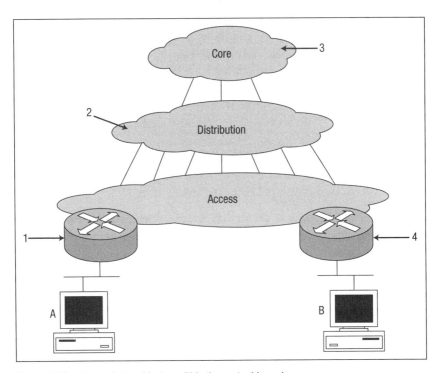

Figure 11.5 Access list positioning within the router hierarchy.

(where each router has plenty of processing power) and managing a single list (or at least fewer lists) in the distribution routers. In the latter case, the distribution routers would do more processing but it would be much easier to manage the access lists.

Notice in Figure 11.5 that you could place extended access lists at position 1 or 2 based on the comments made previously about processing power and list management issues. You should not place access lists of either type at location 3, in the core. To maximize efficiency, you should do the filtering before the traffic enters the backbone. Figure 11.5 and this discussion also show how important it is to have a hierarchical network design. If the network were fully meshed at the lower levels, you would have to place extended access lists in several locations to prevent access from device A to device B when routing tables change. Not only would this require more work for you (the administrator) and the router, but it would also add to the complexity and increase the probability of error.

Permitting or Denying Telnet Access Using Access Classes

You can use standard IP access lists to prevent Telnet connections to (inbound) or from (outbound) a Cisco router. You could configure inbound traffic filters to prevent Telnet access from any source to each router interface, but doing so is cumbersome. Another drawback is that access lists won't block traffic that originates from within the router itself. That is, Telnet traffic passing through the router can be filtered with extended IP access lists, but you cannot block outbound Telnet traffic (originating from "this" router) with a traffic filter. You would much rather keep Telnet sessions from specified sources (to this router) from starting or restrict Telnet sessions originating in this router to specified destinations. The way to do it is by using an *access class*, an IOS feature that's specifically designed for controlling Telnet access into and out of a router. It's not so much for traffic control as it is to supplement security.

The procedure is to code an access list that permits or denies traffic from particular devices, subnets, or networks. Then, you create an access class that's associated with the virtual terminals (vtys). Essentially, before any security check is run— for example, password checks or Terminal Access Control Access Control System (TACACS)—traffic coming into a vty is checked. Only if the traffic is permitted is a login authentication message presented.

The same access class feature allows you to block Telnet access to other locations from within "this" router. Listing 11.16 shows an example of just such a configuration. The same access class feature allows you to block Telnet access originating in the router you're configuring to other routers.

Listing 11.16   Using an access class to control Telnet traffic to and from the router.

```
access-list 30 permit 172.16.5.0 0.0.0.255
access-list 31 deny any
!
line vty 0 4
access-class 30 in
access-class 31 out
login
password cisco
```

The access list number 30, when applied inbound, allows only 172.16.5.X source addresses to telnet into this router. The access list number 31, when applied outbound, denies all outbound Telnet traffic from this router.

You must configure all vty lines (0 through 4 by default) identically in order for the access class security to work properly. Use the **line vty 0 4** command to apply the configuration to all vty lines simultaneously.

An Alternative to Access Lists

In any situation when you need to prevent all traffic from reaching a remote portion of the network, you can use a very efficient alternative to an access list. You can statically route to a null interface all packets bound for a specific destination network. Essentially a bit bucket, the null interface simply is a logical software destination interface that drops the packet. An advantage is that routing to the null interface is a normal routing process, so you can use fast switching to dispose of unwanted traffic. The null interface works for protocols other than IP as well.

A sample configuration that an ISP can use to block private addresses from accidentally reaching the Internet is shown in Listing 11.17.

Listing 11.17   Using null interfaces.

```
ip route 172.16.0.0 255.240.0.0 null 0
ip route 10.0.0.0 255.0.0.0 null 0
ip route 192.168.0.0 255.255.0.0 null 0
```

The statements in Listing 11.17 are equivalent to those in Listing 11.18 but with much less overhead.

Listing 11.18   Access list equivalent to the null interface command.

```
access-list 101 deny ip any 172.16.0.0 0.15.255.255
access-list 101 deny ip any 10.0.0.0 0.255.255.255
access-list 101 deny ip any 192.168.0.0 0.0.255.255
```

No ICMP messages are returned when the null interface is used. An advantage is reduced traffic. The disadvantage is that no indication is given of the drop. For example, if someone in network management were doing connectivity tests with pings, the pings would simply disappear.

Helper Addresses

Routers will segment a broadcast domain. In other words, routers do not, by default, forward broadcast traffic. There are times when you might want to forward broadcasts selectively. Sometimes it is not so important to filter all broadcasts. Instead, it is desirable to provide a way for certain broadcasts to be passed through a router. If hosts don't know a destination, they attempt to use a local broadcast (255.255.255.255) to obtain a service such as DHCP (Dynamic Host Configuration Protocol), DNS (Domain Name Service), or TFTP. Routers block local broadcasts, which is usually considered to be good. However, placing servers on every LAN segment so that local broadcasts will reach them may be cumbersome.

IP helper addresses are a feature that allows traffic sent to local broadcast addresses to be readdressed to a unicast (single destination) address. Once this is done, the packet may be routed just like any other.

It is not usually desirable to forward all broadcasts. When you use the IP helper address on an interface command, only traffic from certain UDP ports (on that particular inbound interface) is forwarded by default. Table 11.6 shows a list of UDP ports.

If you need to forward other ports, include an **ip forward-protocol UDP** statement for that port. To forward only DNS, for example, you should enter a **no ip forward-protocol [*protocol*]** statement (where [*protocol*] represents the protocols you do not wish to forward) for each protocol to be blocked. The general format of the **ip forward-protocol** statement is shown in Listing 11.19.

Table 11.6 UDP ports forwarded by default when the IP helper address is used.	
Port Number	**Description**
37	Time
49	TACACS
53	DNS
67	BootP client
68	BootP server (DHCP)
69	TFTP
137	NetBIOS Name Service
138	NetBIOS Packet Service

Listing 11.19   Syntax of the **ip forward-protocol** statement.

```
[no] ip forward-protocol { udp [port] | nd | sdns }
```

The **nd** keyword refers to an old Sun protocol for diskless workstations: network disk. The **sdns** keyword refers to Network Security Protocol.

Examples of IP Helper Address Usage

When you want to use helper address functionality, you must consider three scenarios: a single server at a remote location, multiple servers that share a remote subnet, and multiple servers on multiple remote subnets. Use Figure 11.6 along with the following listings to view helper address functionality.

Listings 11.20, 11.21, and 11.22 show how to code the Denver router, shown in Figure 11.6.

Listing 11.20   Adding UDP port 5000 to those being forwarded.

```
!
ip forward-protocol udp 5000
```

Listing 11.21   Not forwarding NetBIOS name requests.

```
no ip forward-protocol udp 137
!
interface Ethernet 0
ip address …
```

Listing 11.22   Pointing the broadcasts to a single remote server on a single LAN segment.

```
ip helper-address 10.0.1.1
```

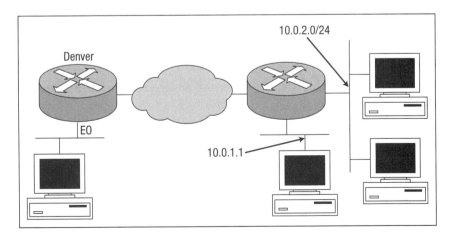

Figure 11.6   Helper address operation.

If other servers are available on other segments, put an address in for them also. In this case, there are redundant servers on the same subnet, so use a directed broadcast, as shown in Listing 11.23.

Listing 11.23   Using an IP helper address to forward to a directed broadcast address.

```
ip helper-address 10.0.2.255
```

Tunnels

As IP networks evolve, islands of legacy protocols (IPX, AppleTalk, DECnet, and so on) are left at the edges of the network. In some cases, you can migrate these protocols to IP. In others, you can use a method that allows the users to continue using the environments they want while keeping the core of the network running only IP. The term for this is *tunneling*, and you accomplish it by causing the source protocol's packets to be wrapped in an IP coating.

Tunneling offers many advantages, including:

➤ An IP-only core means simpler configuration, less training required for core personnel, fewer routing updates in the core, and smaller routing tables in the core.

➤ The hop count between islands of tunneled protocols is reduced to 1.

➤ You have less conversion to worry about.

➤ Client departments can continue to run protocol suites with which they are familiar.

Figure 11.7 illustrates the value of tunneling. The tunnel allows the noncontiguous islands of whatever protocol to appear to be a much smaller network. A smaller number of routers and circuits will make the island protocol more manageable.

Figure 11.8 shows a sample tunneling configuration.

Listings 11.24 and 11.25 show the code for configuring the tunnel shown in Figure 11.8.

Listing 11.24   The code for the router on the left side of Figure 11.8.

```
interface Ethernet 1
ipx network 1000
appletalk cable-range 1000-1000
appletalk zone Denver
!
interface Ethernet 0
```

```
ip address 172.17.7.2 255.255.255.0
!
interface Tunnel 0
ipx network 1500
appletalk cable-range 1500-1500
appletalk zone Backbone
tunnel source E0
tunnel destination 172.16.5.1
tunnel mode gre ip
```

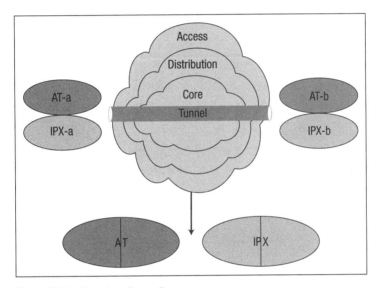

Figure 11.7   The value of tunneling.

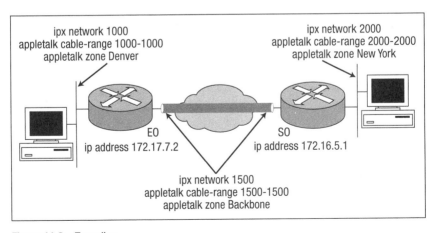

Figure 11.8   Tunneling.

Listing 11.25   The code for the router on the right side of Figure 11.8.

```
interface Ethernet 0
ipx network 2000
appletalk cable-range 2000-2000
appletalk zone New York
!
interface Serial 0
ip address 172.16.5.1 255.255.255.0
!
interface Tunnel 0
ipx network 1500
appletalk cable-range 1500-1500
appletalk zone Backbone
tunnel source S0
tunnel destination 172.17.7.2
tunnel mode gre ip
```

The *tunnel source* is the IP address of any active interface on this router. It is easier to use an interface name and number on this end (for example, loopback 0, serial 0). The other end of the tunnel (for example, the tunnel destination) is any IP address on an active interface on the remote router. One option that's not illustrated is the *tunnel encapsulation mode*. The default is Generic Routing Encapsulation in IP (**tunnel mode gre ip**) and it's the one normally used. Cisco also supports AppleTalk tunneling protocols such as AppleTalk Update-Based Routing Protocol (AURP) and Cayman, which you can use to connect with other AppleTalk routers. See the Cisco Web site (**www.cisco.com**) for other tunneling modes.

 Remember to filter unnecessary traffic before it goes into the tunnel. Routers along the path see only IP, and all traffic types being tunneled go to the same IP address.

 You must specify the tunnel source, destination, and mode. You will then apply tunneled protocol attributes to the tunnel interface (for example, IPX network number, AppleTalk cable range, and so on). Do not put an IP address on the tunnel interface.

Useful Commands

To see the results of your work, the following commands will be most useful:

➤ **show ip route**—Shows the content of the forwarding database, including the next hop, metric, and such routing sources as Routing Information Protocol (RIP), Open Shortest Path First (OSPF), Enhanced Interior Gateway Routing Protocol (EIGRP), or Interior Gateway Routing Protocol (IGRP).

➤ **show access-lists**—Displays the access lists that are active and the number of times each line in the list has been used

➤ **show [ip •••] interface** [*type port*]—Displays the protocol-specific values, such as whether an access list is associated with a particular interface, what number it is, and whether it functions on the inbound or outbound path

➤ **debug access-list**—Displays hits to a line in the access list as they occur

 Be sure to be familiar with access lists, SAP filters, and tunneling. The routing examination will probably have several questions on these topics.

Practice Questions

Question 1

The following access list has been inserted in a router and correctly tied to an interface, but it isn't working. Why?

```
access-list 1 deny 172.16.5.0 0.0.0.255
access-list 1 permit 172.16.5.1 0.0.0.0
access-list 1 permit any
```

○ a. It works as coded.

○ b. The line that permits host 172.16.5.1 is in the wrong sequence.

○ c. The second line should have been configured as ... host 172.16.5.1.

○ d. The **deny** statement's position blocks all traffic.

Answer b is correct. The second line should have been first. Always go from the most specific to the most general. Answer a is incorrect because the access list does not work; either line 2 should not be in the list or it must come first. Although you may use the configuration in answer c, its lack of use is not why the access list failed. Answer d is incorrect because the **deny** blocks only one subnet. The **permit any** in line 3 allows all traffic that does not originate from the 172.16.5.0 subnet.

Question 2

The following access list has been inserted in a router and correctly tied to an interface, but it isn't working. Why?

```
access-list 1 deny host 172.16.5.1
access-list 1 permit 255.255.255.255 0.0.0.0
```

○ a. It works as coded.

○ b. It works because of the **permit any** used as the last line of the list.

○ c. It doesn't work because the **permit any** has been coded as a **permit local broadcast**.

○ d. It doesn't work because the first line requires a wildcard mask.

Answer c is correct. Line 2 should have been **0.0.0.0 255.255.255.255** or **any**. Answer a is incorrect because the list essentially denies all traffic. Answer b is incorrect because line 2 is not a **permit any**. Answer d is incorrect for two reasons. First, by using the **host** keyword before the IP address, the result is the same as coding the wildcard mask 0.0.0.0. Second, the default wildcard mask is 0.0.0.0.

Question 3

The following access list has been inserted in a router and correctly tied to an interface, but it isn't working. Why?

```
access-list 1 permit host 172.16.5.1
access-list 1 deny 172.16.5.0
access-list 1 permit any
access-list 1 deny 0.0.0.0 255.255.255.255
```

○ a. It works as coded.

○ b. It doesn't work. The line that denies the 172.16.5.0 subnet doesn't work because the default wildcard mask is 0.0.0.0, and no packet would contain a source address with a zero for the host number.

○ c. The **deny any** statement must come before the **permit any**.

○ d. The **deny** statement's position blocks all traffic.

Answer b is correct, for the reason given in the answer. Answer a is incorrect because the list does not block the 172.16.5.0 subnet. Answer c is incorrect because you should not code a **permit any** and a **deny any** in the same access list. Whichever statement comes first ends the access list as far as traffic is concerned. Answer d is incorrect because the **deny any** follows the **permit any** and is never reached when the code is executed.

Question 4

The following access list has been inserted in a router and correctly tied to an interface, but it isn't working. Why?

```
access-list 1 deny 172.16.6.1 255.255.255.255
access-list 1 deny host 172.30.18.4
access-list 1 permit any
```

- ○ a. It works as coded.
- ○ b. It doesn't work because line 2 should have been coded as 172.30.18.4 0.0.0.0.
- ○ c. It doesn't work because line 1 is essentially a **permit any**.
- ○ d. It doesn't work because line 1 is essentially a **deny any**.

Answer d is correct. The mask shown causes all bits in the source address to be considered "don't care bits." A **show access-lists** command on the router would show the statement as **access-list 1 deny any**. Answer a is incorrect because it is essentially a **deny any**. Answer b is incorrect because line 2 is correctly coded but would never have been executed because all traffic source addresses will match the **deny any** in line 1. Answer c is backwards: Line 1 is a **deny any** not a **permit any**. The coding causes line 1 to be a **deny any**, which renders every other line in the access list ineffective.

Question 5

Access lists can have significant overhead processing. Is there a way to reduce it? [Choose the three best answers.]

- ❑ a. Use a static route to a loopback interface.
- ❑ b. Use standard rather than extended access lists.
- ❑ c. Use a static route to the null interface.
- ❑ d. Place the access list on the outbound side of the router if possible.

Answers b, c, and d are correct. Answer b is correct because standard access lists use only the source address and result in less processing. Answer c is correct because the null interface is a bit bucket that is designed to allow traffic to be fast switched into oblivion. Answer d is correct because inbound access lists process every packet before it is routed. It's probably a good idea for you to use an input (rather than an output) traffic filter if the primary reason for the list is security. However, doing so results in unnecessary processing for packets that would not have been filtered. Answer a is incorrect because the loopback interface is a place to keep addresses that must always be up. You cannot shut down the loopback interface.

Question 6

> You don't want some people to be able to use the virtual terminal (Telnet) interface to your router. How might you prevent them from doing so? [Choose the two best answers.]
>
> ❏ a. Apply inbound standard IP access lists on every interface for every interface on the router.
>
> ❏ b. Apply inbound extended access lists on every interface for every interface in the router that blocks inbound Telnet.
>
> ❏ c. Apply IP access lists that block access except from desired hosts, subnets, or networks and that are applied as an inbound access class to all vty lines.
>
> ❏ d. Leave the vtys configured as the IOS is delivered by Cisco.

Answers c and d are correct. Answer c is the best answer because it allows the administrator to be selective. This means that unless the address is one from your network management subnet, you won't even be presented with a login prompt on the router. Answer d works well if no one is to be allowed Telnet access to the router because Cisco's default is to place a login process on the vty with no password. Essentially, when Telnet is attempted, the source receives a message such as **password required but none set.** . . . Answer a is incorrect for several reasons. First, it causes the administrator too much work, and there's too much overhead on the router. Second, all access to the router (such as TFTP, SNMP, and ICMP) would be blocked. Answer b is incorrect for the same reasons as answer a. However, answer b would be a better choice than answer a because TFTP and the other protocols could reach the router.

Question 7

> You have DECnet in your system and it won't go away. You're trying to opti-
> mize the backbone and hold down training costs for your technicians by
> using only IP in the backbone. What can you do?
>
> ○ a.   Set up fully meshed GRE IP tunnels between the disparate groups
>   of DEC users.
>
> ○ b.   Hire new technicians directly out of college and train them in
>   DECnet. Don't use high-end 12000 GSR routers; they're too
>   expensive anyway.
>
> ○ c.   Tunneling won't work with DECnet. Use the solution in answer b.
>
> ○ d.   Build a separate DEC-only network. That way, you can have an
>   optimized solution for both groups of users.

Answer a is correct because it is the best solution. Answer b is incorrect because
training new folks would be a waste of time. Answer c is incorrect because tunneling does work with DECnet. Answer d is incorrect because building a separate DEC-only network isn't necessary.

Question 8

> Which access list will deny traffic for the host 172.16.1.10?
>
> ○ a.   access-list 1 deny 172.16.1.10
>
> ○ b.   access-list 1 deny host 172.16.1.10
>
> ○ c.   access-list 1 deny host ip 172.16.1.10
>
> ○ d.   access-list 1 deny 172.16.1.0 0.0.0.255

Answer b is correct. This standard access list will deny all traffic for host
172.16.1.10. The three wrong answers could easily trick you. Answer a is incorrect because it is missing the "host" portion of the list, which designates that a
host is being specified, so that a mask does not need to accompany this command. Answer c is incorrect because it includes the word "ip" in the command,
and protocols cannot be specified in standard access lists. Answer d is incorrect
because this access list denies traffic for the entire range of addresses in the
172.16.1.0 network instead of just the host as stated in the question.

Need to Know More?

 Caslow, Andrew Bruce. *Cisco Certification: Bridges, Routers, and Switches for CCIEs*. Prentice Hall PTR. Upper Saddle River, NJ, 1998. ISBN 0-13-082537-9. Chapters 24 through 26 have good in-depth information on different types of access lists.

 Doyle, Jeff. *CCIE Professional Development: Routing TCP/IP Volume 1*. Macmillan Technical Publishing. Indianapolis, IN 1998. ISBN 1-57870-041-8. Appendix B has a tutorial on access lists.

 Larson, Bob, Corwin Low, and Michael Simon. *CCNP Routing Exam Prep*. The Coriolis Group. Scottsdale, AZ, Fall 2000. ISBN 1-57610-778-2. This book, an Exam Prep for the CCNP exam, covers each related subject in great detail.

 For information on access lists and the other topics in this chapter, check out the Cisco Web site at **www.cisco.com**.

Optimizing Routing Updates

. . . .

Terms you'll need to understand:

✓ Static routes

✓ Passive interfaces

✓ Default routes

✓ Route filtering

✓ Redistribution between different routing protocols

Techniques you'll need to master:

✓ Configuring and using static routes

✓ Understanding and configuring passive interfaces

✓ Configuring and using default routes

✓ Understanding and applying IP route filters

✓ Applying route redistribution to multiple routing protocols

✓ Using various techniques to prevent loop development when redistributing

So far in this book, you've seen how various routing protocols propagate routing update information through the network. Sometimes, however, you may want to prevent routing information from flowing into or out of a router. For example, when a low-bandwidth wide area network (WAN) link connects two parts of a network, there may be no useful information to gain by filling the bandwidth with routing updates. Therefore, you should not send them; instead, you should use static or default routes. This chapter explores update optimization through the use of passive interfaces, route filters, and route redistribution.

Controlling Routing Information

How you design your WAN network profoundly affects your ability to manipulate routing updates as well as network reachability. At the same time, a good design makes configuration and troubleshooting significantly easier. A combination of static routes, passive interfaces, default routes, and route filters can provide full reachability while eliminating redundant routing information. Two of the tools for manipulating routing information include static routes that are permanent and hand-coded routes used to override normal routing protocol-learned routes. Default routes are just a special case of static routes used when a large number of routes may be left out of the routing table without sacrificing reachability. The best example of a default route is the path from your company's network to the Internet. There is no value gained by having thousands of extra routes in each of your company's routers when all your company's data goes through a single router on its way to the Internet. Route filters, which are implemented using the **distribute-list** command, are used to hide routes by blocking their inclusion in routing updates in or out of interfaces and other routing protocols.

Network Topology

The network's topology (its physical layout) is a key concern in your design. How you implement your WAN links profoundly affects the internetwork's operations. Cisco uses a three-tier hierarchy as its network model. At the bottom of the hierarchy are access routers, which are small routers with features used in controlling single LANs or dial access. The distribution routers occupy the middle tier in the hierarchy. Their function is to shape traffic and to steer traffic toward the appropriate backbone or access router. Access lists might be used in access or distribution routers to eliminate useless traffic or keep undesirable traffic away from the core routers (backbone). The third and highest tier contains the core routers. These are usually very large machines connected over very fast links in a meshed pattern (distribution and access routers are not meshed) for redundancy and to provide for quality of service and differentiation of paths across the network. Switching may be used at the access and core levels to speed network operation, but routers are required to give the network form (hierarchy) and scalability.

(Remember, switching is bridging—there are limits to how many devices may be successfully bridged). Although this isn't a design course, remember that correct design will allow the tools to work properly. One quick, good example of the kind of problem you encounter if you mesh access routers might be where to put the access lists. If the hierarchy is well laid out and maintained, your traffic is always flowing toward or away from the backbone. If it's meshed, there are many possible directions. Therefore, you need more and longer access lists to keep the traffic where you want it.

Full-Mesh Networks

Full-mesh networks are those networks in which all hosts have a direct connection to all other hosts across the WAN. This type of layout is not very common because it is very expensive to maintain the full mesh. To calculate the number of circuits you'll need to facilitate the full-mesh network, use the formula n(n-1)/2. In other words, for a 20-router full-mesh network, you'll need to configure 190 circuits, which requires a significant amount of time and other resources. Some degree of meshing is common in the core, where the need for redundancy overrides cost.

Hub-and-Spoke Networks

Possibly the most common WAN topology is known as *hub and spoke*. In this layout, the central hub router connects to multiple spoke networks (sometimes referred to as *stub networks*). The magic of this design is that no alternate routes exist to the remote sites. Although this may mean a loss of service when the network fails, it alleviates any fear of routing loops. One issue that arises with this type of implementation is, of course, redundancy.

Notice in Figure 12.1 that all spoke sites connect only to the central hub. As a result, a spoke site's only path to the rest of the world is through the hub. In this scenario, there is no benefit in filling the bandwidth between the central hub and spoke sites with routing updates. The reason is simply reachability. To get to any remote network, the spoke router must forward all traffic to the hub router. The hub router knows about all routes in each spoke router. These routes are wasted resources because they point to the hub router for all destinations except for those that are local.

Static Routes and Passive Interfaces

If you don't want your spoke routers to hold all known routes in the internetwork, you do have a number of alternatives. One of them is static routes—that is, permanent, hand-coded routes that are used to preclude the need for routing updates. The problem is this: How do the routers in the main network find the correct router to forward traffic to the stub networks? You configure static routes

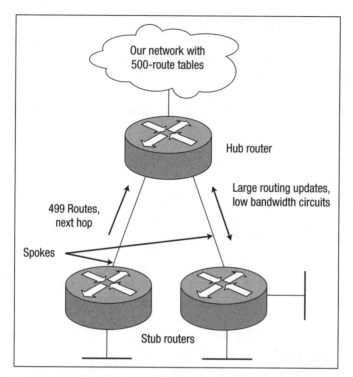

Figure 12.1 A hub and spoke network.

to remote stub networks in the hub router that point to the appropriate spoke site as a next-hop address. The static routes in the hub are added to its outgoing routing updates via route redistribution (covered later in this chapter) and are propagated to all other routers in the main part of the network cloud.

Just because you use static routes doesn't mean the routing protocol will not try to advertise routes out of an interface; for that you need either an outbound route filter (distribute list) or a **passive-interface** command. The **passive-interface** command keeps the routing protocol that's running in the hub router from wasting the bandwidth by sending the routing updates to the stub sites. The effect of this command differs depending on the routing protocol with which it is used. For Routing Information Protocol (RIP) and Interior Gateway Routing Protocol (IGRP), it has a "listen, but don't talk" effect. In other words, it accepts but does not send updates from that interface. For Open Shortest Path First (OSPF) and Enhanced Interior Gateway Routing Protocol (EIGRP), it has a "don't talk, don't listen" effect. In other words, these two protocols require a neighbor relationship to be established before they can exchange updates. The router cannot accept these routing updates because the neighbor relationship cannot be established through a passive interface. You can use the **passive-interface** command with all routing protocols.

When you are using the **passive-interface** command with OSPF and EIGRP, the "don't talk" prevents even hellos from being sent. See Chapters 6, 7, and 8 for more information on hello operation with OSPF and EIGRP.

Figure 12.2 illustrates the use of static routes and passive interfaces, and Listing 12.1 details their configuration.

Listing 12.1   Hub router configuration.

```
interface serial 0
ip address 172.16.4.1 255.255.255.0
!
interface serial 1
ip address 172.16.3.1 255.255.255.0
!
interface serial 2
ip address 172.16.3.1 255.255.255.0
!
ip route 172.16.5.0 255.255.255.0 Serial 0
ip route 172.16.7.0 255.255.255.0 Serial 1
ip route 172.16.8.0 255.255.255.0 Serial 2
!
router rip
network 172.16.0.0
passive-interface Serial 0
passive-interface Serial 1
passive-interface Serial 2
```

Note: You do not need to use a redistribute static command because the static routes point to interfaces on the local router and have the administrative distance of a connected route. You must redistribute static routes when they do not point to an interface on this router because the administrative distance would be greater than zero (the administrative distance of a connected route) and would therefore not automatically be redistributed.

Static Route Command Syntax

Static routes have several interesting features. The static route syntax and the parameter definitions are shown in Listing 12.2.

Listing 12.2   Static route command syntax.

```
ip route destination-network [network-mask]
     {next hop ip address | interface}
     [administrative distance] [permanent]
```

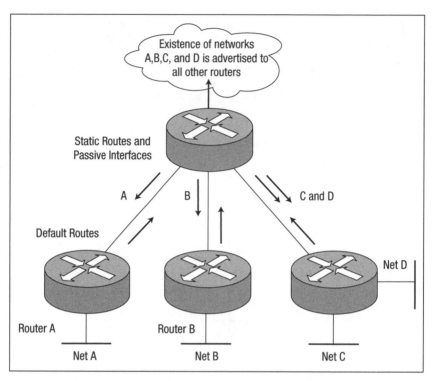

Figure 12.2 Using static routes and **passive-interface** commands.

Here are the parameter definitions from Listing 12.2:

➤ **destination-network** and **network-mask** point to the final destination. These parameters indicate the direction in which packets should be forwarded. If the next step is a serial interface or subinterface, specifying the outbound interface on this router does the trick. If the outbound interface is a multiaccess network (such as Ethernet or token ring), you must indicate exactly which address on the multiaccess network represents the next hop for the packet on its way to the end destination network.

➤ **administrative distance** (discussed in the next section) allows you to position a route above others to the same destination. If multiple routes to the same destination network are available for insertion into the routing table (such as a dynamic routing protocol and one or more static routes to the same destination that point to different interfaces), the route with the lowest numeric value for its administrative distance will be selected.

➤ The **permanent** keyword is used to keep the route active even if the next hop becomes unavailable. Normally, if an attached route goes down, the router removes the static route from consideration as the route for the forwarding database. Using the **permanent** keyword forces the router to keep the route in the forwarding base, thus causing any packets for that destination to be dropped. This might be useful in an encryption device being used on a very secure path. Should the encryption device or the path become unusable, the permanent static route will not allow the packets to follow another less-secure path.

Administrative Distance

The router must decide what routes should be included in its forwarding database. *Forwarding database* is a new term that has moved into the Cisco vernacular. The term *routing table* is not specific enough when many sources of routing information exist simultaneously. For example, you might have a static route or two, a Routing Information Protocol (RIP) route, an Enhanced Interior Gateway Routing Protocol (EIGRP) route, and an Open Shortest Path First (OSPF) route to the same destination network. Which route should be inserted into *the* routing table? The problem is that each protocol creates its own set of routes to all destinations and therefore can be considered to have a routing table. To remove some of the confusion, Cisco uses the term *forwarding database*, which is the component that the routed protocol uses to forward actual traffic.

 You may find the terms *routing table* and *forwarding database* used at different times.

The forwarding database is constructed from the best routes each protocol offers. Which route actually ends up in the forwarding database depends on the believ-ability—or *quality*—of the route based on its administrative distance. Cisco uses an internal value called *administrative distance* to judge the relative believability of the route. When more than one route to a single destination network is available from multiple routing sources, the route with the lowest administrative distance is preferred.

You can alter administrative distances for individual routing protocols or individual routes when a less-believable protocol offers a better path. Remember that routing is similar to the situation in statistics: What is true for the population in general (the relative believability or quality of a particular routing source) is not necessarily true when you look at a single case (one route). Figure 12.3 shows administrative distance selecting the wrong path.

Router A advertises network A to both routers B and C. Assume that router C advertises network A to router B (before router B was advertising it to router C). Router B installs the Interior Gateway Routing Protocol (IGRP) route to router C

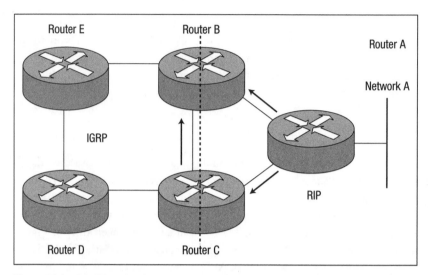

Figure 12.3 Administrative distance selecting the wrong path.

as being the next hop for network A (the destination). You can remedy this problem by making router C's interface passive or by filtering information from router C. However, by filtering the IGRP route to network A, you remove the IGRP alternate path if the primary path to network A through router A fails.

The best long-term solution is to alter the administrative distance so that the router's routing protocol can fix the network after a failure. A way to adjust administrative distance is by using the **distance** command. Listing 12.3 shows its syntax.

Listing 12.3 The distance command's syntax.

```
distance weight [address wildcard-mask
      [access-list number | name]]
```

The parameters used with the **distance** command are shown here:

➤ **weight**—Administrative distance with a range of 10 through 255 (0 through 9 are reserved for internal use)

➤ **address**—IP address in dotted-decimal notation (optional)

➤ **wildcard-mask**—Wildcard mask (optional)

➤ **access-list number | name**—Standard IP access list used to select the routes that will use the **weight** parameter

Listing 12.4 shows how you can use the **distance** command to alter the routing table.

Listing 12.4 Using the **distance** command to change a route's believability.

```
router igrp 200
network 172.31.0.0
redistribute rip
default-metric 100 400 255.1 1500
distance 130 0.0.0.0 255.255.255.255 99
!
access-list 99 permit 172.16.5.0 0.0.0.255
```

Use of the 0.0.0.0 255.255.255.255 in the **distance** command allows **access-list 99** to select which networks need changes.

Adjusting administrative distance is a good technique for correcting single route problems because it provides for an automatic alternate path if the primary path fails.

Default Routes

If your network has a large number of routes, static routes might not buy you much due to the trade-off between simplifying the routing updates and the constant manual changing of the static routes as the network configuration changes in each router. If you don't want to use static routes, default routes (which are known as *gateways of last resort*) present another option. If the routing table does not have a route to a destination network, the default route will be used. For example, going back to the hub and spoke scenario, to enable a default route, simply define in each spoke router a default route that points back to the hub router for unknown traffic. Listings 12.5 and 12.6 show how to configure each spoke router shown in Figure 12.2 to have an Internet Protocol (IP), or other protocol, address on its local area network (LAN) segment. However, it uses a default route that points in the direction of the bigger cloud. Notice the configurations of the spoke sites.

Listing 12.5 Configuring the router attached to network A.

```
interface Serial 0
ip address 172.16.4.2 255.255.255.0
```

Listing 12.6 Configuring the default route that points toward the hub.

```
ip route 0.0.0.0 0.0.0.0 Serial 0
```

Note that the other router configurations are identical to this router's configuration, except for the addresses on the serial interfaces.

A default route is actually a static route to network 0.0.0.0 with a 0.0.0.0 mask. This 0.0.0.0 form of default route is used with RIP and OSPF to indicate a "none of the above routes" path. If no routes exist in the forwarding database for the destination IP address in the datagram, the router forwards it in the direction of the default route.

Referring back to Figure 12.2, the default route of router A points to an interface on the local router. This configuration works on links where nothing further is required to indicate the next-hop address. The default route of router B— although not required in Figure 12.2—shows a configuration you could use on a multiaccess network segment where you need to point to a specific router. The form of the default route for IGRP and EIGRP is **ip default-network** *x.x.x.x*, where *x.x.x.x* is the actual network address. Obviously, you must have a valid route to the destination network. In all other ways, the default routes of routers A and B work the same way.

Here's how traffic would flow from network A to network D in Figure 12.2: The router attached to network A attempts to match the packet's destination IP address with that of one of the destinations in its forwarding database. If it can't find a matching entry, the router forwards the packet upstream along the default path toward the hub (but only if the default route is present). The hub has a next-hop address for network D due to the static route included in the configuration and forwards the traffic properly. The return traffic follows the same path in the reverse order.

Deciding When to Use Static or Default Routes

Because static and default routes (a *default route* is a special case of the static route) don't change even when the network breaks, it is important to point out that the best use of static routes is when only one path exists between source and destination. Because no alternate path exists (due to the network design), no confusion will result when the primary—actually the *only*—path goes down. Notice in Listings 12.5 and 12.6 that the static route is more specific and points from the "big" cloud to the "little" cloud. The placement decision is easy because all routers in the bigger cloud need to learn the route to the stub network (or networks), and the stub router will intentionally not be advertising its connected routes. By adding a static route that points to the stub network, the router at the edge of the larger network will redistribute the static routes to provide the necessary routing information. The default route, being the "none of the above" choice, points from the little cloud toward the big one. This approach keeps the size of the stub router's forwarding database to a minimum while providing full connectivity and minimizing the routing overhead. If you use default routes, you'll probably use two defaults: one from the stub site to the rest of the organization and the other in the big cloud pointing to the Internet. An Internet Service Provider (ISP) would likely use a static route to your organization's network to allow the rest of the Internet to find you.

For more information on ISPs, see Chapters 9 and 10.

Remember that RIP and IGRP are classful routing protocols. It is often necessary to use the **ip classless** command if you are planning to reach destinations of unrecognized subnets of directly connected networks. By default, the Internetwork Operating System (IOS) will discard the packets received for a subnet that numerically falls within its subnet if there is no such subnet number in the routing table and there is no default route. When the **ip classless** command is used, the IOS will forward these packets to the best supernet route or the default route.

Distribute Lists

Passive interfaces are great for blocking all routing updates from departing through a specific interface. However, you may want to limit distribution of only some specific routes. To accomplish specific route filtering, use distribute lists (also known as *route filters*), which are simply access lists used on routing updates rather than on traffic. For more information on access lists, see Chapter 11. Notice in Figure 12.4 that you can decide to hide routes from one part of the network or another because default and static routes may make having all routes in a forwarding database undesirable. Listing 12.7 details the configuration of a route filter.

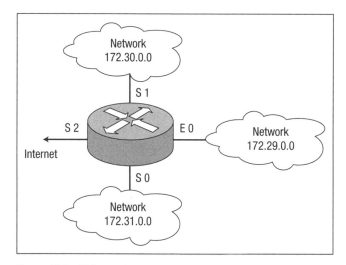

Figure 12.4 Hiding routes.

Listing 12.7   Route filtering.

```
interface Ethernet 0
ip address 172.29.5.1 255.255.255.0
!
interface Serial 0
ip address 172.31.14.1 255.255.255.0
!
interface Serial 1
ip address 172.30.3.1 255.255.255.0
!
interface Serial 2
ip unnumbered Ethernet 0
!
ip route 0.0.0.0 0.0.0.0 S2
!
router rip
network 172.29.0.0
network 172.30.0.0
network 172.31.0.0
distribute-list 99 out Serial 0
distribute-list 98 out Serial 1
!
access-list 99 permit 172.30.0.0 0.0.255.255
!
access-list 98 permit 172.31.0.0 0.0.255.255
```

The listing illustrates that every device can reach the Internet from the router shown in Figure 12.4; however, the 172.29.0.0 network will remain unknown to the 172.30.0.0 and 172.31.0.0 networks. The forwarding databases of the routers within 172.30.0.0 and 172.31.0.0 would be reduced in size, thus providing faster routing table lookups, a smaller forwarding database, and smaller routing up-dates. However, with the default route going through the router shown in Figure 12.4, traffic would still flow to and from the 172.29.0.0 cloud because the router actually knows all the routes for all networks plus the default route to the Internet. If security, not the size of the routing tables, is your primary concern, you need access lists to block traffic. You can code standard IP access lists exactly the same way you did in Chapter 11. This time, however, use the **access-list** command with the **distribute-list** command to filter routing update traffic.

Syntax of the **distribute-list** Command
Listing 12.8 shows the full syntax of the **distribute-list** command.

Listing 12.8   Syntax of the distribute-list command.

```
[no] distribute-list {access-list | name} in [ interface-name]

[no] distribute-list {access-list | name} out [ interface-name ]
| routing-process | autonomous-system number ]
```

The parameter descriptions are as follows:

➤ **access-list number | name**—Associates an IP access list with this statement.

➤ **out | in**—Describes the direction in which the filter acts. Notice that inbound distribute lists apply only to interfaces.

➤ **interface-name | routing-process | autonomous-system number**—Describes what routing destination is to be filtered. If this parameter is not specified, the default is for all interfaces.

Using More Than One Protocol

The real power of routers is found in the dynamic routing protocol, where lost routes can be circumvented and newly added routes can be discovered and added to the forwarding database. It is better—and easier—to support only one routing protocol per routed protocol; however, you must sometimes run multiple routing protocols in the same router at the same time.

Here are some situations where you would run multiple routing protocols in one router:

➤ You are migrating or converting your network from one routing protocol to another.

➤ Two organizations share common routers and need to share certain routes to each other; however, for political reasons, the organizations want to keep most of the network's routes separate and private.

➤ There are multiple vendor interoperability issues or incompatible protocols.

➤ You have some application-specific need. For example, you might need to convert from RIP to OSPF to gain convergence fast enough to support IBM Systems Network Architecture (SNA) traffic.

➤ You need to support legacy protocols. Unix systems commonly run RIP, but you want your core backbone routers to run EIGRP or OSPF.

Route Redistribution

Redistribution is the term used to describe the action of a routing protocol when the routing protocol advertises (redistributes) its routing information to another routing protocol running on the same router. When two or more protocols are running simultaneously in the same router, each protocol learns and maintains its own routes. The router must build a single forwarding database from multiple sources of routing information. If only one route exists (for example, only one of several routing protocols is reporting that route) to a destination, that route is installed in the forwarding database. If more than one choice for a route to a particular destination exists (that is, more than one routing source has a route to it), which route should be used? A vendor may simply write code to select the "best" route from the multiple sources. Cisco uses *administrative distance* as a way to grade routes on their "believability."

The router has access to each protocol's routes but only the most believable routes are added to the forwarding database. When it comes time to redistribute the routes, each individual routing protocol advertises only routes it has learned. A protocol will not include routes from another routing protocol unless you specifically tell the other routing protocol to share or redistribute its routes. The metrics that the routing protocols use are completely different and incompatible (the notable exception being IGRP and EIGRP). Therefore, you need to help the routing protocol by telling it what metric values to use when redistributing routes from another source of routing information.

Route redistribution must be done with care considering issues related to the mixing of routes from different routing sources. For example, consider that each part of the network will reconverge at a different rate, which results in routes that are aging out and being replaced at different rates. If you connect the network parts with a single router even though you might be using a protocol that converges quickly in one part of the network, its new source of information may not be correct (that is, current enough). The problem is much worse if routes are being shared from multiple routers. Redistribution adds a great opportunity to share conflicting information throughout your internetwork. That is what this chapter is about.

A single routing protocol has features to produce consistent, loop-free topologies. The fact to keep in mind is that when redistributing, you— the administrator—are the one who must keep things straight, both logically and physically, to prevent loops.

Routing Metrics

Metrics extract the best pathway to a specific destination. They vary based on the routing protocol(s) active on the router. Incompatible route selection information is one problem that occurs with route distribution. RIP, OSPF, and EIGRP/IGRP all have different ideas as to what a good metric is. As a result, you must set *seed metrics* (the metrics used when routes are redistributed) when redistributing. In addition, because the router uses administrative distance to rate the believability of different routing sources, you have a good source for misunderstanding about what the *real* route into and out of the internetwork should be. There is no way to directly map either the hop count metric of RIP to the cost-routing metric that OSPF uses or the composite metrics that IGRP and EIGRP use. You must manually plug in metric values for the redistributed routes.

Each protocol begins building its metric from the autonomous system boundary router (ASBR), which is based on the initial seed value. It is a good idea to set the seed metric for a redistributed route to a larger value than the metric value derived locally for a route to the same destination. This way, if routes from your network are redistributed back at you (called *route feedback*, discussed later in this chapter), they will be perceived as being farther away than any local protocol metric and therefore not used.

This technique of setting the seed metric higher for redistributed routes than any local metric has a very big advantage over filtering routes to prevent route feedback. If your local route to a network fails, that backup route through the nonlocal protocol may still be available. If the routes were simply filtered, no alternative path would be available.

Figure 12.5 shows how using a low value for the seed metric produces suboptimal paths.

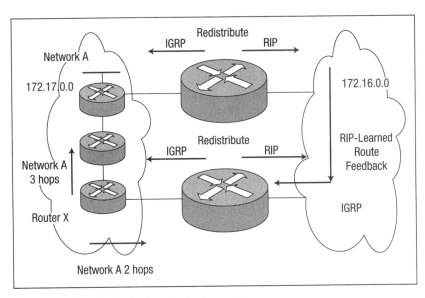

Figure 12.5   Routing feedback with suboptimal paths.

Notice at the lower left what happens when the routes come back through. Assume that 1 is the seed metric for IGRP routes (which are, in actuality, the earlier redistributed RIP routes the route update information is looping) being redistributed into the RIP cloud. RIP begins growing the metric value as if the RIP to IGRP to RIP (again) routes are one hop from the ASBR. The lower-left router sees router X as being three hops along the internal path. However, because a low metric value is attached coming back from the IGRP cloud, network X appears to be closer via the IGRP cloud. The result is an inaccurate routing decision.

What are possible solutions to the problem? One approach is to always apply a metric higher than the maximum in the local cloud. For example, if the maximum diameter in the RIP cloud is 5 hops, assign a metric of 6 to routes coming from the IGRP cloud. Doing so keeps RIP feedback originating within the IGRP cloud from seeming to provide better paths than natural RIP paths. Manipulating seed metrics is better than filtering routes because if router X became unreachable through the normal RIP cloud and if a real path did exist through the IGRP cloud, it would become the pathway of choice through normal route selection. If the routes are filtered, no alternative paths through the other network are available.

The primary command used to establish the seed metric is **default-metric**. There are two versions of the command's syntax. Listing 12.9 shows the syntax for RIP and OSPF; Listing 12.10 shows the syntax for IGRP and EIGRP.

Listing 12.9   Configuring **default-metric** for RIP and OSPF.

```
[no] default-metric <number>
```

For RIP, you must provide a hop count. For OSPF, you need to provide a path cost, which is simply a number based on the link's bandwidth.

Listing 12.10   Configuring **default-metric** for IGRP and EIGRP.

```
[no] default-metric <bandwidth> <delay> <reliability> <load> <mtu>
```

For IGRP and EIGRP, you need to use the more complex components used for these protocols. Refer to Listing 12.11, later in this chapter, for a good example of **default-metric** usage.

Single Router between Two Networks

Several distinct scenarios exist for the use of a single router with multiple networks. There are also several tools available to aid you in the configuration of those scenarios. Some solutions fit better than others in given situations. Figure 12.6 illustrates a simple but common problem of having one router between two different routing clouds.

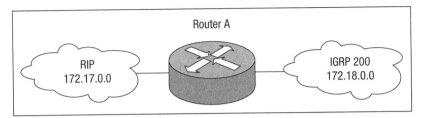

Figure 12.6   Multiple routing protocols in one router.

On the left is a RIP cloud, and on the right is IGRP. Router A's forwarding database contains routes from both RIP and IGRP. As a result, all networks are reachable from router A. The RIP process in router A advertises only RIP-learned routes (only those not learned through the interface that's directly connected to the RIP cloud) back into the RIP cloud due to split horizon. *Split horizon* is a loop-avoidance technique that prevents distance-vector protocols from advertising a route back to the router interface from which it was learned.

The IGRP routing process in router A advertises only IGRP's route information, again taking split horizon into account for outbound updates. To make the routing processes advertise each other's routes, you must configure additional statements (one for each protocol that needs redistribution) that specifically authorize each protocol to redistribute routes learned from the other protocols.

 Split horizon is an important concept. You must understand that split horizon does affect the outcome of passing routing updates from a router.

Listings 12.11 and 12.12 show how to handle redistribution for the scenario shown in Figure 12.6.

Listing 12.11   IGRP configuration.

```
router igrp 200
network 172.17.0.0
redistribute rip
default-metric 10000 2000 255 1 1500
```

Notice the IGRP/EIGRP-style seed metric. The 10000 represents the bandwidth in kilobytes (for example, 10,000K is 10Mbps), and the 2000 is the approximate serialization delay for an Ethernet frame at 10Mbps. *Serialization delay* is simply how long it takes to put the bits onto the circuit at a given speed. For example, an 8,000-bit record being sent on a 64Kbps link would take 8,000/64,000 of a second to leave the router's interface. The 255 represents the link's reliability as a ratio, with 255 as the denominator; therefore, a 100-percent reliable link would be

255/255. The 1 represents the current load factor, again as a ratio, with 1/255 indicating a not-busy link. Finally, the 1500 represents the MTU size for the link.

Listing 12.12   RIP configuration.

```
router rip
network 172.18.0.0
redistribute igrp 200
default-metric 3
```

The seed metric for RIP is in hops.

The statements authorize each protocol to advertise routes from the forwarding database that the other protocol originally learned. Notice that the **default-metric** statements provide values in each protocol's native metric format to allow the routing protocol to compare routes. This method of providing a metric is necessary because RIP and IGRP use totally different metric types. There is no realistic way to translate RIP's hop count to IGRP's complex metric. Therefore, you must provide the **default-metric** before any information can be passed between the two protocols.

Note that there is only one point of connection between the two networks. In this situation, you would gain little by redistributing all routes in both directions. Rather than adding additional entries into all routing tables on both sides of the cloud, consider redistributing all routes into one protocol (into either the core or the surviving protocol during a conversion) and injecting a default route into the other side. Listings 12.13 through 12.15 show such a scenario.

Listing 12.13   Redistributing routes in one network and using the default in the other.

```
router igrp 200
network 172.18.0.0
redistribute rip
default metric 10000 2000 255 1 1500
```

Listing 12.14   Configuring a static route that points to the RIP side of the network.

```
ip route 0.0.0.0 0.0.0.0 Serial 0
```

Listing 12.15   RIP configuration.

```
router rip
network 172.16.0.0
redistribute static
default-metric 3
```

This example didn't need to show the **redistribute** command for static routes, but we included it for clarity. Notice that we sent the default route into only the RIP side of the network. There isn't really an effective way to generate a default route into both protocols from within the same router unless a common default route exists for both. Figure 12.7 shows an example of a default route to a third network (in this case, the Internet).

In Figure 12.7, you could send a default route to both the RIP and OSPF routing domains because they both want to reach destinations on the Internet. This scenario works because the router that runs the multiple protocols is also the router that connects to the Internet. If, for example, another router were the default to the Internet, redistribution in one direction with a default route in the other direction is more typical.

 Redistributing in one direction and using a default route in the other is a good strategy when you have a single router between two clouds. When multiple points of redistribution (multiple routers) between two or more clouds exist, the problem requires you to combine route filtering, metric, or administrative distance manipulation strategies.

Route Feedback

Redistributing routes in one direction and employing a default route in another direction works well in the situation shown in Figure 12.7. Unfortunately, a new problem arises—routing feedback, which causes suboptimal paths and/or routing loops. Figure 12.8 shows route feedback. Feedback was discussed in earlier sections. However, additional detail is warranted.

Two (or more) connections between the clouds are desirable, so routes redistributed originally from the RIP cloud to the IGRP cloud attempt to return to the

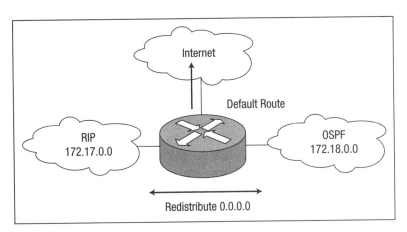

Figure 12.7   Default route to a third network.

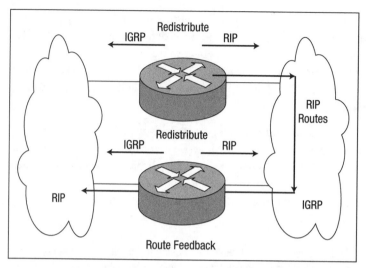

Figure 12.8 Route feedback.

RIP cloud from IGRP. The more connections there are, the bigger the problem. We highly recommend that you avoid having multiple equal-cost routes out of your autonomous system (AS). If your traffic is departing your network via one router and returning via a different router, you have created a routing loop that could cause massive instability in your internetwork. This problem is troublesome, causing routing loops and "funny" routes that provide strange paths to the destinations. You can use the following strategies (alone or in combination) to handle route feedback:

➤ Redistribute in one direction only using a default route in the other cloud.

➤ Redistribute in both directions but filter routes in both directions.

➤ Redistribute but make certain the seed metric is higher than any local metric. For example, if the maximum number of hops in the RIP cloud is 7, set the default metric to 8. This approach provides a backup through the "other" cloud if all paths through this network are down.

➤ Redistribute and change metrics or administrative distance on specific routes.

Configuring Redistribution

The best of all worlds would be to run only one routing protocol, but when you must redistribute, keep the following in mind:

➤ Don't run overlapping protocols.

➤ Decide where a new protocol should be added.

> Try to always have a sharp, distinct border (an edge) between sections of the network that are running different protocols. Usually the edge is a short-term position. The edge is just a way for you to better visualize the redistribution situation.

> Determine which protocol will be the edge (the one being eliminated) and which will be the core (the one to remain). A good strategy is to redistribute into the core (or backbone) and filter or use default routes to reach the core from the edge protocol.

> Select the ASBR(s) carefully. Decide which routes will be injected in which direction and the strategy for blocking their return.

Designating the edge device may be permanent due to necessity, as with a group of Unix machines running RIP (not capable of any other protocol) and connecting to a backbone that runs OSPF. It is feasible, however, that the edge might be temporary and movable for a migration. Figures 12.9, 12.10, and 12.11 show what "keeping a defined edge" means.

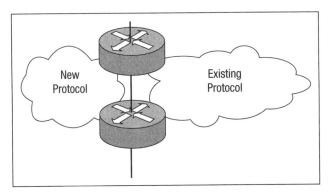

Figure 12.9   Keeping an edge.

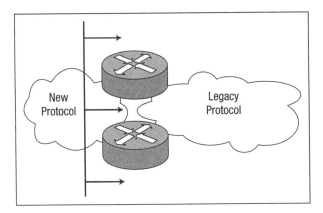

Figure 12.10   Moving the edge in discrete steps.

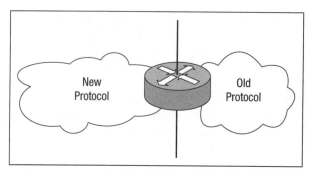

Figure 12.11 Establishing the end position.

Testing the Configuration

The commands most most often used in testing the configuration deal with the forwarding table. However, all the following commands will be useful:

➤ **show ip route**—Shows the content of the forwarding database, including the next hop, metric, routing source (such as RIP, OSPF, EIGRP, and IGRP), administrative distance, and route aging information.

➤ **show [ip •••] protocols**—Displays which protocols are currently running in the router, what the routing update sources are (other routers), and the default administrative distance for the protocol. In this command, "•••" represents the name of the routed protocol whose information you want to see.

➤ **traceroute**—Shows the path taken by traffic for a particular destination.

Migration Strategies

Plan migrations from one network and routing protocol to another carefully. Sometimes you can do a small network conversion as a one-shot conversion (called a *flash cut*), where there is no edge. Often, however, you must plan the migration to occur over several steps. When you plan it, it's important to have in mind a good idea of what you expect to happen. Nothing can replace what you know about your current network. Study the network extensively and carefully; then plan the steps. Use one or more of these strategies to keep things working:

➤ If you have access to planning tools, such as Cisco NetSys, or if you have a lab where you can try a pilot implementation of the solution before putting it into a live network, by all means do so.

➤ Show your design to everyone you can. Sometimes, someone—too often a guy on the job for fewer than two weeks—will see a problem you missed. Even if the other members of your team don't notice a problem, they'll all understand what's about to happen and when; if something goes a little off the mark, they'll be more prepared to help.

➤ When you make the changes, be ready to reinstall the original network configuration. One way this could be accomplished is with TFTP servers with the original router configurations. Another approach is to simply make changes to running RAM only, not saving the changes to Non-Volatile Random Access Memory (NVRAM). That way, a reload will fix the problem.

➤ Hopefully, you can make any necessary changes during nonproduction hours.

Some other issues you may face include special statements for dealing with IGRP and EIGRP. These protocols employ a different kind of default route coding from other protocols.

Practice Questions

Question 1

> Why would two routing protocols be used in the same router? [Choose all that apply.]
>
> ❑ a. Because a conversion or migration is being performed from one protocol to another.
>
> ❑ b. Because you need to support legacy routing protocols.
>
> ❑ c. Because of political boundaries within the organization.
>
> ❑ d. Due to multivendor interoperability or host-based routers.

Answers a, b, c, and d are correct. All answers provide possible scenarios when you may need or want to consider using multiple protocols.

Question 2

> What is an ASBR?
>
> ○ a. A type of route used to connect autonomous systems.
>
> ○ b. A router that runs OSPF.
>
> ○ c. A router that runs two different routing protocols simultaneously.
>
> ○ d. A different vendor's router.

Answer c is correct. An ASBR is a router that runs two different routing protocols at the same time, although the definition is usually expanded to include that the protocols share routes. Answer a is incorrect because ASBR is not a route; this is where the trick is. The trick is in the wording. Most people will read the answer in a quick manner and their brains will register route as *router* in most cases. Cisco uses this technique to ensure that people read the questions thoroughly. Answer b is incorrect because although the term ASBR is commonly used with OSPF, the definition of an ASBR is more general. Answer d is incorrect because with ASBR, no differentiation is made regarding another vendor's router.

Question 3

> What is an administrative distance?
>
> ○ a. A Cisco-specific mechanism for deciding which protocol is more believable or has a better-quality route.
>
> ○ b. A metric used by OSPF.
>
> ○ c. An identifier that describes routers under common administration.
>
> ○ d. A type of access list used to filter routes.

Answer a is correct. An administrative distance is used when more than one routing source has a route to a single destination. The route associated with the lowest numeric value administrative distance is the one inserted into the forwarding database. Answer b is incorrect because the OSPF metric is known as *cost*. Answer c is incorrect because an identifier that describes routers under common administration defines an AS. Answer d is incorrect because the access list used to filter routes is called a *distribute list*.

Question 4

> What is the command to display the administrative distance associated with an IP route?
>
> ○ a. **show ip route**
>
> ○ b. **show ip protocols**
>
> ○ c. **show interface**
>
> ○ d. **show administrative distance**

Answer a is correct. The routing table lists for each nonconnected route the metric, administrative distance, age, next hop, and outgoing interface. Although **show ip protocols** shows the administrative distance for the protocol, it does not show whether a route has had its administrative distance changed. Therefore, answer b is incorrect. Answer c is incorrect because **show interface** doesn't show administrative distance at all. Answer d is incorrect because this command doesn't exist.

Question 5

What is a disadvantage of using a route filter or filters to eliminate a route from the routing table?

○ a. There are no disadvantages; using a route filter is the best way to avoid route feedback.

○ b. A route filter becomes almost the reverse of a static route. If the route you're filtering represents a possible alternative route, filtering it prevents it from ever being an alternate route.

○ c. It changes the administrative distance on the route.

○ d. It changes the seed metric associated with a route.

Answer b is correct. A route filter will not adapt just because the network changes. It works like a static route that won't allow the network to heal because you're overriding the ability of the routing protocol to fix itself. Answer a is incorrect because although using a route filter is one way to avoid route feedback, there are better ways to avoid it. Although you can use an access list to select traffic for these types of changes, the route filter allows (**permit**) or blocks (**deny**) routing update contents. Therefore, answers c and d are incorrect because they have nothing to do with route filters.

Question 6

Which of the following techniques is a loop avoidance mechanism?

○ a. Default route

○ b. Split horizon

○ c. Event horizon

○ d. Loopback interface

Answer b is correct. Split horizon is a loop-avoidance technique that prevents distance-vector protocols from advertising a route back to the router interface from which it was learned. Answer a is incorrect because a default route specifies a route traffic should take in the event that there is not a more specific route in the routing table. Answer c is incorrect because not only is event horizon a term used in association with the formation of black holes, but it is a pretty good sci-fi movie. Answer d is incorrect because a loopback interface is a logical interface that is configured on a router to provide a stable network address that can be used with certain routing protocols.

Question 7

When using a **passive-interface** in conjunction with OSPF or EIGRP, the interface will not send hello packets.

○ a. True

○ b. False

Answer a is correct. When an interface is associated with the **passive-interface** command, the "don't talk" mechanism will also prevent hello packets from being transmitted.

Need to Know More?

 Cheek, Andrea, H. Kim Lew, and Kathleen Wallace. *Cisco CCIE Fundamentals: Network Design and Case Studies.* Cisco Press. Indianapolis, IN, 1998. ISBN 1-57870-066-3. This is a great book for even more information on CCIE fundamentals.

 Doyle, Jeff. *CCIE Professional Development: Routing TCP/IP Volume I.* Macmillan Technical Publishing. Indianapolis, IN, 1998. ISBN 1-57870-041-8. Chapters 11 through 13 discuss related topics.

 Larson, Bob, Corwin Low, and Michael Simon. *CCNP Routing Exam Prep.* The Coriolis Group. Scottsdale, AZ, Fall 2000. ISBN: 1-57610-778-2. This book, an Exam Prep for the CCNP exam, covers each related subject in great detail.

 Cisco's Web site (**www.cisco.com**) includes white papers and router documentation about redistribution and route filtering.

Implementing
Scalable Addresses

Terms you'll need to understand:

✓ Variable-length subnet masks (VLSMs)

✓ Route summarization

✓ Scalability

✓ Hierarchical addressing

✓ Network Address Translation (NAT)

Techniques you'll need to master:

✓ Developing a hierarchical addressing scheme

✓ Deploying a hierarchical addressing scheme

✓ Assigning addresses

✓ Using VLSMs

✓ Implementing route summarization

This chapter discusses some specifics for addressing and certain features that can be implemented to ensure address scalability. Network addressing is one of the most important tasks when designing and implementing an internetwork. With this information, you should be able to make informed decisions regarding addressing and how it can be used in different situations to provide you with an overall addressing scheme that meets all your goals. This logical design is a useful tool you can use to ensure that the process of moving from the design stage to the physical implementation of equipment goes as smoothly as possible.

IP Address Scalability

When beginning any network project, it's very important that you incorporate a robust and scalable addressing scheme. Hierarchical addressing is a model for applying a structured and robust addressing scheme to an internetwork design. When this addressing model is properly implemented, it can easily facilitate the proper deployment of network addresses.

Hierarchical Addressing

One of the best-known addressing hierarchies is post office addressing. Suppose you want to mail a letter to your parents. Once your letter hits the post office, it is sorted based on Zip code, state, city, and local address. That's what hierarchical addressing is all about: Start out big and work your way down, smaller and smaller, until you get to your destination. This practice is also used in addressing internetworks across the world. You start with a large area and work your way down to the network, subnetwork, and finally the end station for completion of the data transfer. There are several benefits to hierarchical routing:

➤ *Efficient address allocation*—When utilizing this type of addressing scheme, you are able to optimize the use of available address space on the network. With random address assignments, you may be unable to use entire blocks of addresses due to addressing conflicts.

➤ *Reduction in routing table entries*—One of the main goals in a network design is to minimize the size of a routing table by using route summarization. This allows for a single IP address and supernet mask to represent a group of networks, thus reducing the amount of entries in the router.

Several other solutions have been developed that can be used in correlation with hierarchical addressing. They can assist in the depletion of valuable address space. The following is a brief list of these solutions and their function:

➤ *Variable-length subnet masking*—This was developed to add multiple levels of subnetworked address space within a single network. This topic is covered in more detail in Chapter 4.

➤ *Allocation of private network addresses*—This was developed for organizations that do not need much access to the Internet. Any network can utilize these privately assigned IP addresses within their organization, rather than using a public address.

➤ *Network Address Translation (NAT)*—This was developed for organizations that use private addressing. (Private addressing is covered in great detail in RFC 1918.) This strategy enables an organization to access the Internet with a valid public address, without having to reassign the private address that's in place. NAT is covered in more detail in Chapter 4.

By following a solid hierarchical scheme, you can improve a network's performance by optimizing routes and reducing CPU cycles involved with routing calculations as well as reducing memory usage and requirements.

Address Assignment

Network addresses should be thoroughly planned and documented to ensure that the addresses are utilized optimally and not duplicated on the network. A clearly documented addressing scheme can assist in troubleshooting and managing any network. Addresses can be administered from a central information technology (IT) section in a company, by authorized systems administrators who are assigned throughout an organization, or by using a dynamic addressing procedure such as Dynamic Host Configuration Protocol (DHCP). It doesn't matter who assigns the addresses that are being used, but it is important that the established addressing scheme is adhered to and followed. Otherwise, any problems that arise during troubleshooting or when installing a new system will be compounded.

Note: BOOTP is a protocol that is used in resolving an IP address based on a layer 2 MAC address. BOOTP was the predecessor to DHCP and has lost popularity as DHCP has become more widely used.

The following is a list you can use to help you successfully design and implement a hierarchical addressing scheme:

➤ *Hierarchical scheme*—Designing a hierarchical scheme should be accomplished in the following order: autonomous system, area, networks, subnets, and end stations. The exact hierarchy you use depends on which routing protocol(s) you decide to use.

➤ *Route summarization*—Route summarization reduces the number of routes present in your routing tables, which reduces the amount of memory utilized on the router and allows for faster retrieval of routing information.

➤ *Low-level hierarchy*—When the high-level design is complete, there will be a need for lower-level addressing and naming. For instance, if your customer has offices in different regions or cities, this would allow you to use established guidelines for addressing and naming.

➤ *Special device addressing*—To assist in troubleshooting, special devices such as routers, servers, switches, and any other high-priority devices should be given a host address within a certain range. For instance, if you give all your routers host addresses of .1 to .30, switches .31 to .50, and servers .51 to .100, you'll be able to tell what kind of device is not operating properly during troubleshooting just by looking at the IP address. This is an easy standardization that can save you and your customer a lot of wasted time trying to figure out what a device is. However, as with everything in networking there is a major drawback that goes along with this easy solution. By implementing a standardized method of addressing, you increase the possibility of an intruder being able to find these high-priority resources, as this type of addressing is typical in today's networks and is easily predicted.

➤ *User station addressing*—To meet scalability requirements, it's suggested that user station addresses be dynamically assigned whenever possible. By using a dynamic addressing product, you ensure optimization of user station addresses and alleviate configuration changes that need to be done if a station is moved to another location.

When implemented properly, this list can save you and your customer time, effort, and possibly money in the long run. By adhering to these guidelines, you can ensure that you have properly designed a network in a hierarchical manner that's sure to meet your customer's business and technical goals.

Implementing Scalability Features

The capability to extend your internetwork is determined, in part, by the scaling characteristics of the routing protocols used and the quality of the network design.

As stated earlier in this book, network scalability is limited by two factors: operational issues and technical issues. Typically, operational issues are more significant than technical issues. Operational scaling concerns encourage the use of large areas or protocols that do not require hierarchical structures. When hierarchical protocols are required, technical scaling concerns promote the use of small areas. Finding the right balance is the art of network design.

Routing protocols scale best if their resource utilization grows at a slower pace than that of the network. Three critical resources are used by routing protocols: memory, central processing unit (CPU), and bandwidth. Here's a detailed description of each:

➤ *Memory*—Routing protocols use memory to store routing tables and topology information. Route summarization cuts memory consumption for all routing protocols. Keeping areas small reduces the memory consumption for hierarchical routing protocols.

➤ *CPU*—CPU usage is protocol dependent. Some protocols use CPU cycles to compare new routes to existing routes. Other protocols use CPU cycles to regenerate routing tables after a topology change. In most cases, the latter technique will use more CPU cycles than the former. For link-state protocols, keeping areas small and using summarization reduces CPU requirements by reducing the effect of a topology change and by decreasing the number of routes that must be recomputed after a topology change.

➤ *Bandwidth*—Bandwidth usage is also protocol dependent. Three key issues determine the amount of bandwidth a routing protocol consumes:

➤ *When routing information is sent*—Periodic updates are sent at regular intervals.

➤ *What routing information is sent*—Complete updates contain all routing information.

➤ *Where routing information is sent*—Flooded updates are sent to all routers.

These resources are ones that can be addressed fairly easily if your organization has the money or resources to purchase more bandwidth or higher-end routers with more memory and more CPU power. Those organizations that don't have the means necessary to purchase these expensive machines when problems start to arise have to look to alternative ways to meet their scalability issues without the added expense. Two of these alternatives involve using variable-length subnet masks and route summarization. The following sections are brief overviews of these topics. For more detailed information on these topics you can refer back to Chapter 4 of this book.

VLSM

VLSM was covered in detail in Chapter 4; therefore it will only be briefly touched upon here. VLSM, defined in RFC 1009, has been around the internetworking industry for a number of years. It is far from a new technology. It is a methodology for reducing the amount of wasted IP address space on small networks, specifically point-to-point serial links.

The first point that needs to be stressed is that not all routing protocols support the use of VLSM. In order for VLSM to be supported, the routing protocol must be able to pass the prefix in routing updates. Protocols such as Routing Information Protocol (RIP) and Interior Gateway Routing Protocol (IGRP) do not include the prefix (for example, subnet mask, remember?) in their routing updates. Therefore, they cannot advertise varied-length masks.

As mentioned earlier, the routing protocol must include the prefix in routing updates in order to support VLSM. If your routing protocol does not support passing the prefix, you cannot use VLSM. Open Shortest Path First (OSPF), Enhanced Interior Gateway Routing Protocol (EIGRP), and Intermediate System to Intermediate System (IS-IS) are a few examples of protocols that can include prefix information in routing updates.

Route Summarization

Route summarization focuses on reducing the routing tables of all routers in the network. It is generally performed at the edge routers at the border between two address domains. Otherwise, all routers would have to keep all networks in their routing tables, thus increasing CPU and memory utilization. Summarization is based on finding a bit boundary where multiple addresses share a common bit pattern. As with VLSM, the routing protocol must be able to support passing the network prefix in order to support route summarization.

Practice Questions

Question 1

What are the benefits of using a hierarchical addressing scheme? [Choose two.]

❏ a. Decreased memory utilization

❏ b. Network organization

❏ c. Reduced routing table size

❏ d. Optimized addressing algorithm

Answers a and c are correct. By using a hierarchical addressing scheme, you are able to decrease the memory usage on your router. A hierarchical addressing design can be used to minimize the size of a routing table by using route summarization. This allows for a single IP address to represent a group of networks, thus reducing the number of entries in the routing table. Answer b is incorrect because hierarchical addressing does not guarantee that your network will be organized, but it is a step in the right direction. Answer d is incorrect because there is no addressing algorithm associated with hierarchical addressing.

Question 2

When developing an addressing scheme, which step defines that user station addresses be dynamically assigned whenever possible?

○ a. User station addressing

○ b. Low-level hierarchy

○ c. Special device addressing

○ d. Route summarization

Answer a is correct. To meet scalability requirements, it is suggested that user station addresses be dynamically assigned whenever possible by using DHCP or Boot Protocol (BOOTP). BOOTP is a protocol used to resolve an IP address to a layer 2 Media Access Control (MAC) address, and DHCP is the Microsoft version of BOOTP. By using a dynamic addressing product, you can ensure optimization of user station addresses and alleviate configuration changes that need to be done if a station is moved to another location. Answer b is incorrect because low-level hierarchy is used when the high-level design is completed and there is a need for lower-level addressing and naming. Answer c is correct because with this step, it is suggested that special devices such as routers, servers, switches, and any other high-priority devices be given a host address within a certain range. Answer d is incorrect because route summarization reduces the amount of routes present in your routing tables. This also reduces the amount of routing update traffic that travels across your network.

Question 3

What are the three critical resources used by routing protocols? [Choose three.]

❑ a. CPU utilization

❑ b. Bandwidth usage

❑ c. Number of router interfaces

❑ d. Memory usage

Answers a, b, and d are correct. Three critical resources are used by routing protocols: memory, central processing unit (CPU), and bandwidth. Routing protocols use memory to store routing tables and topology information. Route summarization cuts memory consumption for all routing protocols. Keeping areas small reduces the memory consumption for hierarchical routing protocols. CPU usage is protocol dependent. Some protocols use CPU cycles to compare new routes to existing routes. Other protocols use CPU cycles to regenerate routing tables after a topology change. In most cases, the latter technique will use more CPU cycles than the former. For link-state protocols, keeping areas small and using summarization reduces CPU requirements by reducing the effect of a topology change and by decreasing the number of routes that must be recomputed after a topology change. Bandwidth usage is also protocol dependent. Answer c is incorrect because the number of interfaces is not identified as a critical resource. If there are many connections on a router and memory is scarce, then the number of router interfaces could have an effect, but this would fall under memory utilization.

Question 4

> What is required for a routing protocol to support VLSM or route summarization?
>
> ○ a. An exchange of prefix information
>
> ○ b. A classless routing protocol
>
> ○ c. An exchange of network updates
>
> ○ d. A classful routing protocol

Answer a is correct. In order for VLSM to be supported, the routing protocol must be able to pass the prefix information in the routing updates. As with VLSM, the routing protocol must be able to pass the network prefix in order to support route summarization. Answer b is incorrect because a router requires that a classless routing protocol be used for VLSM or summarization. The trick is that the router requires a classless protocol, but the protocol itself requires the exchange of prefix information. Answer c is incorrect because all routing protocols are capable of exchanging network updates, whether the protocol includes the prefix information or not. Answer d is incorrect because a classful routing protocol does not exchange prefix information, so it cannot support VLSM or route summarization.

Question 5

> What feature allows a private address to be exchanged for a valid address when attempting to gain access to the Internet?
>
> ○ a. Route summarization
>
> ○ b. Hierarchical addressing
>
> ○ c. Network Address Translation
>
> ○ d. None of the above

Answer c is correct. NAT enables an organization to access the Internet with a valid public address, without having to reassign the private address that's in place. NAT is covered in more detail in Chapter 4. Answer a is incorrect because route summarization reduces the number of routes present in your routing tables. Answer b is incorrect because hierarchical addressing represents a tiered-structure approach to addressing. Answer d is incorrect because answer c is correct.

Question 6

> What does route summarization accomplish when implemented? [Choose all that apply.]
>
> ○ a. Reduce address space
>
> ○ b. Reduce routing table size
>
> ○ c. Reduce memory utilization
>
> ○ d. Reduce CPU utilization

Answers b, c, and d are correct. You will reduce the size of the routing tables on all routers that route summarization is configured on, thus reducing the memory and CPU utilization. Answer a is incorrect because VLSM must be used to reduce address space.

Question 7

> What are the three critical resources that are utilized by routing protocols? [Choose three answers.]
>
> ❑ a. Memory
>
> ❑ b. Bandwidth
>
> ❑ c. Type of protocol
>
> ❑ d. CPU

Answers a, b, and d are correct. Routing protocols use memory to store routing tables and topology information. CPU usage is protocol dependent. Some protocols use CPU cycles to compare new routes to existing routes. Other protocols use CPU cycles to regenerate routing tables after a topology change. Bandwidth usage is also protocol dependent. The amount of bandwidth a routing protocol consumes depends on whether periodic updates are sent at regular intervals. This is true whether complete updates contain all routing information, or if updates that are sent are flooded to all routers.

Need to Know More?

Doyle, Jeff. *CCIE Professional Development: Routing TCP/IP Volume 1.* Cisco Press. Indianapolis, IN 1998. This core textbook takes you from a basic understanding of routers and routing protocols through a detailed examination of each of the IP routing protocols.

Larson, Bob, Corwin Low, and Michael Simon. *CCNP Routing Exam Prep.* Coriolis Publishing. Scottsdale, AZ, Fall 2000. ISBN 1-57610-778-2. This book, an Exam Prep on the CCNP exam, covers each related subject in great detail.

Oppenhiemer, Priscilla. *Top Down Network Design.* Cisco Press. Indianapolis, IN 1999. ISBN 1-57870-069-8. This book describes hierarchical design and scalability issues and provides you with a full understanding of network design concepts.

Visit Cisco's Web site at **www.cisco.com** and perform a search on any of the concepts discussed here, such as IP addressing, VLSM, and route summarization.

Sample Test

This chapter provides pointers to help you develop a successful test-taking strategy, including how to choose proper answers, how to decode ambiguity, how to work within the Cisco testing framework, how to decide what you need to memorize, and how to prepare for the test. The end of the chapter includes 69 questions on the subject matter that pertains to Cisco Exam 640-503, "Routing 2.0." In Chapter 15, you'll find the answer key to this test. Good luck!

Questions, Questions, Questions

There should be no doubt in your mind that you are facing a test full of specific and pointed questions. The version of the Routing 2.0 exam that you'll take is a variable-length test, so it will include a pool of questions to pull from. You can get anywhere from 60 to 70 questions, and you'll be allotted 75 minutes to complete it. Because this is a variable-length test, the minimum passing score will vary depending on the number of questions you get.

For this exam, questions belong to one of four basic types:

➤ Multiple choice with a single answer

➤ Multiple choice with multiple answers

➤ Simulations (that is, you must answer a question based on a picture of a network scenario)

➤ Drag and drop

Always take the time to read a question at least twice before selecting an answer, and always look for an Exhibit button as you examine each question. Exhibits include graphics information that's related to a question. An exhibit is usually a screen capture of program output, a list of commands to choose from, or GUI information that you must examine to analyze the question's contents and to formulate an answer. The Exhibit button brings up graphics and charts used to help explain a question, provide additional data, or illustrate page layout or program behavior.

Not every question has only one answer; many questions require multiple answers. Therefore, it's important to read each question carefully to determine how many answers are necessary or possible as well as to look for additional hints or instructions when selecting answers. Such instructions often occur in brackets immediately following the question itself (as they do for all multiple-choice, multiple-answer questions). Unfortunately, some questions do not have any right answers and you are forced to find the "most correct" choice.

Picking Proper Answers

Obviously, the only way to pass any exam is to select enough of the right answers to obtain a passing score. However, Cisco's exams are not standardized like the SAT and GRE exams; they are far more diabolical and convoluted. In some cases, questions are strangely worded, and deciphering them can be a real challenge. In those cases, you may need to rely on answer-elimination skills. Almost always, at least one answer out of the possible choices for a question can be eliminated immediately because it matches one of these conditions:

➤ The answer does not apply to the situation.

➤ The answer describes a nonexistent issue, an invalid option, or an imaginary state.

➤ The answer may be eliminated because of the question itself.

After you eliminate all answers that are obviously wrong, you can apply your retained knowledge to eliminate further answers. Look for items that sound correct but refer to actions, commands, or features that are not present or not available in the situation that the question describes.

If you're still faced with a blind guess among two or more potentially correct answers, reread the question. Try to picture how each of the possible remaining answers would alter the situation. Be especially sensitive to terminology; sometimes the choice of words (*remove* instead of *disable*) can make the difference between a right answer and a wrong one.

Only when you've exhausted your ability to eliminate answers, but remain unclear about which of the remaining possibilities is correct, should you guess at an answer. An unanswered question offers you no points, but guessing gives you at least some chance of getting a question right; just don't be too hasty when making a blind guess.

Decoding Ambiguity

Cisco exams have a reputation for including questions that can be difficult to interpret, confusing, or ambiguous. In our experience with numerous exams, we consider this reputation to be completely justified. The Cisco exams are tough, and they are deliberately made that way.

The only way to beat Cisco at its own game is to be prepared. You'll discover that many exam questions test your knowledge of things that are not directly related to the issue that a question raises. This means that the answers you must choose from, even incorrect ones, are just as much a part of the skill assessment as the question itself. If you don't know something about most aspects of routing, you may not be able to eliminate obviously wrong answers because they relate to a different area of routing than the one that the question at hand is addressing. In other words, the more you know about the software and hardware, the easier it will be for you to tell right from wrong.

Questions often give away their answers, but you have to be Sherlock Holmes to see the clues. Often, subtle hints appear in the question text in such a way that they seem almost irrelevant to the situation. You must realize that each question is a test unto itself and that you need to inspect and successfully navigate each question to pass the exam. Look for small clues, such as the mention of times, group permissions and names, and configuration settings. Little things like these can point at the right answer if properly understood; if missed, they can leave you facing a blind guess.

Another common difficulty with certification exams is vocabulary. Be sure to brush up on the key terms presented at the beginning of each chapter. You may also want to read through the Glossary at the end of this book the day before you take the test.

Working within the Framework

The test questions appear in random order, and many elements or issues that receive mention in one question may also crop up in other questions. It's not uncommon to find that an incorrect answer to one question is the correct answer to another question, or vice versa. Take the time to read every answer to each question, even if you recognize the correct answer to a question immediately. That extra reading may spark a memory or remind you about a Cisco router Internetwork Operating System (IOS) feature or function that helps you on another question elsewhere in the exam.

Deciding What to Memorize

The amount of memorization you must undertake for an exam depends on how well you remember what you've read and how well you know the software by heart. The tests will stretch your recollection of the router's commands and functions.

At a minimum, you'll want to memorize the following kinds of information:

➤ The basics of Enhanced Interior Gateway Routing Protocol (EIGRP) and how it selects routes.

➤ The basic functions and configuration of Open Shortest Path First (OSPF). Know how to spot a bad configuration example.

➤ The basic functions and configuration of Border Gateway Protocol (BGP) and how it selects routes.

➤ How redistribution operates and how to configure it using all the routing protocols mentioned previously in the list.

➤ The various **show** commands that allow you to see the status of the subjects mentioned throughout the book.

If you work your way through this book while sitting at a Cisco router (actually you may need a group of routers) and trying to manipulate this environment's features and functions as they're discussed throughout, you should have little or no difficulty mastering this material. Also, don't forget that the Cram Sheet at the front of the book is designed to capture the material that is most important to memorize; use this to guide your studies as well.

Preparing for the Test

The best way to prepare for the test—after you've studied—is to take at least one practice exam. We've included one here in this chapter for that reason; the test questions are located in the pages that follow (and unlike the preceding chapters in this book, the answers don't follow the questions immediately; you'll have to flip to Chapter 15 to review the answers separately).

Give yourself 75 minutes to take the exam, keep yourself on the honor system, and don't look at earlier text in the book or jump ahead to the answer key. When your time is up or you've finished the questions, you can check your work in Chapter 15. Pay special attention to the explanations for the incorrect answers; these can also help to reinforce your knowledge of the material. Knowing how to recognize a correct answer is good, but understanding why incorrect answers are wrong can be equally valuable.

Taking the Test

Relax. Once you're sitting in front of the testing computer, there's nothing more you can do to increase your knowledge or preparation. Take a deep breath, stretch, and start reading that first question.

There's no need to rush; you have plenty of time to complete each question. Both easy and difficult questions are intermixed throughout the test in random order. Because you're taking a variable-length test, don't cheat yourself by spending too much time on a hard question early on in the test, thereby depriving yourself of the time you need to answer the questions at the end of the test.

That's it for pointers. Here are some questions for you to practice on.

Sample Test

Question 1

RIP supports VLSM.

○ a. True

○ b. False

Question 2

OSPF supports VLSM.

○ a. True

○ b. False

Question 3

What is the principle on which routers make forwarding decisions?

○ a. Classless routing

○ b. VLSM

○ c. Longest match

○ d. None of the above

Question 4

Where in the internetwork is summary routing generally performed?

○ a. On the edge routers between dissimilar networks

○ b. On all routers

○ c. Nowhere

○ d. On point-to-point serial links

Question 5

What is the process of mapping private internal addresses to registered public addresses known as?

- ○ a. Network Address Translation
- ○ b. Subnet masking
- ○ c. Address summarization
- ○ d. Classless Interdomain Routing

Question 6

The command _____ will show all interfaces configured for IP.

- ○ a. **show interfaces ip**
- ○ b. **show ip interfaces**
- ○ c. **display ip**
- ○ d. **show protocol ip**

Question 7

What type of connection does BGP use for the transport of routing updates?

- ○ a. FTP
- ○ b. UDP
- ○ c. TCP
- ○ d. LSA

Question 8

Which statements are true regarding EIGRP? [Choose the two best answers.]

- ❏ a. It supports areas.
- ❏ b. It supports VLSM.
- ❏ c. It requires considerably more configuration than OSPF.
- ❏ d. It keeps all protocols in one table.
- ❏ e. It sends notifications to only the systems that are affected by a change.

Question 9

If your network uses RIP, how do you prevent the distribution of routes without using access lists?

○ a. By using default routes

○ b. By using passive interfaces

○ c. By using static routes

○ d. By using routing update filters

Question 10

The command to _____ will reset a specific BGP connection.

○ a. **clear ip route**

○ b. **clear ip route ***

○ c. **clear ip route [*address*]**

○ d. **clear ip bgp [*address*]**

Question 11

Why is OSPF better than RIP in a large network? [Choose the two best answers.]

❑ a. OSPF has virtually no reachability limits.

❑ b. OSPF is less complex than RIP.

❑ c. OSPF has fewer tables to manage.

❑ d. OSPF selects the best path using cost based on bandwidth as a metric.

Question 12

How many class C addresses can be summarized with the route 192.12.172.0/20?

○ a. 4

○ b. 8

○ c. 16

○ d. 20

○ e. 32

Question 13

What is a group of neighbors with the same update policies called?

○ a. Neighbors

○ b. Peer groups

○ c. Area

○ d. Network

Question 14

Which of the following situations would require BGP routing? [Choose the two best answers.]

❑ a. You need to make a decision based on the source and destination of internal traffic within an AS.

❑ b. You need to make connections to different Internet Service Providers.

❑ c. Security concerns require that you filter all but three networks from the Internet.

❑ d. The ISP you connect to uses BGP to connect to the NAP.

Question 15

Which problems can be associated with a high number of routers in an OSPF area? [Choose the two best answers.]

❑ a. Excess LSA traffic

❑ b. Frequent table recalculation

❑ c. Frequent adjacency table recalculation

❑ d. More reachability errors

Question 16

What has to happen for BGP to load balance?

○ a. Identical routing information must be received from the same provider.

○ b. A connection to multiple providers must be established.

○ c. Identical routing information must be received from multiple providers.

○ d. Identical routing metrics must be established between multiple providers.

Question 17

Which options are available on IP extended access lists but are not available for standard access lists? [Choose the three best answers.]

❑ a. Session layer information

❑ b. Destination IP

❑ c. Application port number

❑ d. Source host IP

Question 18

Which of the following is true about nonroutable protocols?

○ a. There is no FCS in the header.

○ b. There is no network layer addressing.

○ c. They use broadcasts to determine the best route.

○ d. They should not be used with WAN links.

Question 19

In what situation would you use a null interface instead of an access list?

○ a. When an access list does not provide the necessary functionality.

○ b. When you want to use hostnames rather than IP addresses.

○ c. When you need to conserve CPU resources.

○ d. When you cannot filter nonroutable protocols.

Question 20

Which address ranges are private? [Choose the two best answers.]

❑ a. 192.167.2.0

❑ b. 172.16.0.0

❑ c. 172.68.0.0

❑ d. 192.168.1.0

Question 21

The command _____ specifies generic route encapsulation to carry traffic through an IP tunnel.

○ a. **tunnel mode ip**

○ b. **tunnel mode gre**

○ c. **tunnel mode gre-ip**

○ d. **tunnel mode gre ip**

Question 22

Which statement about EIGRP is true?

○ a. It keeps a copy of its neighbors' tables.

○ b. It uses forward broadcasts to discover routers.

○ c. Adjacencies exist between master routers (MRs).

○ d. It provides support for other network layer protocols such as IPX AppleTalk and IP.

Question 23

Which of these descriptions of OSPFs features are true? [Choose the three best answers.]

❑ a. It can span more than 15 hops.

❑ b. Its path can be based on throughput.

❑ c. It sends a full routing table on updates.

❑ d. Its routing updates are multicast.

❑ e. It effectively replaces RTMP, IPX, RIP, and IP RIP.

Question 24

When is it suggested that you use BGP to connect to an ISP?

○ a. When you have the same routing policies

○ b. When you have differing routing policies

○ c. When you need more bandwidth to your ISP

○ d. When you need a faster connection to your ISP

Question 25

The summary address 10.10.8.0/22 represents which range of IP addresses?

○ a. 10.0.0.0 to 10.255.255.255

○ b. 10.10.0.0 to 10.10.255.255

○ c. 10.10.8.0 to 10.10.11.255

○ d. 10.10.8.0 to 10.10.10.255

Question 26

What is the private autonomous system (AS) range for BGP?

○ a. 64000 to 65000

○ b. 64500 to 65500

○ c. 64535 to 65512

○ d. 64512 to 65535

Question 27

The BGP community attribute is restricted according to what?

○ a. Autonomous system (AS)

○ b. Path

○ c. Peer group

○ d. None of the above

Question 28

Why is OSPF better than RIP in large networks? [Choose the two best answers.]

❑ a. It uses less RAM on the router.

❑ b. It has no reachability limits.

❑ c. It is less complex than RIP.

❑ d. It supports VLSMs.

Question 29

What does Cisco use for route filtering that can be used with BGP to control and modify routing information and define when routes are redistributed between routing domains?

○ a. Route maps

○ b. Route reflectors

○ c. Passive interfaces

○ d. Redistribution

Question 30

The command _____ will display OSPF interfaces that are configured to each area and all the adjacent neighbor names.

○ a. **show ip ospf neighbors**

○ b. **show ip ospf neighbor**

○ c. **show ip ospf**

○ d. **show ospf neighbors**

Question 31

Which statements are true about the following configuration? [Choose the two best answers.]

```
interface Ethernet 0
ip address 172.16.1.77 255.255.255.0
ip helper-address 172.16.90.255
```

❑ a. Host 172.16.90.255 is a backup router for 172.16.1.77.

❑ b. TFTP broadcasts on interface Ethernet 0 will be forwarded to network 172.16.90.0.

❑ c. All nonroutable protocol traffic will be forwarded to network 172.16.90.0.

❑ d. NetBIOS broadcasts from network 148.19.90.0 will be sent as directed broadcasts to the 172.16.90.0 network.

Question 32

What command is necessary to configure OSPF?

○ a. **router ospf network ; <*address-mask*> <*area-id*>**

○ b. **router ospf <*process id*> network <*address-mask*> <*area-id*>**

○ c. **router ospf <*process id*>; network <*address*> <*wildcard-mask*> <*area area-id*>**

○ d. None of the above

Question 33

What feature is essential when implementing routing policies?

○ a. Static routes

○ b. Route filtering

○ c. Default routes

○ d. Dynamic routes

Question 34

The command _____ is used to show EIGRP routing tables.

○ a. **show ip route eigrp**

○ b. **show ip router eigrp**

○ c. **show router eigrp**

○ d. **show ip eigrp route**

Question 35

Through what process can a single IP represent many IP addresses?

○ a. Default routes

○ b. Static routes

○ c. Route summarization

○ d. Route expansion

Question 36

Which of the following statements regarding the sample configuration are true? [Choose the two best answers.]

```
router EIGRP 100
network 12.0.0.0
network 13.0.0.0
```

- ❑ a. AS 100 is invalid.
- ❑ b. The EIGRP process is running in autonomous system 100.
- ❑ c. The **network** statements are missing the **netmask** statement.
- ❑ d. Network 12.0.0.0 is included in autonomous system 100.

Question 37

What is the full command to display access list 190?

- ○ a. **show access-list**
- ○ b. **show access list 190**
- ○ c. **show access-list 190**
- ○ d. **show access-lists 190**

Question 38

What type of routing protocol is BGP?

- ○ a. Link state
- ○ b. Distance vector
- ○ c. Path vector
- ○ d. None of the above

Question 39

Cisco refers to a default route as what?

○ a. Static route

○ b. Default gateway

○ c. Gateway of last resort

○ d. Static gateway

Question 40

Which routing protocols are IGPs? [Choose all that apply.]

❑ a. OSPF

❑ b. IGRP

❑ c. EIGRP

❑ d. All of the above

Question 41

Which of these are tables kept by EIGRP routers? [Choose the three best answers.]

❑ a. Protocol

❑ b. Topology

❑ c. Neighbor

❑ d. Routing

Question 42

If you cannot connect an OSPF area directly to area 0, what must you configure?

○ a. Route summarization

○ b. Static routes

○ c. Virtual link

○ d. Designated router

Question 43

What is the command to view EIGRP routers with which you have established neighbor relationships?

- ○ a. **show ip neighbors**
- ○ b. **show ip eigrp neighbors**
- ○ c. **show eigrp neighbors**
- ○ d. **show ip eigrp neighbor**

Question 44

What is the best route to any destination in an EIGRP routing table called?

- ○ a. Feasible successor
- ○ b. Current successor
- ○ c. Adjacency
- ○ d. DUAL

Question 45

The command _____ will force EIGRP to stop summarizing routes to normal classful boundaries.

- ○ a. **no summary**
- ○ b. **no auto-summary**
- ○ c. **no auto summary**
- ○ d. **no summary auto**

Question 46

Which BGP attribute is a list of AS paths that a route has traveled to reach its destination?

- ○ a. AS sequence list
- ○ b. AS route attribute
- ○ c. AS path attribute
- ○ d. AS sequence attribute

Question 47

What command displays the status of all BGP connections?

○ a. **show bgp connections**

○ b. **show ip bgp summary**

○ c. **show ip bgp route**

○ d. **show bgp summary**

Question 48

What command allows routers using one routing protocol to know about routes from another routing protocol?

○ a. **redistribute protocol [*process id*]**

○ b. **redistribute routes protocol [*process id*]**

○ c. **redistribute protocol protocol [*process id*]**

○ d. None of the above

Question 49

Which networks are represented by the summarized address of 172.15.168.0/21?

○ a. 172.15.168.0 - 172.15.169.0

○ b. 172.15.168.0 - 172.15.175.0

○ c. 172.15.168.0 - 172.15.171.0

○ d. 172.15.0.0 - 172.15.168.0

Question 50

Which of the following are pieces of information that OSPF requires to establish and maintain a neighbor relationship? [Choose the three best answers.]

❑ a. Hello/dead interval

❑ b. Routing table

❑ c. Router priority

❑ d. Designated router ID

Question 51

What is the command under the **router rip** configuration that would stop RIP updates from leaving via interface Ethernet 3?

○ a. **passive interface ethernet 3**

○ b. **passive-interface ethernet 3**

○ c. **passive-interfaces**

○ d. **passive-interfaces ethernet 3**

Question 52

What command sets a default static route via interface Serial 0?

○ a. **ip route 0.0.0.0 0.0.0.0 serial 0**

○ b. **static route 0.0.0.0 0.0.0.0 serial 0**

○ c. **ip route 0.0.0.0 255.255.255.255 serial 0**

○ d. **ip route 255.255.255.255 0.0.0.0 serial 0**

Question 53

A standard access list is used in route filtering with distribute lists.

○ a. True

○ b. False

Question 54

What BGP function allows for multiple BGP routers to peer with a central point router?

○ a. BGP confederation

○ b. BGP reflector

○ c. BGP concentration

○ d. Route reflector

Question 55

EIGRP is known as what type of routing protocol?

○ a. Link state

○ b. Distance vector

○ c. Advanced distance vector

○ d. Path vector

Question 56

What are the default metrics that EIGRP uses? [Choose two answers.]

❑ a. Bandwidth

❑ b. Reliability

❑ c. Delay

❑ d. MTU size

Question 57

You configure a stub router in an area that has an ASBR.

○ a. True

○ b. False

Question 58

What type of OSPF area only accepts intra-area and default routes?

○ a. Backbone area

○ b. Stubby area

○ c. Standard area

○ d. Totally stubby area

Question 59

What BGP function is based on breaking an AS into multiple sub-ASes?

- ○ a. Confederation
- ○ b. Route reflector
- ○ c. BGP concentration
- ○ d. AS concentration

Question 60

What is the designation given to routers at the top of your network hierarchy?

- ○ a. Distribution
- ○ b. Access
- ○ c. Primary
- ○ d. Core

Question 61

Which command displays all the directly connected OSPF routers?

- ○ a. **show ip ospf neighbor**
- ○ b. **show neighbors**
- ○ c. **show cdp neighbor detail**
- ○ d. **show ip route**

Question 62

What command displays all currently active routing protocols for IP?

- ○ a. **show ip route**
- ○ b. **show ip protocols**
- ○ c. **show ip routing protocols**
- ○ d. **show protocols**

Question 63

Which summarized address best covers the networks 10.10.4.0 through 10.10.7.0?

○ a. 10.10.4.0/24

○ b. 10.10.4.0/22

○ c. 10.10.7.0/22

○ d. 10.10.0.0/16

Question 64

What is the process of configuring dissimilar routing protocols to share information?

○ a. Summarization

○ b. ISDN

○ c. Adjacency

○ d. Redistribution

Question 65

Where should an IP helper address be placed?

○ a. On the outbound interface of the broadcasting router

○ b. On the inbound interface of the broadcasting router

○ c. On the outbound interface of the router that receives the broadcast request

○ d. On the inbound interface of the router that receives the broadcast request

Question 66

Place the term next to the appropriate description.

Term	Description
	Used by link-state to exchange information about neighbors and path costs.
	Multicast packet that is used by certain routing protocols for neighbor discovery and recovery.
	OSPF router that generates LSAs for multiaccess networks and has other responsibilities in the OSPF process.
	Logical collection of network segments and their attached devices.

Designated Router (DR)

Link-State Advertisement (LSA)

Hello Packet

Area

Question 67

Based on the following diagram, what is the most correct summarization address for router A?

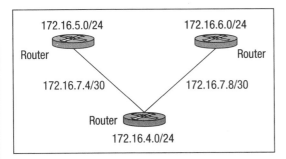

172.16.5.0/24   172.16.6.0/24

Router   Router

172.16.7.4/30   172.16.7.8/30

Router

172.16.4.0/24

○ a. 172.16.0.0/16

○ b. 172.16.0.0/24

○ c. 172.16.8.0/22

○ d. 172.16.4.0/22

Question 68

Place the hierarchical design terms in the appropriate places in the following diagram. Not all labels will be used.

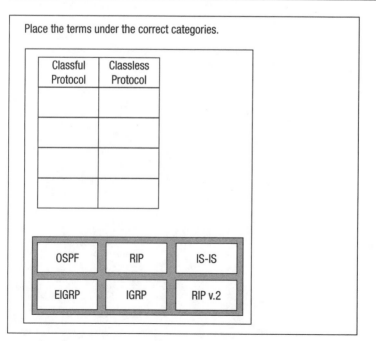

Core layer

Access layer

Backbone layer

Distribution layer

Question 69

Place the terms under the correct categories.

Classful Protocol	Classless Protocol

OSPF   RIP   IS-IS

EIGRP   IGRP   RIP v.2

Answer Key

For asterisked items, please see textual representation of answer on the appropriate page of this chapter.

1. b	19. c	36. b, d	53. a
2. a	20. b, d	37. c	54. d
3. c	21. d	38. c	55. c
4. a	22. d	39. c	56. a, c
5. a	23. a, b, d	40. d	57. b
6. b	24. b	41. b, c, d	58. d
7. c	25. c	42. c	59. a
8. b, e	26. d	43. b	60. d
9. b	27. d	44. b	61. a
10. d	28. b, d	45. b	62. b
11. a, d	29. a	46. c	63. b
12. c	30. b	47. b	64. d
13. b	31. b, d	48. a	65. d
14. b, c	32. c	49. b	66. *
15. a, b	33. b	50. a, c, d	67. d
16. a	34. a	51. b	68. *
17. a, b, c	35. c	52. a	69. *
18. b			

Question 1

Answer b is correct. RIP does not support VLSM, route summarization, or classless routing in any way. It cannot include the prefix in routing updates.

Question 2

Answer a is correct. OSPF, unlike RIP, can pass the prefix in routing update information.

Question 3

Answer c is correct. Longest match is based on the number of bits of a destination address that correspond to entries in the routing table. The entry that matches the most contiguous bits should be the proper entry on which to base a forwarding decision. Answer a is incorrect because classless routing is what allows you to perform route summarization and VLSM. It does not describe the method the router uses to make a forwarding decision. VLSM is basically a type of classless routing implementation. Therefore, answer b is incorrect. Answer d is incorrect because a correct answer is given.

Question 4

Answer a is correct. To get an idea of how you might use a border between dissimilar networks, consider the OSPF implementation of separate area hierarchies as a great example of where to summarize. If you summarize at the area borders, you need only a single route to provide reachability to all networks outside the local area. Refer to Chapters 6 and 7 for more information on OSPF. Answer b is incorrect because summarization is not performed on all routers; it would be ineffective to do so. Summarization makes a difference only between dissimilar networks. If you summarize on every router, the routers in similar address space could misdirect traffic flow and create routing inconsistencies or routing loops. Answer c is incorrect because in order for summarization to work, it must be properly configured at the proper points. Answer d is incorrect because point-to-point serial links are a transport mechanism, not a summarization scheme.

Question 5

Answer a is correct. NAT is used specifically to allow access to the public Internet without an administrator having to readdress the existing network. Subnet masking is the process of dividing up the address space you have internally. Therefore, answer b is incorrect. Address summarization—otherwise known as *route summarization*—is the process of reducing the routing table by aggregating addresses based on a common bit boundary. Therefore, answer c is incorrect. CIDR allows you to conserve address space by giving you as close as possible the number of addresses you need, rather than wasting addresses needlessly. Therefore, answer d is incorrect.

Question 6

Answer b is correct. **show ip interfaces** gives you the information of all IP-configured interfaces currently active on the router. Answers a, c, and d are incorrect because they are not valid commands.

Question 7

Answer c is correct. BGP uses a connection-oriented protocol (TCP) to ensure that routing updates are delivered. Answer a is incorrect because FTP is a file transport protocol and cannot be used for routing updates. Answer b is incorrect because UDP is a connectionless protocol. Answer d is incorrect because LSAs are used in OSPF, not BGP.

Question 8

Answers b and e are correct. EIGRP does support VLSM in environments where it is necessary. In addition, when there is a change in the network, an update is sent to the directly connected neighbors because they will also be affected by the change in reachability. Answer a is incorrect because EIGRP does not support a hierarchical area structure such as OSPF. Answer c is incorrect because a basic EIGRP configuration is much simpler in nature than that of OSPF. EIGRP does not require the use of a wildcard mask to specify network statements. Therefore, answer d is incorrect. EIGRP can route multiple layer 3 protocols, but it keeps separate neighbor, topology, and routing tables for each protocol.

Question 9

Answer b is correct. Passive interfaces tell RIP and other routing protocols not to send updates out of the specified interface(s). Answer a is incorrect because default routes are placed in the routing table by an administrator or by a redistribution of routing information. They do not stop RIP updates. Answer c is incorrect because static routes are placed in the routing table by an administrator and will be advertised only in certain circumstances. Answer d is incorrect because routing update filters require the use of access lists to function.

Question 10

Answer d is correct. By specifying the protocol (BGP) and the address of the network that you want to reset, you will clear only that route. Answer a is incorrect because it is an invalid command. Answer b is incorrect because it would reset the entire routing table. Answer c is incorrect because it is an invalid command.

Question 11

Answers a and d are correct. RIP has a 15-hop reachability limitation. This is one of the reasons for the creation of OSPF in the beginning. RIP uses hop count as a metric, whereas OSPF's route calculation takes into account the bandwidth of the pathway to the destination. OSPF is a more intelligent routing protocol than RIP. Answer b is incorrect because RIP's configuration is actually much less complex than OSPF's configuration. Answer c is incorrect because OSPF actually builds more tables than RIP. OSPF builds a topology database, an SPF tree, and a routing table. It also must build a table to track neighbor and adjacency relationships.

Question 12

Answer c is correct. A natural class C address is automatically summarized to 24 bits. However, when you take away four bits from the natural network portion, you have to make a calculation of 2^4, which is 16. No other answer mathematically works out properly when you're looking at 20 bits with a class C address.

Question 13

Answer b is correct. Peer groups are groups of BGP neighbors that can be configured to have the same update policies. Answer a is incorrect because neighbors are routers that have established an adjacency; this does not mean that they have the same update policies. Answer c is incorrect because an area is a logical grouping of routers that breaks up the number of devices affected by routing changes and is associated with OSPF. Answer d is incorrect because a network statement would only associate a network under a routing protocol that it is to be routed through.

Question 14

Answers b and c are correct. Connecting to multiple ISPs requires you to manipulate local preference or the multiexit discriminator attributes in order to choose the preferred route out of your AS. It is not desirable for your traffic to leave your

AS via one ISP and return via the other. In order for you to implement security in your network, you'll need to be in charge of what information comes into and goes out of your network. Should you want to filter networks at the ISP connection, you'll need to do so with the protocol that allows the two ASes to communicate—BGP. Answer a is incorrect because IGP, not BGP, should make your internal AS routing decisions. Answer d is incorrect because the method by which your ISP connects to the tier above it is irrelevant to your connection to that ISP.

Question 15

Answers a and b are correct. The reasons for creating areas are to cut down on the number of route calculations that must be made as well as to cut down on the impact of routing updates. If the area gets too big, changes in the network can have a profound effect on the router's ability to keep up with the changes. By cutting down the amount of LSA traffic, you'll reduce the frequency of routing table recalculations. Answer c is incorrect because the routing table gets recalculated, not necessarily the adjacencies. Without the adjacency relationship, there is no other router to which to send LSA traffic. Answer d is incorrect because reachability is the reason for the LSA traffic. If the traffic is being received and alternative routes are available, reachability should not be affected to a great degree.

Question 16

Answer a is correct. For load balancing to occur with BGP, it has to receive identical routing updates from the same service provider. Answers b, c, and d are all incorrect because they all mention connecting to multiple service providers, which cannot occur for load balancing to work.

Question 17

Answers a, b, and c are correct. IP extended access lists can filter based on the session layer protocols TCP or UDP. They can filter based on source and destination IP address as well as an application port number. Answer d is incorrect because IP standard access lists can filter only on a source address.

Question 18

Answer b is correct. Nonroutable (also called *layer 2*) protocols do not contain network layer information that is associated with IP/IPX/AppleTalk. In other words, there is no *network.node* relationship in a layer 2 protocol. Answer a is incorrect because the layer 2 framing does have an FCS. Answer c is incorrect because some nonroutable protocols use explorer frames to find routes rather than using broadcasts. Answer d is incorrect because many times you may have no other choice but to send these protocols across a WAN link.

Question 19

Answer c is correct. Using a null interface has a similar effect to using access lists without the additional CPU overhead associated with access lists. The router simply makes a routing decision and routes packets destined for the specified network into a nonexistent logical interface. No error message is generated because the use of the null interface is a valid routing decision. Answer a is incorrect because an access list actually provides more functionality than a null interface. Answer b is incorrect because the use of hostnames has nothing to do with actual network routing decisions. In any event, a hostname must be resolved to an IP address, so you'd have to use both the hostname and the IP address. Answer d is incorrect because using a null interface is a routing decision. Nonroutable protocols are not supported in these layer 3 decisions.

Question 20

Answers b and d are correct. RFC 1918 defines the private internetwork address space. The class A range is 10.0.0.0 through 10.255.255.255. The class B range is 172.16.0.0 through 172.31.255.255. The class C range is 192.168.0.0 through 192.168.255.255. Answers a and c do not fall within any of these ranges and are therefore incorrect.

Question 21

Answer d is correct. This is the default mode for a tunnel interface. Therefore, you should not have to type it. However, it might be worth the time involved in learning the command. Answers a, b, and c are all incorrect because they are invalid commands.

Question 22

Answer d is correct. EIGRP provides routing support for IP, IPX, and AppleTalk. Answer a is incorrect because EIGRP does not keep a copy of its neighbors' routing tables. It does keep track of the destinations the neighbors know about, but not their actual routing tables. Answer b is incorrect because EIGRP does not use broadcasts to forward routing updates. Answer c is incorrect because there is no master router relationship in EIGRP.

Question 23

Answers a, b, and d are correct. OSPF does not have the limitation of 15 hops as does RIP. It uses a cost based on bandwidth to select the best routes, and all routing updates go out as multicast traffic, not broadcast traffic. Answer c is incorrect because OSPF updates go out on an as-needed basis and then only the changes are sent, not the full routing table. Answer e is incorrect because OSPF is an IP-only routing protocol.

Question 24

Answer b is correct. It suggests that you only use BGP when connecting to a service provider that has differing routing policies than your own. Answers a, c, and d are incorrect because these are issues that should not affect the decision of whether to use BGP.

Question 25

Answer c is correct. This summary address that was used represented a subnet mask of 255.255.252.0. This means that there are four subnets within that range. Answer a is incorrect because that is the entire class A range. Answer b is incorrect because that is the range for an entire class B range of address space. Answer d is incorrect because it is not a valid range of address space.

Question 26

Answer d is correct. The private range of AS numbers is 64512 to 65535. Answers a, b, and c are incorrect because they are invalid number ranges.

Question 27

Answer d is correct. The community attribute is not restricted by any boundary or physical restrictions. Answers a, b, and c are incorrect because they are not valid boundaries.

Question 28

Answers b and d are correct. OSPF is a more intelligent routing protocol than RIP. It does not suffer from the 15-hop limitation, as does RIP. In addition, it supports VLSM. Answer a is incorrect because the trade-off to having additional functionality is more resource utilization in the router. Answer c is incorrect because the OSPF configuration parameters tend to be somewhat complex, whereas RIP configuration is very simple.

Question 29

Answer a is correct. By using route maps with BGP, you can manipulate and filter traffic to meet your needs. Answer b is incorrect because route reflectors are a central point for multiple BGP routers to peer with. Answer c is incorrect because passive interfaces restrict routing updates from exiting through a specific interface. Answer d is incorrect because redistribution will allow one routing protocol to be injected into another routing protocol.

Question 30

Answer b is correct. The **show ip ospf neighbor** command will display all OSPF neighbors that a router is established with. You'll be able to monitor neighbor relationships for the OSPF process using this command. Answers a, c, and d are incorrect because they are all invalid commands.

Question 31

Answers b and d are correct. **ip helper-address** enables the forwarding of specific broadcast traffic via unicast, multicast, or (in the case of answers b and d) directed broadcast. Answer a is incorrect because this is not a backup scenario. Answer c is incorrect because the use of **ip helper-address** is not a bridging technique. It simply enables the forwarding of selected broadcasts, not all layer 2 protocols.

Question 32

Answer c is correct. OSPF configuration requires the process to be initialized on the router by using the **router ospf <process id>** command. The **id** is a locally significant number that sets one OSPF process apart from other OSPF processes that may be running on this particular router. Answers a and b do not specify the appropriate information. Therefore, they are incorrect. Answer d is incorrect because a correct answer is given.

Question 33

Answer b is correct. By implementing route filtering, you are able to manipulate traffic to meet your policy needs. Answer a is incorrect because static routes can only specify a limited control of network traffic. Answer c is incorrect because default routes are used to route traffic that does not have a more specific route in the routing table. Answer d is incorrect because dynamic routes are routes that are learned through a routing protocol.

Question 34

Answer a is correct. This command will display only the EIGRP routes within the routing table. Answers b, c, and d are incorrect because they are invalid commands.

Question 35

Answer c is correct. Route summarization is the method by which a single address can be used in the routing table to represent any number of addresses. Answer a is incorrect because default routes serve only as gateways of last resort for traffic that cannot be adequately associated with any destination network in the routing table. Answer b is incorrect because static routes do not provide summarization. You can use static routes to override what the dynamic routing protocol has chosen for a pathway. Answer d is incorrect because route expansion is not a valid internetworking term.

Question 36

Answers b and d are correct. The commands are specifying that the EIGRP process should be a part of AS 100. They also state that any interface that includes an address of 12.X.X.X or 13.X.X.X should be included in the EIGRP routing process. Answer a is incorrect because 100 is a perfectly valid AS number for your internal private routing domain. Answer c is incorrect because EIGRP configurations do not require or make use of a netmask.

Question 37

Answer c is correct. This is the correct command to display the information associated with access list 190. Answers a, b, and d are incorrect because they are invalid commands.

Question 38

Answer c is correct. BGP has some of the characteristics of both link-state and distance-vector routing protocols, but by using AS path information it is deemed a path-vector routing protocol. Answers a and b are incorrect because even though

BGP has some of the features of each, it is not categorized as either. Answer d is incorrect because answer c is correct.

Question 39

Answer c is correct. Cisco refers to default routes as *gateways of last resort*. Answers a and b are incorrect because these items are only known by their names. Answer d is incorrect because this is not a valid category.

Question 40

Answer d is correct. Interior Gateway Protocols (IGPs) include any routing protocol that is used to route internal networks. This includes RIP, RIPv2, IGRP, EIGRP, OSPF, IS-IS, and many others. Answers a, b, and c are incorrect because answer d was more correct.

Question 41

Answers b, c, and d are correct. EIGRP routers keep a topology table, a neighbor table, and a routing table for IP, IPX, and AppleTalk. Each of these tables is a separate entity. Answer a is incorrect because the router does not keep a protocol table.

Question 42

Answer c is correct. OSPF virtual links are required when a non-area 0 must connect to the network via another non-area 0. Virtual links should be avoided. Answer a is incorrect because, although route summarization takes place at area borders, it is not the connection between the two. Answer b is incorrect because static routes exist in various places throughout an area but do not connect areas. Answer d is incorrect because a designated router is an OSPF router with a high priority and/or a high-router ID on a broadcast multiaccess network such as Ethernet.

Question 43

Answer b is correct. This command will show all IP EIGRP neighbors and their associated information. Answers a, c, and d are incorrect because they are invalid commands.

Question 44

Answer b is correct. The current successor is the route with the lowest feasible distance. Answer a is incorrect because the feasible successor is the second-best route. Answer c is incorrect because adjacency refers to the forming of a neighbor relationship. Answer d is incorrect because DUAL refers to the algorithm that EIGRP uses for route selection.

Question 45

Answer b is correct. The **no auto-summary** command is the correct answer when typed under the router eigrp configuration mode. This will disable EIGRP summarization at the classful boundary. Answers a, c, and d are incorrect because they are invalid commands.

Question 46

Answer c is correct. The AS path attribute begins with the AS that originated the route. The AS path will then add its own AS number and then each AS that the route travels will add its AS number to the beginning of the path list. Answer a is incorrect because this is a final list that represents all the autonomous systems that a route has traveled, with the originating AS at the end of the list. This is the product of the AS path attribute. Answers b and d are incorrect because they are invalid BGP attributes.

Question 47

Answer b is correct. This command will display the status of all BGP neighbor connections. Answers a, c, and d are all incorrect because they are invalid commands.

Question 48

Answer a is correct. By issuing this command, a router will redistribute the protocol in question into another routing protocol. Answers b, c, and d are incorrect because they are invalid commands.

Question 49

Answer b is correct. The summarized address of 172.15.168.0/21 is also represented as 172.15.168.0 255.255.248.0, which dictates that there are eight networks available for use. Thus, 172.15.168.0 through 172.15.175.0 would be the correct number of networks represented by the summarized address. Answer a is incorrect because this range of addresses is represented by /23 or 255.255.254.0. Answer c is incorrect because this range is represented by a /22 or 255.255.252.0. Answer d is incorrect because it is an invalid range and would have to be represented by more than one summarized address.

Question 50

Answers a, c, and d are correct. OSPF routers must keep track of neighbors as they come up on and drop off of the network. This is done through a Hello protocol. The Hello protocol keeps track of a dead interval. The *dead interval* is how long a router will wait before purging the neighbor entry once it has ceased responding to and sending Hello packets. The router priority is used in the election of a designated router. It is important to know what the DR for a particular network segment happens to be at any point in time. Answer b is incorrect because the neighbor relationship must be maintained in order to pass routing updates so the routing table can be built. Although it is important to maintain the routing table, it is not necessary to the formation and/or maintenance of the neighbor relationship.

Question 51

Answer b is correct. Issuing the **passive-interface ethernet 3** command will stop the updates from leaving the router via the Ethernet 3 interface. Answers a, c, and d are all incorrect because they are invalid commands.

Question 52

Answer a is correct. The command **ip route 0.0.0.0 0.0.0.0 serial 0** will set the default route and assume it to be directly connected to Serial 0. Answers b, c, and d are incorrect because they are invalid commands.

Question 53

Answer a is correct. Standard access lists are used to define permitted or denied networks for distribute lists.

Question 54

Answer d is correct. A route reflector will allow multiple BGP neighbors to peer with a central focal point; this central router will then peer with other route reflectors so that all BGP routers will be seen as peers. Answer a is incorrect because a BGP confederation is a function in which you can create multiple subautonomous systems from a single AS. Answers b and c are incorrect because they are invalid functions of BGP.

Question 55

Answer c is correct. EIGRP used to be known as a "hybrid" routing protocol because it used some of the functionality of both link-state and distance-vector routing protocols. Cisco has changed this terminology recently to reflect the fact that EIGRP is more closely related to distance-vector protocols than link-state protocols, so it adopted the name *advanced distance vector*. Answer a is incorrect because link-state routing protocols use the Dijsktra algorithm for route determination, whereas EIGRP uses the Diffused Update Algorithm (DUAL). Answer b is incorrect because distance-vector routing protocols use the Bellman-Ford algorithm for route determination. Answer d is incorrect because path vector is associated with BGP because of its path attributes.

Question 56

Answers a and c are correct. Bandwidth and delay are the two default metrics EIGRP uses for route determination. If there are multiple routes with the same metric, the other metrics are measured to break the tie. Answers b and d are incorrect because they are not the default metrics used for route determination. They are, however, used for route selection in the event of a tie between multiple routes.

Question 57

Answer b is correct. You cannot configure a stub router into an area that has an ASBR, due to the fact that the stub router will not accept any Type 5 LSAs. You would have to configure the entire area as a stub area to block these LSAs, which the ASBR will not allow because it is redistributing all those redistributed routes since, which are treated as Type 5 LSAs.

Question 58

Answer d is correct. A totally stubby area is an area that only received intra-area and default routes. If it has to route to a network that is not in its area, it will forward the traffic to its default route. Answer a is incorrect because a backbone area is required to process all types of traffic. This allows for traffic to flow from multiple areas freely across the backbone area. Answer b is incorrect because a stubby area will receive intra-area, interarea, and default routes. A stubby area will not directly receive external routes from a separate routing protocol or any redistributed routes. Answer c is incorrect because a standard area will receive all types of LSA traffic; therefore, it will know about all routes in OSPF.

Question 59

Answer a is correct. A confederation is a function of BGP that allows you to create multiple subautonomous systems from a single AS. Answer b is incorrect because a route reflector is a central focal point that allows multiple BGP routers to peer with one single router. This route reflector will then peer with other route reflectors so that all BGP neighbors will become peers. Answer c and d are incorrect because they are invalid functions of BGP.

Question 60

Answer d is correct. Core routers exist at the top of your routing hierarchy. They are also known as *backbone routers*. Answer a is incorrect because distribution routers exist just below the core routers in the hierarchy. Answer b is incorrect because access routers exist below distribution routers in the network. Answer c is incorrect because primary is not a term to denote placement in the routing hierarchy.

Question 61

Answer a is correct. OSPF keeps a table of its neighbors, and at times you need to view their status. Answer a is the only one that shows the proper use of the command. Answer b is incorrect because it does not specify what neighbors to show. It is not a valid command. Answer c is incorrect because the Cisco Discovery Protocol (CDP) neighbor commands are used to view any directly connected routers whether OSPF neighbor relations have been established or not. Answer d is incorrect because it shows the routing table, not neighbors.

Question 62

Answer b is correct. The **show ip protocols** command will display the status of all currently active IP routing protocols. Answer a is incorrect because **show ip route** will display the contents of the router's routing table. Answers c and d are incorrect because they are invalid commands.

Question 63

Answer b is correct. This summarized network represents the network range of 10.10.4.0 thru 10.10.7.255, since the subnetmask of /22 or 255.255.252.0 allocates four subnets in that range. Answer a is incorrect because the /24 subnet mask will only allow for the subnet 10.10.4.0. Answer c is incorrect because this address range would contain the networks 10.10.7.0 thru 10.10.10.255. Answer d is incorrect because it represents the address range of 10.10.0.0 thru 10.10.255.255. Even though this covers the range that was specified it is not the "best" way to achieve the goal.

Question 64

Answer d is correct. Route redistribution is the configuration of routers to share information learned via routing protocol processes. Answer a is incorrect because summarization is the process of aggregating routes in order to reduce the number of routing table entries. Answer b is incorrect because ISDN is simply a high-tech phone call. Answer c is incorrect because adjacency refers to the establishment of a relationship between two routers running a common routing protocol.

Question 65

Answer d is correct. An IP helper address forwards selected broadcasts that it receives to a unicast address specified in the command. The IP helper address should be placed on the inbound interface of the router that receives the broadcast. Answers a, b, and c are incorrect because they do not illustrate the proper placement of the IP helper address. Placing the address anywhere other than as described in answer d is ineffective.

Question 66

Term	Description
Link-State Advertisement (LSA)	Used by link-state to exchange information about neighbors and path costs.
Hello Packet	Multicast packet that is used by certain routing protocols for neighbor discovery and recovery.
Designated Router (DR)	OSPF router that generates LSAs for multiaccess networks and has other responsibilities in the OSPF process.
Area	Logical collection of network segments and their attached devices.

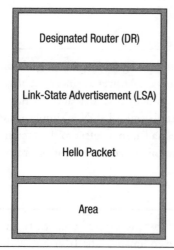

Designated Router (DR)

Link-State Advertisement (LSA)

Hello Packet

Area

Question 67

Answer d is correct. The route 172.16.4.0/22 will encompass networks 172.16.4.0 through 172.16.7.0. Answer a is incorrect because it would encompass the range of 172.16.0.0 through 172.16.255.0, which would work but wouldn't be the best solution in this instance. Answer b is incorrect because it only counts the range of 172.16.0.0. Answer c is incorrect because this statement would encompass the range of 172.16.8.0 through 172.16.11.0

Question 68

Backbone layer is not used because it is not a hierarchical design term.

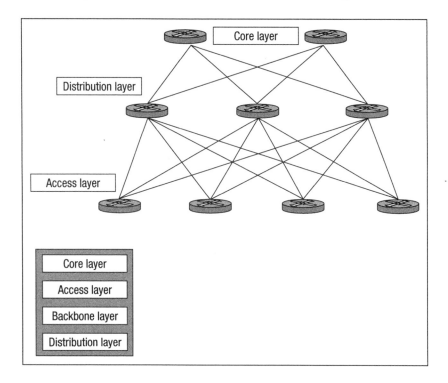

Question 69

Classful Protocol	Classless Protocol
RIP	OSPF
IGRP	EIGRP
	IS-IS
	RIP v.2

RIP and IGRP are classful routing protocols because they do not pass prefix information in routing updates. Thus, these protocols route based on the class of the address. OSPF, EIGRP, IS-IS, and RIP v.2 are classless routing protocols because they are not limited to route based on the class of the address. As classless routing protocols, they are capable of passing prefix information in the routing updates, which allows them to support VLSM.

Glossary

. . . .

ABR (Area Border Router)
In OSPF, this is any router that has interfaces configured to be a part of multiple areas.

access-class
A method of restricting Telnet access to and from a router using access lists.

access-group
When an access list is created, it must be associated with a physical interface. **access-group** is the association of the access list to the interface.

access-list
A method of permitting and/or denying traffic based on predefined criteria for a particular protocol.

access router
Any router that exists at the lowest levels of a network hierarchy.

ACK (Acknowledgment)
A response returned to a traffic source to inform that source that the transmitted data has been received.

adjacency
In a link-state or hybrid routing protocol, this is a relationship that is formed to facilitate the passing of routing updates.

administrative distance
A number between 0 and 255 that specifies the believability of a route derived by one routing protocol versus a route to the same destination derived by another routing protocol. Administrative distance is based on the routing protocol's selection criteria (such as the metric) or manual administrator manipulation.

advanced distance-vector routing protocol
A routing protocol that employs the characteristics of both distance-vector and link-state protocols to attempt to exploit the positive aspects of each.

advertised distance
In EIGRP, this is the metric advertised by a directly connected neighbor for a specific destination network.

AppleTalk

A network-layer protocol developed by Apple Computer to facilitate communication between Macintosh desktop computers.

application layer

The top layer of the OSI model. It only generates data for transmission across a network.

area

In OSPF, this is a logical grouping of routers that breaks up the number of devices affected by routing changes, thereby reducing convergence time.

area border router

See ABR (area border router).

area id

Refers to the OSPF area that is to be associated with the OSPF address range.

ARIN (American Registry for Internet Numbers)

ARIN is a nonprofit organization established for the purpose of administration and registration of Internet Protocol (IP) numbers.

ARP (Address Resolution Protocol)

A protocol used in the association of a network-layer address (layer 3) to a data link-layer address (layer 2 or MAC address) to facilitate transmission of information across various media types.

AS (autonomous system)

The collective name for the grouping of all routers under a single administration.

ASBR (autonomous system boundary router)

In OSPF, this is a router that is a part of the area hierarchy but that also has a connection to an external AS, such as an ISP.

ATM (Asynchronous Transfer Mode)

A high-speed switching technology based on the transmission of a fixed-size cell rather than variable-sized frames.

attributes

A set of parameters that describes the characteristics of a route.

AURP (AppleTalk Update-Based Routing Protocol)

This is a method for encapsulating AppleTalk traffic in the header of a foreign protocol, which allows the connection of two or more noncontiguous AppleTalk networks. This forms an AppleTalk WAN structure and maintains the routing tables for the entire AppleTalk WAN by exchanging routing information with exterior routers.

backbone area

Part of an OSPF network that acts as the primary path for traffic that is destined for other areas throughout the network. This area is designated as Area 0.

backbone router

In OSPF, this is any router that is connected to Area 0.

bandwidth

The total amount of throughput available on a given interface.

BDR (backup designated router)

In OSPF, when multiple routers are connected to broadcast media segments (such as an Ethernet), specific routers are elected as representatives (one primary and one backup) of the network to receive and transmit routing updates on that segment. The election is based on priority and/or router ID. The BDR is the backup router on that segment.

Bellman-Ford algorithm

The process by which distance-vector routing protocols exchange updates on a periodic timer. This process is generally characterized by low memory utilization and slow convergence time. It is also known as *routing by rumor*.

BGP (Border Gateway Protocol)

A dynamic routing protocol used to connect external ASes and to implement routing policy throughout the network. BGP can be implemented internally or externally.

bit

Binary digit used in the binary numbering system. This number is represented as either a 1 or 0.

BOOTP (Boot Protocol)

A protocol used in resolving an IP address based on a layer 2 MAC address.

bottleneck

Any point in an internetwork where the amount of data being received exceeds the data-carrying capacity of the link. (See also *congestion*.)

BPDU (Bridge Protocol Data Unit)

A Spanning Tree Protocol update entity used in path determination between bridges.

bridge

A device used to break up a collision domain and make forwarding decisions between the segments based on a MAC address.

broadcast

A transmission sent to all nodes on a particular media segment.

byte

Used to refer to a series of consecutive binary digits (bits) that are operated on as a unit, such as an eight-bit byte.

CERT

A major reporting center for Internet security problems. CERT provides technical assistance and coordinates responses to security compromises, identifies trends in intruder activity, works with other security experts to identify solutions to security problems, and disseminates information to the Internet community. It also analyzes product vulnerabilities, publishes technical documents, and presents training courses. CERT was formerly known as the *Computer Emergency Response Team*.

CHAP (Challenge Handshake Authentication Protocol)

An encrypted user-verification algorithm that uses a mathematical riddle based on the predefined username and password of the calling device. The actual password is not passed over the wire.

CIDR (classless interdomain routing)

An effective method to curb the allocation of IP address space, thus reducing the routing tables on the Internet. CIDR is documented in RFCs 1517, 1518, 1519, and 1520.

class A address

Any IP address with a first octet value between 1 and 126.

class B address

Any IP address with a first octet value between 128 and 191.

class C address

Any IP address with a first octet value between 192 and 223.

class D address

Any IP address with a first octet value between 224 and 239. This class of address is used for multicast operations.

class E address

Any IP address with a first octet value between 240 and 247. This class of address is used for research purposes only and is not currently deployed in existing internetworks.

classful routing

Routing based on information derived from the natural boundaries of the different classes of IP ad-dresses. Routing table information for networks that are not directly connected is kept only based on that natural network because the subnet masks of the remote networks are not contained in the routing update.

classless routing

Routing based on information derived from routing updates that include subnet mask information (such as prefix information). Routing table information shows all known networks and their accompanying prefix information.

confederation

A BGP confederation is based on the concept that an AS can be broken into multiple sub-ASes.

congestion

A condition that arises when the data being passed across a circuit exceeds the data-carrying capacity of that circuit.

console

A physical port used in the configura-tion of a router. The console is the default source for configuration information.

convergence

The exchanging of routing updates by routers that participate in dynamic routing protocol activities to form a consistent perspective of the network. When all routers know of all possible destinations in the network, the network has converged.

core router

Any router attached to the highest level of network hierarchy, usually the core backbone of the network.

cost

In OSPF, this is the metric used for route calculation. This calculation is based on the bandwidth of the link in question.

CPU (central processing unit)

The core decision-making device in a router.

CRC (cyclic redundancy check)
A calculation performed on an inbound frame to verify its validity.

CSMA/CD (Carrier Sense Multi-Access/Collision Detection)
The nature of a network to be based on contention for the use of resources on a physical media segment. An example of this is Ethernet technology.

current successor
In EIGRP, this is the existing best route to a particular destination network.

custom queuing
A Cisco proprietary strategy for prioritizing traffic output from a router interface, usually a low-speed serial interface.

data link layer
The layer in the OSI model at which hardware signals and software functions are converted. This is also known as *layer 2* of the OSI model. This layer is logically subdivided into two parts: the MAC sublayer and the logical link control (LLC) sublayer. The MAC portion is where the burned-in hardware address is stored. The LLC discriminates between protocols to ensure proper passage of various network-layer protocol traffic types.

DDR (dial-on-demand routing)
This is a technique where a router can automatically initiate and close a circuit-switched session based on interesting traffic on the network.

dead interval
This mechanism is used in OSPF to determine topology changes. If a router fails to receive an OSPF Hello packet from its neighbor within this timeframe, the neighbor is assumed down. This mechanism is configurable using the interface command **ip ospf dead-interval** *time* command. The dead interval has a default setting of forty seconds.

debug
Any of the many commands used in diagnosing router problems, or simply watching router operation processes.

DECnet
A group of communications equipment developed by the Digital Equipment Corporation. The most recent iteration is called *DECnet Phase V* or *DECnet/OSI* and supports both OSI protocols and proprietary Digital protocols.

dedicated circuit
A data circuit, generally point to point, that is available at all times between two routers.

default route
A route that signifies a gateway of last resort for traffic destined for remote networks for which a router does not have specific reachability information.

delay
A calculation based on the bandwidth of a link to determine the amount of time it takes to transmit data from across that link. This value is an amount of time expressed in milliseconds.

destination protocol address
The layer 3 address of the intended recipient of a specific packet.

DHCP (Dynamic Host Configuration Protocol)

A Microsoft Corporation implementation of the BootP protocol used for dynamic assignment of IP addresses on the network.

digital

In networking technologies, this is a string of electrical signals that take on the characteristics of one of two discrete binary states.

directed broadcast

A layer 3 term for a data transmission destined to all hosts in a specific subnet.

distance-vector routing protocol

Any dynamic routing protocol that uses the Bellman-Ford algorithm for routing update exchange that employs the use of metric addition to derive a measurement of a route to a particular destination network. Commonly referred to as *routing by rumor*.

distribute list

A configuration option that allows for the filtering of reachability information (such as routing information) using **access-list** commands to permit and/or deny routes.

distribution router

Any router in your internetwork hierarchy that connects lower-level access routers to the higher-level core routers.

Diyjkstra's algorithm

The process that many link-state routing protocols employ to keep reachability information in a current state. Generally characterized by high memory usage and very fast convergence time.

DNS (Domain Name Service)

A service that runs on an IP-capable server that resolves IP addresses to private or registered names.

DR (Designated Router)

In OSPF, this is the primary router elected to receive and send link-state updates to all routers that share a broadcast media segment. This election is based on the router priority and then router ID as a tiebreaker.

DUAL (Diffusing Update Algorithm)

The algorithm for routing update exchange and maintenance that EIGRP employs.

dynamic routes

Routes that adjust automatically to network topology or traffic changes.

EBGP (External Border Gateway Protocol)

A BGP implementation that connects external ASes.

EGP (Exterior Gateway Protocol)

A dynamic routing protocol that connects two external ASes.

EIGRP (Enhanced Interior Gateway Routing Protocol)

A Cisco proprietary dynamic routing protocol that attempts to combine the positive traits of distance-vector and link-state protocols. EIGRP is sometimes referred to as a *hybrid routing protocol* or an *advanced distance-vector routing protocol.*

Ethernet

A framing convention used in CSMA/CD networks.

ExChange state

This state occurs when master and slave routers exchange one or more database description packets.

ExStart state

This is the state that is achieved after the DR and BDR have been elected.

extended access list

Any access list that is meant to employ more than basic functionality of traffic filtering. In IP, an extended access list can filter on source address, destination address, protocol, and port.

external route

In OSPF, this is a route received from any source outside of the local area.

FCS (Frame Check Sequence)

A function performed on inbound frames to determine whether they are valid entities and are worthy of further processing.

FDDI (Fiber Distributed Data Interface)

A dual-ring, token-passing technology that employs the use of fiber-optic cable.

feasible distance

In EIGRP, this is the metric associated with each piece of routing information entered into the routing table.

feasible successor

In EIGRP, this is the second best route to a particular destination network. The feasible successor is selected only if the advertised distance of the second-best route is lower than the feasible distance of the best route.

FIFO (first in, first out)

A queuing strategy that dispatches traffic in the order in which it was received. In other words, FIFO is the absence of queuing.

flash memory

Physical storage space in a router in which the router's operating system is stored.

frame

Any entity generated at the data link layer.

Frame Relay

A serial technology that employs the use of frame switching, usually through a telco provider's switching facility.

FTP (File Transfer Protocol)

A TCP-based file upload/download protocol that allows for security and authentication procedures.

full state

After the LSRs have been satisfied for a given router, the adjacent routers are considered synchronized, or in a full state.

giant

An Ethernet frame in excess of the maximum transmittable unit size of 1,518 bytes.

gigabit

One billion bits.

HDLC (High-Level Data Link Control)

A Cisco proprietary serial framing convention that allows for the use of multiple protocols across a serial link. This is the default encapsulation for serial interfaces on Cisco routers.

Hello protocol
A means of communication between two hosts on a network that require constant and continued connectivity to each other. The two devices exchange these hello messages at a specified interval.

helper address
An address used to forward selected broadcasts by converting them to unicasts or directed broadcasts.

holdtime
A general term that refers to how long a device waits before purging an entry in a routing table, neighbor table, topology table, and so on. Once the holdtime expires, the entry, whatever the type, is purged.

hop
The crossing of a router in an internetwork.

host
A specific end station that exists on a subnet.

hub
A nonintelligent physical-layer device used in connecting Ethernet clients.

hybrid routing protocol
See *advanced distance–vector routing protocol*.

IBGP (Internal Border Gateway Protocol)
An implementation of BGP between routers inside the same AS.

ICMP (Internet Control Message Protocol)
An IP status protocol that returns status, error, and message notifications to a specified host. Ping is an example of ICMP implementation.

IEEE (Institute of Electronic and Electrical Engineers)
A standards body comprised of electronic and electrical engineers charged with creating physical and data link layer standards.

IGP (Interior Gateway Protocol)
Any routing protocol employed within an AS.

IGRP (Interior Gateway Routing Protocol)
A Cisco proprietary routing protocol that functions on a 90-second update timer.

inter-area route
In OSPF, this is any route to a destination outside of the local area.

internal router
In OSPF, this is any router in which all interfaces configured for OSPF operation are in the same area.

Internet
A public IP-based internetwork that facilitates communications on a global scale.

intra-area route
In OSPF, this is a route to a destination network within the local area.

IOS (Internetwork Operating System)
Cisco's router operating system software that provides the intelligence and functionality of Cisco routers.

IP (Internet Protocol)

A layer 3 protocol based on a 32-bit address, some portion of which is known as *network* and the remainder of which is known as *host*.

IP address

A 32-bit address consisting of network and host portions that is used in data communications.

IPX (Internetwork Packet Exchange)

A layer 3 protocol employed by Novell NetWare clients and servers.

IPX address

An 80-bit address that consists of network and host portions. The host portion of the address is usually the MAC address of the end station.

IPX RIP (IPX Routing Information Protocol)

A Novell NetWare distance-vector routing protocol based on delay (ticks) in the network.

ISDN (Integrated Services Digital Network)

A digital telephony technology that allows the use of a dialed phone call to provide data connectivity across geographical separations.

IS-IS (Intermediate System to Intermediate System)

IS-IS is an OSI link-state hierarchical routing protocol that is based on work originally done by the Digital Equipment Corporation for DECnet Phase V.

ISP (Internet Service Provider)

A company that specializes in providing individuals, companies, and corporations with access to the public Internet.

K Values

In IGRP and EIGRP, these are the values of bandwidth, delay, reliability, load, and MTU.

keepalive

A message passed across a link in order to keep an active, constant conversation with a node on the remote end.

kilobit

One thousand bits.

LAN (local area network)

A network meant to interconnect physically co-located devices and to enable the sharing of local resources.

layer 1

See *physical layer*.

layer 2

See *data link layer*.

layer 3

See *network layer*.

layer 4

See *transport layer*.

layer 5

See *session layer*.

layer 6

See *presentation layer*.

layer 7

See *application layer*.

link-state routing protocol

Any dynamic routing protocol that employs the Diykstra algorithm for passing and maintaining routing information.

load

A value between 1 and 255 that specifies the saturation level of a link.

loading state

Occurs when link-state requests (LSR) are sent to neighbors asking for recent advertisements that have not yet been discovered. The router then builds several lists to ensure all links are up-to-date and have been acknowledged.

logical AND

The process of deriving an IP network address by associating the address with a subnet mask and performing this Boolean function on the pair.

longest match

The methodology behind route selection and data forwarding decisions within the router. The more bits a router can match when comparing the destination address and the routing table, the better the chance of reaching that destination.

loopback interface

The use of a loopback interface enables you to assign the router ID for certain routing protocols, such as OSPF and BGP. This is beneficial because the loopback interface is logical and will not go down unless specified by the administrator, or if the router itself goes down.

LSA (link-state advertisement)

A routing update flooded through the network by routers that participate in a link-state routing protocol.

LSR (link-state request)

Requests pieces of the topological database from neighbor routers. These messages are exchanged after a router discovers that parts of its topological database are out-of-date.

LSU (link-state update)

Responds to an LSR packet. These messages are also used for the regular dispersal of LSAs. Several LSAs can be included within a single LSU packet.

MAC (Media Access Control) address

A layer 2 address associated with LAN interfaces. This is also referred to as a *burned-in address* (BIA).

megabit

One million bits.

metric

A unit of measure to facilitate the selection of the best route to a given destination.

MIB (Management Information Base)

A network information database installed on an end station that is used and maintained by a network-management protocol such as SNMP or CMIP.

MTU (maximum transmittable unit)

The largest entity that can be forwarded by any given layer 2 encapsulation.

multicast

A transmission onto a network segment that is destined for multiple, but not all, hosts on a destination network. In OSPF, this is the means by which routing updates are passed. Only OSPF routers respond to OSPF multicasts.

NAP (National Access Provider)
A corporation responsible for larger portions of the public Internet. NAPs are in charge of providing public Internet access to ISPs and to efficiently manage scarce IP address space.

NAT (Network Address Translation)
A technology that allows for the static and/or dynamic mapping of private, internal IP addresses to registered public IP addresses for communication via the public Internet.

NBMA (nonbroadcast multiaccess) network
NBMA networks are very similar to multiaccess networks, with the exception that they do not allow broadcast traffic.

neighbor
Routers that have interfaces to a common network are deemed *neighbors*. Neighbors can be either dynamically discovered or manually configured.

neighbor table
In nondistance-vector routing protocols, this is a listing of routers that share directly connected links.

NetBIOS
A connectionless, data link-layer protocol that utilizes broadcasts for communications.

network layer
The layer in the OSI model at which path determination for layer 3 protocols (IP, IPX, AppleTalk, and so on) is performed. The network layer is the primary focus of routing operations.

NIC (network interface card)
A module that provides network communication capabilities to and from a computer system.

NLSP (NetWare Link Services Protocol)
A dynamic, link-state routing protocol developed by Novell to replace IPX RIP, for use in IPX internetworks.

null interface
A logical software interface in a router used as an alternative to access lists to deny traffic. Traditionally, a static route is configured to specify the null interface as the outbound interface for traffic destined for the denied network.

NVRAM (Non-Volatile Random Access Memory)
Static memory space in the router where the router's configuration is stored. NVRAM, as the name implies, does not require power to keep its contents in storage.

octet
One of four 8-bit divisions of an IP address.

OSI model
A model devised by the International Standards Organization to divide the task of networking into separate

modules to facilitate accelerated evolution of each individual component.

OSPF (Open Shortest Path First)
A standardized dynamic-link state routing protocol designed to overcome the limitations of RIP by utilizing a hierarchical area structure.

OSPF database
This is the topological database that the router maintains. This database contains information such as the Process ID and LSA types.

packet
A logical grouping of information that includes a header containing control information and user data. Packets are most often used to refer to network-layer units of data.

PAP (Password Authentication Protocol)
An authentication method that utilizes clear text usernames and passwords to permit and deny access to remote users and/or routers.

passive-interface
This command prevents all routing updates for a given routing protocol from being sent to or received from a network via a specific interface.

peer group
A BGP peer group is a group of BGP neighbors that share the same update policies. Instead of defining policies for each individual neighbor, you can create a peer group and assign policies to the group itself.

periodic update
A routing update dispatched at a specified interval.

physical layer
The lowest layer of the OSI model. It deals with physical media and connectivity.

port number
In IP, this is a service access point between the transport layer and the upper application layers.

PPP (Point-to-Point Protocol)
An access protocol designed for use by remote clients (such as end users and/or routers) to access the centralized network resources.

prefix
The bits in an IP address that comprise the network portion.

presentation layer
The layer of the OSI model that deals with file format.

priority queuing
A Cisco queuing strategy that allows the prioritization of various traffic based on its importance in the network.

private internetwork address space
Any IP addresses that exist in space defined by RFC 1918 (consisting of network 10.0.0.0 through 10.255.255.255, 172.16.0.0 through 172.31.255.255, and 192.168.0.0 through 192.168.255.255).

protocol
A set of rules that define a method of communication.

public internetwork address space
Any IP addresses that exist outside of the private address space. Public address space is normally under the

control of a registration authority in charge of assigning these addresses to companies and/or individuals that require them.

queuing
The process of prioritizing traffic output on a serial interface.

QoS (Quality of Service)
The measure of performance for a transmission system that reflects its transmission quality and service availability.

RAM (Random Access Memory)
Volatile memory space in a router in which the running configuration is stored. Without power applied, the contents of RAM will be lost.

RARP (Reverse Address Resolution Protocol)
A process that dynamically provides addressing information to end clients that know only their MAC address. This process is similar to BootP and/ or DHCP.

redistribution
See *route redistribution*.

redundancy
The process of providing failsafe connectivity for hardware and/or software.

reliability
A measurement of dependability of a link on a scale of 1 to 255, with 255 being highly dependable.

repeater
A physical-layer device that only regenerates a bit stream. No intelligence is associated with a repeater.

RIP (Routing Information Protocol)
A standardized distance-vector dynamic routing protocol. RIP uses a number of hops to a destination network as a metric to measure the attractiveness of a route.

route
Information in a router regarding reachability of a particular destination network.

route feedback
Occurs when one routing protocol learns routes from another routing protocol, thus creating routing loops.

route filter
A configuration, employing access lists, used to control the networks being advertised out of or into a router.

route map
A method of controlling the redistribution of routes between routing domains.

route redistribution
The sharing of routing information between two separate routing protocols. Redistributed routes are propagated throughout the network as routes derived by the protocol receiving the shared information.

route reflector
A concept based on the idea of specifying a concentration router to act as a focal point for internal BGP sessions. Multiple BGP routers can peer to a central router, and then multiple route reflectors can peer together.

route summarization

The process of condensing the number of routes in a routing table by configuring a single entry to represent multiple destination networks.

routed protocol

Any of the layer 3 protocols that can be implemented on a routed interface. Examples of routed protocols are IP, IPX, AppleTalk, DECnet, and VINES.

router ID

Used to identify a router. The highest IP address on an active interface is used as the router ID. This information is important in establishing neighbor relationships and coordinating messages between routers on the network. The router ID is also used to break ties in the election of the DR and BDR in an OSPF network.

router priority

A value that indicates the priority of the router when selecting a designated DR or BDR. The default priority is 1 and can be configured to a higher number to ensure a router becomes the DR.

routing protocol

Any protocol that builds and maintains network reachability information in a routing table.

routing table

A listing of destination networks, metrics necessary to reach those networks, a next-hop address, and an outbound interface through which to depart the router to reach that destination network.

RTMP (Routing Table Maintenance Protocol)

Apple's proprietary routing protocol. RTMP establishes and maintains the routing information that is required to route datagrams from any source socket to any destination socket in an AppleTalk network. By using RTMP, routers dynamically maintain routing tables to reflect changes in topology.

runt

Any frame transmitted that is smaller than the minimum transmittable unit.

SAP (Service Advertising Protocol)

A Novell NetWare protocol used in providing service reachability for NetWare clients. All devices in a NetWare network that are capable of offering particular services issue SAP updates regarding those services.

scalable internetworks

Networks connected together by interconnectivity devices that are reliable, secure, accessible, and adaptable to the evolving needs of the network.

serial interface

Any interface designed to access WAN services. Typical serial interfaces include V.35, EIA/TIA 232, and EIA/TIA 449.

session layer

The layer of the OSI model that deals with interhost communications. This layer is considered to be one of the higher application layers.

single point of failure

Any point in the network that exists without redundancy. If this point fails, much, or all, of the network suffers an outage as well.

SMTP (Simple Mail Transfer Protocol)
In TCP/IP implementations, this is a protocol that deals specifically with the propagation of electronic mail.

SNA (System Network Architecture)
A nonroutable IBM protocol usually associated with mainframe connectivity.

SNMP (Simple Network Management Protocol)
In TCP/IP implementations, this is a protocol that deals specifically with the monitoring, configuration, and management of various internetwork devices.

source protocol address
The layer 3 address of the originating host.

Spanning Tree Protocol (STP)
A bridging protocol employed by bridges to elect a root bridge and calculate the lowest-cost pathway to that root bridge. Should two bridge interfaces be connected to the same networks, the bridge with the lowest-cost path to the root bridge services that network. The other bridge interface is placed into a blocking mode and does not forward traffic.

split horizon
A routing technique in which information about routes is prevented from exiting the router interface through which that information was received. This mechanism is useful in preventing routing loops.

standard access list
An access list of limited functionality, generally used to permit or deny access to/from hosts and networks.

standard area
An area in OSPF that can accept link updates and route summaries.

static route
A route that an administrator places in the routing table to override or augment the dynamic routing process.

stub area
In OSPF, this is an area that is allowed only a single point of access. Stub areas know only of the routes within the local area and summary routes to other areas.

stub area flag
Stub areas will set a flag (E-bit) in their Hello packet to 0. The stub routers will not accept any Hello packets from a router where the E-bit is set to 1.

subnet
A logical layer 3 network.

subnet mask
In IP, this is the information that specifies the distinction between the network and host portions.

switch
An internetworking device that makes forwarding decisions based on a layer 2 address.

TACACS (Terminal Access Control Access Control Server)
An application used to provide remote authentication services for network access.

TCP (Transmission Control Protocol)

A transport-layer connection-oriented protocol that exists to provide reliable services for the IP protocol suite.

Telnet

An IP application that provides connection-oriented virtual terminal access to other IP hosts and/or servers.

TFTP (Trivial File Transfer Protocol)

A connectionless file-sharing protocol that requires no authentication for uploading and/or downloading of files.

topology table

A listing of known destination networks and the number of pathways known to reach those individual destinations.

totally stubby area

In OSPF, this is an area that contains only a single exit point, routes for the local area, and a default route out of the area. No external routes are known at a totally stubby area.

transport layer

The layer of the OSI model that deals with flow control and optional reliability of data transfer.

triggered update

A routing update spawned as a result of a topology change. These updates are not sent out regularly. They go out on an as-needed basis only.

TTL (time to live)

A field in an IP header that indicates how long a packet is considered valid.

tunnel

A logical configuration of the encapsulation of one layer 3 protocol inside the payload of another layer 3 protocol. Tunnel configuration requires the configuration of the source, destination, and encapsulation mode of the tunnel as well as encapsulated protocol attributes on the logical tunnel interface.

tunnel destination

The termination point of a logical tunnel.

tunnel interface

A logical interface to which encapsulated protocol attributes are assigned. The tunnel's source, destination, and mode are defined here as well.

tunnel mode

The encapsulation method used for a tunnel configuration. The default is **gre ip**.

tunnel source

The origination point of a logical tunnel.

UDP (User Datagram Protocol)

A transport-layer connectionless protocol used in providing transport services for the IP protocol suite.

variance

Used in IGRP and EIGRP, the **variance** command determines which routes are feasible for unequal-cost load balancing. The term *variance* defines a multiplier by which a metric may differ, or vary, from the metric of the lowest-cost route.

virtual link

In OSPF, this is a link that must be configured when a non-Area 0 area must be connected directly to another non-Area 0 area. The virtual link transits the non-Area 0 area that is connected to Area 0 to create a logical connection of the new area to Area 0.

VLSM (variable-length subnet mask)

A subnet mask that does not remain constant throughout the internetwork for a given classful network.

VTY (virtual terminal)

A logical port that provides a means of accessing a router through the use of a Telnet session.

WAN (wide area network)

Any of the various network technologies employed to cover wide geographical expanses.

WFQ (Weighted Fair Queuing)

A Cisco queuing strategy employed to give low-volume traffic the priority for output consideration. Also called *last bit in, first out* (LBIFO).

wildcard mask

A four-octet mask used in the configuration of access lists to specify addresses for permission and/or denial. Also used in defining OSPF area membership.

X.25

A WAN technology used in many parts of the world. X.25 is generally a very low-bandwidth serial technology.

Index

The Coriolis Exam Cram Personal Trainer
An exciting new category in certification training products

The Exam Cram Personal Trainer is the first certification-specific testing product that completely links learning with testing to:
- **Increase your comprehension**
- **Decrease the time it takes you to learn**

No system blends learning content with test questions as effectively as the Exam Cram Personal Trainer.

Only the Exam Cram Personal Trainer offers this much power at this price.

Its unique Personalized Practice Test Engine provides a real-time test environment and an authentic representation of what you will encounter during your actual certification exams.

Much More than Just Another CBT!
Most current CBT learning systems offer simple review questions at the end of a chapter with an overall test at the end of the course, with no links back to the lessons. But Exam Cram Personal Trainer takes learning to a higher level.

Its four main components are:
- The complete text of an Exam Cram study guide in HTML format
- A Personalized Practice Test Engine with multiple test methods
- A database of 150 questions linked directly to an Exam Cram chapter

Plus, additional features include:
- **Hint:** Not sure of your answer? Click Hint and the software goes to the text that covers that topic.
- **Lesson:** Still not enough detail? Click Lesson and the software goes to the beginning of the chapter.
- **Update feature:** Need even more questions? Click Update to download more questions from the Coriolis Web site.
- **Notes:** Create your own memory joggers.

- **Graphic analysis:** How did you do? View your score, the required score to pass, and other information.
- **Personalized Cram Sheet:** Print unique study information just for you.

Windows 2000 Server
Exam Cram Personal Trainer
ISBN: 1-57610-735-3

Windows 2000 Professional
Exam Cram Personal Trainer
ISBN: 1-57610-734-5

Windows 2000 Directory Services
Exam Cram Personal Trainer
ISBN: 1-57610-732-9

Windows 2000 Security Design
Exam Cram Personal Trainer
ISBN: 1-57610-772-8

Windows 2000 Network
Exam Cram Personal Trainer
ISBN: 1-57610-733-7

Windows 2000 Migrating from NT4
Exam Cram Personal Trainer
ISBN: 1-57610-773-6

MCSE Networking Essentials
Exam Cram Personal Trainer
ISBN:1-57610-644-6

A+ Exam Cram Personal Trainer
ISBN: 1-57610-658-6

CCNA Routing and Switching
Exam Cram Personal Trainer
ISBN: 1-57610-781-7

$99.99 U.S. • $149.99 Canada

Available: November 2000

CORIOLIS™
Certification Insider Press

The <u>Smartest</u> Way to Get Certified
Just Got Smarter™

Look for All of the Exam Cram Brand Certification Study Systems

ALL NEW! Exam Cram Personal Trainer Systems

The Exam Cram Personal Trainer systems are an exciting new category in certification training products. These CD-ROM based systems offer extensive capabilities at a moderate price and are the first certification-specific testing product to completely link learning with testing.

This Exam Cram study guide turned interactive course lets you customize the way you learn.

Each system includes:
- A Personalized Practice Test engine with multiple test methods
- A database of nearly 300 questions linked directly to the subject matter within the Exam Cram

Exam Cram Audio Review Systems

Written and read by certification instructors, each set contains four cassettes jam-packed with the certification exam information you must have. Designed to be used on their own or as a complement to our Exam Cram study guides, Flash Cards, and Practice Tests.

Each system includes:
- Study preparation tips with an essential last-minute review for the exam
- Hours of lessons highlighting key terms and techniques
- A comprehensive overview of all exam objectives
- 45 minutes of review questions, complete with answers and explanations

Exam Cram Flash Cards

These pocket-sized study tools are 100% focused on exams. Key questions appear on side one of each card and in-depth answers on side two. Each card features either a cross-reference to the appropriate Exam Cram study guide chapter or to another valuable resource. Comes with a CD-ROM featuring electronic versions of the flash cards and a complete practice exam.

Exam Cram Practice Tests

Our readers told us that extra practice exams were vital to certification success, so we created the perfect companion book for certification study material.

Each book contains:
- Several practice exams
- Electronic versions of practice exams on the accompanying CD-ROM presented in an interactive format, enabling practice in an environment similar to that of the actual exam
- Each practice question is followed by the corresponding answer (why the right answers are right and the wrong answers are wrong)
- References to the Exam Cram study guide chapter or other resource for that topic

Certification Insider Press

The <u>Smartest</u> Way to Get Certified™